2005   Merry Christmas to

Love.
Uncle Kyle + Aunt
Barbara

Thoroughbred Champions

Top 100

RACEHORSES of the 20th CENTURY

Thoroughbred Champions

Top 100

RACEHORSES of the 20th CENTURY

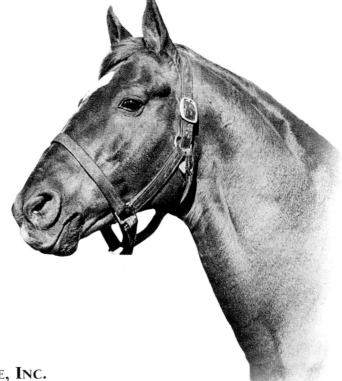

THE BLOOD-HORSE, INC.

LEXINGTON, KENTUCKY

ISBN 1-58150-024-6

Printed in Hong Kong

First Edition: October 1999

6 7 8 9 10

Contents

Foreword 6

Introduction 9

Complete Top 100 List 250

Miscellaneous Lists 252

The Panel/Acknowledgments 255

TOP 20

1	Man o' War	10	**11** Tom Fool	50
2	Secretariat	14	**12** Affirmed	54
3	Citation	18	**13** War Admiral	58
4	Kelso	22	**14** Buckpasser	62
5	Count Fleet	26	**15** Colin	66
6	Dr. Fager	30	**16** Damascus	70
7	Native Dancer	34	**17** Round Table	74
8	Forego	38	**18** Cigar	78
9	Seattle Slew	42	**19** Bold Ruler	82
10	Spectacular Bid	46	**20** Swaps	86

TOP 21-100

21 Equipoise 90	**41** Stymie 130	**61** Omaha 170	**81** Affectionately 210
22 Phar Lap 92	**42** Alysheba 132	**62** Cicada 172	**82** Miesque 212
23 John Henry 94	**43** Northern Dancer .. 134	**63** Silver Charm 174	**83** Carry Back 214
24 Nashua 96	**44** Ack Ack 136	**64** Holy Bull 176	**84** Bimelech 216
25 Seabiscuit 98	**45** Gallorette 138	**65** Alsab 178	**85** Lure 218
26 Whirlaway 100	**46** Majestic Prince 140	**66** Top Flight 180	**86** Fort Marcy 220
27 Alydar 102	**47** Coaltown 142	**67** Arts and Letters ... 182	**87** Gamely 222
28 Gallant Fox 104	**48** Personal Ensign ... 144	**68** All Along 184	**88** Old Rosebud 224
29 Exterminator 106	**49** Sir Barton 146	**69** Noor 186	**89** Bewitch 226
30 Sysonby 108	**50** Dahlia 148	**70** Shuvee 188	**90** Davona Dale 228
31 Sunday Silence 110	**51** Susan's Girl 150	**71** Regret 190	**91** Genuine Risk 230
32 Skip Away 112	**52** Twenty Grand 152	**72** Go for Wand 192	**92** Sarazen 232
33 Assault 114	**53** Sword Dancer 154	**73** Johnstown 194	**93** Sun Beau 234
34 Easy Goer 116	**54** Grey Lag 156	**74** Bald Eagle 196	**94** Artful 236
35 Ruffian 118	**55** Devil Diver 158	**75** Hill Prince 198	**95** Bayakoa 238
36 Gallant Man 120	**56** Zev 160	**76** Lady's Secret 200	**96** Exceller 240
37 Discovery 122	**57** Riva Ridge 162	**77** Two Lea 202	**97** Foolish Pleasure ... 242
38 Challedon 124	**58** Slew o' Gold 164	**78** Eight Thirty 204	**98** Beldame 244
39 Armed 126	**59** Twilight Tear 166	**79** Gallant Bloom ... 206	**99** Roamer 246
40 Busher 128	**60** Native Diver 168	**80** Ta Wee 208	**100** Blue Larkspur ... 248

FOREWORD

FOR ALL THE WORK AND DREAMING that went into it, by all seven panel members who toiled beneath the midnight lamp to create it, one approaches *The Blood-Horse's* list of the Top 100 Racehorses of the 20th Century with a nagging sense of its folly as a rational exercise and of the maddening arbitrariness of its outcome.

Ever since the writer began haunting Chicago racetracks as a young boy in 1955, he has been oft warned of the futility of trying to set horses from one generation against those from another, particularly those who raced decades apart in distinctly different venues. To be sure, a bare-boned truth lies at the core of that age-old admonition. How can one compare horses who broke from a barrier, and were hand-timed, to horses who broke from a starting gate and were electronically timed? Or horses who traveled cross-country by trains with horses who were squirted through time by planes? Or horses who ran over plowed fields, in the early part of the century, with those who competed over modern courses that are watered, harrowed, and manicured like gardens between races? It is as though

they had competed on planets as dissimilar as Earth and Mars. If comparisons are thus always odious, as conventional wisdom teaches, they are also as inevitable as human nature and often as diverting.

Indeed, as the century draws to a close, the concocting of Top 100 lists has become a cottage industry in American culture, the way by which we reference the present to the past, hoping to see a glimpse of the future. Many years ago, Miss Peggy Lee, the singer, was asked on a late-night talk show to name the greatest female jazz vocalist of all time. Not missing a beat, Miss Lee snapped, "You mean besides Ella?" Was James Joyce's novel, *Ulysses* — recently acclaimed the greatest of 100 works of English fiction in this century — grander than *The Great Gatsby*? And were the Beatles, as yet another top 100 list has lately argued, the greatest rock performers ever, over the Rolling Stones?

All such judgments, of course, are entirely subjective, a mixture of whim, wisdom, and whatever prejudices howl through the back of the mind. Man o' War's selection as the leading racehorse of the century is as much a testimony to the stamina of his myth as it is to the vaunted endurance of Big Red himself. None of the panelists who anointed the horse ever saw him run — all there remains, aside from some grainy film footage and a box of still photos, are the immutable names and numbers on his past performances — but he was the standard of the breed for so many generations, such a regally named emblem of the running horse, that he gradually assumed a kind of divine right to be there, looming as large and bold in racing's collective memory as his bronze statue at the Kentucky Horse Park. He certainly defied incalculable odds from birth in staying on top for as long as he did. In fact, what are the odds against America's greatest racehorse of the last 100 years being born in a 1917 crop of only 1,680 foals — the second smallest foal-crop of the century behind the 1,665 born in 1919?

Yet there he is, as fixed and immovable as ever, at the head of the list. Charles Hatton, the aging executive columnist for the *Daily Racing Form*, and trainer Holly Hughes — who saw all the great ones from Old Rosebud (No. 88) through Foolish Pleasure (No. 97) — called Secretariat (No. 2) "the Horse of the Century"

near the close of the colt's career. That pronouncement is arguable, of course, but Secretariat was certainly the most important and charismatic Thoroughbred to perform in the last half of the century — as much a standard to the millions who saw him in the Belmont Stakes as Man o' War was to those who witnessed him in soaring flight. One almost wishes they had finished in a tie, these two magnificent chestnuts, leaving one to represent the first half of the century and the other to stand for the second.

The list is bourbon to the imagination, sending it off spinning here and there, awakening memory and desire, and leaving much to wonder over in the end. Could either Man o' War or Secretariat have really beaten Citation (No. 3) — that is, the Citation who, as a three-year-old in '48, won the Sysonby Mile at Belmont Park on Sept. 29 and then, three days later, galloped off with the two-mile Jockey Club Gold Cup, winning by seven while making light of the four-year-old Phalanx, the winner of the '47 Belmont Stakes? Could any of them have beaten Count Fleet (No. 5)? Sylvester Veitch, the late Hall of Fame trainer, once told this writer that Man o' War and Count Fleet may have been the two best horses he ever saw. "And I think Count Fleet would have run him down," Syl said.

How would the head-strong, free-running Man o' War have handled the head-strong, front-running Dr. Fager (No. 6) over a flat mile at Belmont Park? At his best, Dr.

Fager was like some malevolent wind blowing around American racetracks, charging the air with the crackle of his positive ions, but not far down the list another question looms: could either of them have outrun Triple Crown winner Seattle Slew (No. 9), whose muscles so bulged and rippled in the post parade that he looked like the heavenly tailor had cut him a suit at least one size too small? Forego (No. 8) was a grand old gelding, as generous as any horse that ever lived, but could he really have beaten Slew? Or Spectacular Bid (No. 10) — the greatest horse that ever looked through a bridle at Buddy Delp? Or the great Affirmed (No. 12), who always looked as neat and elegant as Fred Astaire? Or the mighty Swaps (No. 20)? Close your eyes and listen to Hall of Fame trainer Charles Whittingham saying not long ago: "I've never seen a horse who could have beaten Swaps at Hollywood Park in 1956."

On reflection, Ruffian (No. 35) somehow looks too far down the ladder, squeezed unsettlingly between Easy Goer (No. 34) and Gallant Man (No. 36), and the beauty of this list is that it asks you to tinker and putter with one of your own. So let's just move her up and have her switch places with, say, War Admiral (No. 13), a gentlemanly colt who would not mind, and then have the Admiral switch with cranky John Henry (No. 23), who surely would. And what to do about Phar Lap (No. 22)? After Secretariat's triumph in the Triple Crown, the writer asked the elderly Francis Dunne, then a steward in New York, whether Man o' War or Secretariat was the greatest horse that he had ever seen. "Neither," said Francis. "I saw Phar Lap."

What is vastly clear, all opinions aside, is the richness and diversity of the horses in the Top 100: sixty-three colts, twenty-six fillies, and eleven geldings. And fifty-seven bays, twenty-seven chestnuts, ten browns, and six grays. Stylistically, there were all those front-running monsters, from Man o' War to Dr. Fager to Affectionately (No. 81), and those celebrated stretch-runners taking aim at the leaders — from Stymie (No. 41), with his golden head literally rising as he started to kick in, and on to Whirlaway (No. 26), of whom New York *Times* columnist Red Smith once wrote: "When he turned on the heat, you could hear a frying sound."

However one views this long line of horses, whether in peace and contentment — or shock and dismay — together they collectively lit up the landscape of racing and made the sport what it was, giving it much of the beauty, grace, and greatness that it had. May the next one hundred years be as generous and full.

William R. Nack
Washington, D.C.
June 1999

INTRODUCTION

WHEN *THE BLOOD-HORSE* embarked on its millennium exercise, few of us envisioned how satisfying — and democratic — the effort ultimately would be. At the outset, it seemed like a matter of compiling a list, finding the right photographs, and packaging everything neatly between an attractive cover.

But *Thoroughbred Champions: Top 100 Racehorses of the 20th Century* is anything but perfunctory. For starters, we wanted the ranking of the century's best horses to be based on methodical, careful deliberation. Accordingly, we chose seven well-respected racing officials and Turf writers whose individual strengths and collective expertise gave credibility to the undertaking. Our experts honored the solemnity of their task, and by early 1999 we had the most comprehensive list of its kind.

The Top 100 list first appeared as a special issue of *The Blood-Horse* magazine, in February of 1999. Few items in the magazine's history have provoked as much debate, and, in a few instances, sheer outrage, as did that list. To those who still disagree, the list, unfortunately, stands.

For the actual writing of the book, we drew on the skills of the many good writers at *The Blood-Horse* and a few of our very best correspondents. Many eagerly volunteered to write chapters on their favorite horses. Most of the writers also had to write about horses whose exploits occurred in the murky recesses of this century, often relying on stilted accounts and grainy photographs. What great tales they tell. From Man o' War to Blue Larkspur, there is something memorable about every horse.

Thoroughbred Champions is about more than good stories, though. Researchers spent innumerable hours compiling race records and pedigrees. Proofreaders checked and double-checked each fact, occasionally exclaiming over the deeds of a particular horse. An artist revised and refined the design to achieve the most satisfying look. For everyone involved, there was the constant sense of discovery. We hope the reader feels the same. *The Editors*

Man o' War

LEGEND, SENTIMENT, AND FACT co-author an uncommon soliloquy whenever the subject of Man o' War is addressed. Throw the most extravagant adjectives into the mix and history need not blink. Man o' War was eulogized by his groom, Will Harbut, as "de mostest hoss that ever wuz."

None of the descriptions in more formal grammar that have attempted to circumscribe the fame and attraction, the essence, of the great red stallion has improved upon this colloquial gospel-according-to-Will.

Most champions, even great ones, define themselves on the racecourse. We admire and understand their shiny strengths, but in so doing we also come to understand, or suspect, their limits. Those who saw Man o' War apparently never found a hint of limit. At all distances, he was overpowering. He might give a horse thirty pounds or more, but he always arrived at the wire with an expression in muscle and sinew that there was more to give had it been needed. The Man o' War drum roll knew no end, the crescendo reached no terminus.

Man o' War was bred by one of the premiere sportsmen of the American Turf, August Belmont II. It was not Belmont's dream to raise a champion for someone else, for he had been racing his own champions for many years. Late in life, however, Belmont answered the call of his country

and was a Major in the Quartermaster Corps in Spain on behalf of the World War I effort when Man o' War was a youngster. The Belmont yearlings of the crop of 1917 were thus sent up for sale.

Mrs. Belmont, a young actress known as Eleanor Robson before her marriage, conferred upon the handsome son of Fair Play—Mahubah, by Rock Sand, the evocative name Man o' War. At the Saratoga yearling sale of 1918, Ed Buhler (uncle of present day equine artist Richard Stone Reeves) put in the winning bid of $5,000 to secure the handsome colt on behalf of Samuel D. Riddle of Pennsylvania. The sale average was $1,038, and the top price was $15,600, and therein lay a family tale.

The highest-priced colt was purchased for the stable of Walter M. Jeffords Sr., whose wife was Riddle's niece. He was named Golden Broom, and, when they were apprentices, this sorcerer was said to have swept away Man o' War in a private trial. It was his singular flirtation with greatness.

Once trainer Louis Feustel unleashed Man o' War onto the burgeoning post-World War I sports scene, the colt was quick about the business of ensuring that he would rank with such athletes as Babe Ruth, Jack Dempsey, and Red Grange among the hallowed sports figures produced by his era.

At two, Man o' War won nine of ten. The lone defeat came at the hands of H. P. Whitney's Upset, in the 1919 Sanford Stakes. Man o' War was subjected to a bit of racing luck and traffic so bad that to some observers it savored of a possible fix.

Man o' War's feats as a juvenile included carrying 130 pounds in six consecutive races, of which he won five, as well as winning the climactic Futurity Stakes under 127.

Although Riddle and the Jeffords family would forever be connected with Lexington's Faraway Farm, where Man o' War stood, Kentucky was still "the West" to Eastern Turfmen. The Kentucky Derby had received a boost in national prestige four years earlier, when Harry Payne Whitney sent his unbeaten filly, Regret, from the East to win it. Still, it was not such a big deal in Riddle's mind that he was ready to relax his position that one and a quarter miles with 126 pounds in the early spring was too much for a three-year-old.

So, Man o' War, the Kentucky-bred who became a Kentucky legend, never raced in Kentucky — not in the Derby and not in any other race. Instead, he made his return at three in 1920 in the Preakness, which he won handily. This commenced a campaign of eleven victories in eleven starts. The highlights included the Belmont Stakes by twenty lengths; the Dwyer over the audacious effort by John P. Grier to bring him to a drive in the stretch; the Lawrence Realization by a recorded 100 lengths; and the Potomac Handicap under 138 pounds. American time records were scuttled from one mile to one and five-eighths miles.

In his final race, Man o' War galloped home by seven in the Kenilworth Gold Cup over Sir Barton. The previous year, Sir Barton had won the Derby, Preakness, and Belmont, which would later coalesce as the holy grail known as the Triple Crown.

Winner of twenty races in twenty-one starts, Man o' War had earned a record at the time, $249,465.

Although Riddle developed a reputation for mismanaging the big red horse's stud career by not seeing to it that he got appropriately high quality books of mares, Man o' War made a lasting mark in the stud. His best son was probably War Admiral, for whom breeder-owner Riddle relaxed his anti-Kentucky Derby attitude and thus made possible the Triple Crown sweep of 1937.

Man o' War also got the likes of Crusader, American Flag, War Relic, Clyde Van Dusen, Bateau,

RACE and (STAKES) RECORD

YEAR	AGE	STS	1ST	2ND	3RD	EARNED
1919	at 2	10	9(8)	1(1)	0	$83,325
1920	at 3	11	11(11)	0	0	$166,140
Lifetime		21	20(19)	1(1)	0	$249,465

			Spendthrift, 1876	Australian Aerolite
		Hastings, 1893		
	FAIR PLAY,		Cinderella, 1885	Tomahawk Manna
	ch, 1905		Bend Or, 1877	Doncaster Rouge Rose
		Fairy Gold, 1896		
MAN O' WAR,			Dame Masham, 1889	Galliard Pauline
chestnut colt,				
1917			Sainfoin, 1887	Springfield Sanda
		Rock Sand, 1900		
	MAHUBAH,		Roquebrune, 1893	St. Simon St. Marguerite
	b, 1910		Merry Hampton, 1884	Hampton Doll Tearsheet
		Merry Token, 1891		
			Mizpah, 1880	Macgregor Mare by Underhand

Battleship, Edith Cavell, and Frilette among his sixty-four stakes winners (seventeen percent from foals). He was America's leading sire in 1926 and the sire of the dams of 128 stakes winners, including eight champions.

Belmont died in 1924, but his connection to American life lingered in various ways besides his status as the breeder of Man o' War. Eleanor Robson Belmont survived her husband by more than a half-century. When she died a centenarian in 1979, she had become beloved as the Grande Dame of the Metropolitan Opera, in which milieu perhaps most of her admirers had no notion of her connection to a dasher from the dawn of the Roaring Twenties.

Belmont's racing stable was purchased by a partnership made up of two young fellows destined to be remembered away from Turf more than upon it. One was W. Averell Harriman, afterward one of the century's distinguished international statesmen and a governor of New York. The other was George Herbert Walker, whose names were bestowed upon a grandson, President George Bush.

With the impromptu balladeer Harbut as his spiritual gallant for the last sixteen years of his life, Man o' War was embraced by Americana. Thousands ventured to Faraway Farm and fell under the spell of the dual majesties. When Man o' War died at thirty in 1947, his funeral was broadcast nationally over radio. The sculptor Herbert Haseltine had been asked by Riddle more than a half-dozen years earlier to execute the horse's likeness. Named in one world war, Man o' War had survived through the next one. Skilled labor and materials were in such short supply for several years that it was not until a year after the old stallion's death that Haseltine's 3,000-pound, heroic-sized statue was settled down over the grave.

Nearly thirty years later, the sculpture, and remains, were laboriously transferred to the Kentucky Horse Park. There, the high-headed statue surveys the thousands of visitors who still seek the spirit of the horse in their travels to and through Kentucky. The fire has long since died, the voice of Will Harbut silent for a half-century and more, but the likeness of Man o' War as a symbol for speed, and courage, and potency is still appropriate.

"There was something that emanated from that noble animal," sculptor Haseltine mused, "that took my breath away." — E. L. B.

Secretariat

JOCKEY RON TURCOTTE was in for the ride of his life the afternoon of June 9, 1973, at Belmont Park aboard Meadow Stable's Secretariat, and the world of racing would be blessed with an historic moment that would match the magnificence of Don Larson's perfect World Series game, Roger Bannister's sub-four-minute mile, Gene Sarazen's double eagle in the Masters, and Wilt Chamberlain's 100-point game. Coming as it did shortly after Secretariat was featured on the covers of *Time*, *Newsweek*, and *Sports Illustrated* helped stamp it into the nation's consciousness.

The morning before the Belmont, retired Hall of Fame trainer Hollie Hughes was at the track, and he motioned Turcotte over so he could say a few words to him. As a young man, Hughes had sent out George Smith to win the 1916 Kentucky Derby and the list of horses he had seen around that time included the big three from the first part of the century: Sysonby, Colin, and Man o' War.

"He was a man of few words, but he had something to say to me that morning," Turcotte recalled. "He said, 'Son, there is no way you can get this horse beat today — just don't fall off. Believe me, boy, you are riding the greatest horse of all time and I have seen them all.' "

Race day came and the 67,605 fans in attendance and the millions more watching on television witnessed the greatest exhibition of speed and stamina ever seen on the American Turf. Announcer Chic Anderson provided millions of listeners a lasting impression of Secretariat's record performance midway through the one and a half-mile race. "Secretariat is blazing along! The first three-quarters of a mile in 1:09⅘. Secretariat is widening now. He is moving like a tremendous machine!"

Secretariat, and Anderson, didn't let up over the next three-quarters of a mile after disposing of rival Sham. The homebred son of Bold Ruler was in front by seven lengths after a mile in 1:34⅕, by twenty at the quarter pole in the time of 1:59, by twenty-eight with a furlong to go, and finally by thirty-one under the wire in world-record time of 2:24. The time shattered both the track and stakes record of 2:26⅗ set by Gallant Man in 1957 and the American dirt record of 2:26⅕ set by Going Abroad at Aqueduct in 1964.

Few had doubted Secretariat's greatness before the Belmont, and the universal praise after the performance was best expressed by veteran Turf columnist Charles Hatton. "His only point of reference is himself," said Hatton, who also had seen Man o' War run.

Kent Hollingsworth of *The Blood-Horse* wrote, "Two twenty-four flat. I don't believe it. Impossible. But I saw it. I can't breathe. He won by a sixteenth of a mile. I saw it. I have to believe it."

The victory eclipsed to some extent the appreciation of Secretariat's track-record time of 1:59⅖ in the one and a quarter-mile Kentucky Derby and the colt's unofficial record time of 1:53⅖ registered by two veteran *Daily Racing Form* clockers in the one and three-sixteenths-mile Preakness Stakes. The Derby time bettered Northern Dancer's record time by three-fifths of a second, and the 1:53⅖ in the Preakness would have bettered Canonero II's record time by three-fifths of a second if only it had counted. The 1:54⅖ recorded by Pimlico's official timer is listed as the official time.

The Triple Crown pursuit and triumph took a hold on the nation to such an extent that it bestowed a certain amount of stardom on Meadow Stable's Helen (Penny) Chenery. Chenery, who was married at the time to John Tweedy, wore that stardom like a champ.

On behalf of family members, Chenery had taken over the management of the Meadow

Stable operation after her father, farm patriarch Christopher T. Chenery, became ill. She retained that role as manager following her father's death in January of 1973 and spearheaded the deal in which Secretariat was syndicated for breeding purposes for a record $190,000 per share in the first part of his three-year-old season. Secretariat's total value was placed at $6.08 million, and the colt was billed as being worth his weight in gold.

Secretariat was the product of a foal-sharing arrangement between Meadow Stud and breeder owner Ogden Phipps, whose mother, Mrs. Henry Carnegie Phipps, bred and raced the great Bold Ruler. Meadow Stud and Phipps would toss a coin to determine which party

got which foal from the mating of Meadow Stud mares to Bold Ruler. Secretariat's fate was decided at the Saratoga meeting in 1969 when Meadow Stud won the coin toss for the yet unborn foal of Somethingroyal, whose earlier offspring included champion Sir Gaylord. Secretariat, who was foaled at The Meadow near Doswell, Virginia, on March 30, 1970, was bred in the name of Meadow Stud.

The Belmont Stakes might have been Secretariat's defining moment, but it wasn't the last of his great races. After the Belmont, Secretariat was taken to Chicago, where Mayor Richard Daley honored him by declaring June 30 "Secretariat Day." Secretariat easily won the Arlington Invitational at one and one-eighth miles, just missing Damascus' track mark of 1:46⅗ by a fifth of a second. Turcotte later said, "If only I had let him run for two jumps, that would have been another record." The following year, Arlington honored Secretariat by running the Secretariat Handicap, which later gained grade I status. For comparison, it wasn't until 1959 (in New York) when Man o' War was honored with a race.

Secretariat then shocked the racing world by losing the Whitney Stakes at Saratoga. Many blamed Turcotte for keeping Secretariat nearest the rail for much of the trip, but it later was learned that the colt suffered from a fever.

Secretariat redeemed himself in the inaugural Marlboro Cup Invitational Handicap in September, setting a world-record mark of 1:45⅖ for the one and one-eighth miles and winning over older stablemate Riva Ridge, Cougar II, Onion, Annihilate 'em, Kennedy Road, and Key to the Mint. After that, Secretariat lost the Woodward Stakes over a sloppy track while deputizing for Riva Ridge. The loss marked his third defeat in a stakes beginning with the letter W. (The other two were the Whitney and the Wood Memorial in the spring.) About a week later in his turf debut, Secretariat captured the one and a half-mile Man o' War Stakes at Belmont Park in course-record time of 2:24⅕.

Secretariat ran his final race in the Canadian International Championship Stakes at Woodbine in late October. More than a half-century earlier, Man o' War had bidden farewell to racing in Canada, going out a winner over Triple Crown winner Sir Barton.

Secretariat captured the one and five-eighths-mile Canadian International by six and a half lengths for his sixteenth career win from twenty-one starts. He had been trained throughout his career by Lucien Laurin and was ridden by Turcotte in all but his first two starts and his finale. Secretariat was named champion three-year-old male, and picked up his second Horse of the Year title. As a two-year-old in 1972, he had won the Futurity, Hopeful, Garden State Stakes, and Sanford Stakes as well as the Laurel Futurity. He had finished first in the Champagne Stakes, but was disqualified and placed second.

Secretariat arrived for stallion duty at the Hancock family's Claiborne Farm near Paris, Kentucky, in November of 1973, and was placed in the stall once occupied by Bold Ruler. Doubts about his fertility were raised following tests, but nothing ever came of that, and he ended up siring 653 foals, fifty-seven of which became stakes winners. A colt from his first crop of foals was sold for a then-record $1.5 million at the 1976 Keeneland July yearling sale.

Secretariat's stallion career was plagued by the perception that he was a modest stallion because he never sired a runner whose ability matched his, but a list of his added-money winners reveals the names of Horse of the Year Lady's Secret, champion and Preakness/Belmont winner Risen Star, and other good ones. Secretariat's biggest mark came as a broodmare sire, his maternal grandsons including Storm Cat, A.P. Indy, Summer Squall, Gone West, Secreto, Chief's Crown, and Dehere. Secretariat, whose likeness is portrayed in a bronze sculpture at both Belmont Park and the Racing Hall of Fame, was elected to the Hall in 1974. He was euthanized at age nineteen on Oct. 4, 1989, because of complications from laminitis and buried at Claiborne. *Time* magazine ranked Secretariat among the century's ten most influential athletes. — D. S.

		Nearco, 1935	Pharos / Nogara
	Nasrullah, 1940		
BOLD RULER, dk b, 1954		Mumtaz Begum, 1932	Blenheim II / Mumtaz Mahal
		Discovery, 1931	Display / Ariadne
	Miss Disco, 1944		
SECRETARIAT, chestnut colt, March 30, 1970		Outdone, 1936	Pompey / Sweep Out
		Prince Rose, 1928	Rose Prince / Indolence
	Princequillo, 1940		
SOMETHINGROYAL, b, 1952		Cosquilla, 1933	Papyrus / Quick Thought
		Caruso, 1927	Polymelian / Sweet Music
	Imperatrice, 1938		
		Cinquepace, 1934	Brown Bud / Assignation

RACE and (STAKES) RECORD

YEAR	AGE	STS	1ST	2ND	3RD	EARNED
1972	at 2	9	7(5)	1(1)	0	$456,404
1973	at 3	12	9(9)	2(2)	1(1)	$860,404
Lifetime		**21**	**16(14)**	**3(3)**	**1(1)**	**$1,316,808**

Citation

THERE WERE FEW STARS IN THE 1940s to rival Citation and jockey Eddie Arcaro on the nation's sports pages. Baseball had Joe DiMaggio and Jackie Robinson. Boxing had Joe Louis, and football had Slingin' Sammy Baugh. The college football ranks were led by West Point stars Glenn Davis and Doc Blanchard. Not one of them, however, could rival the team of Citation and Arcaro going six furlongs or two miles.

Citation, who was the 1948 Horse of the Year and the last Triple Crown winner for a twenty-five-year period, was the brightest star in the galaxy belonging to Warren Wright's Calumet Farm in the 1940s. Calumet had dominated racing during that decade like no other stable before or since during the 20th Century. Under the management of Hall of Fame trainer Ben A. (Plain Ben) Jones, Calumet captured the money title a record seven years during that ten-year period. Calumet won six Horse of the Year titles with five different horses, all homebreds, and also captured four Kentucky Derbys. Whirlaway, who won the 1941 Triple Crown, captured two of those Horse of the Year titles, but like Calumet Hall of Fame trainer H. A. (Jimmy) Jones pointed out, he was no Citation. Neither was any other horse.

"He was the best horse I ever saw," said Jones, who took over as Citation's trainer from his father, Ben Jones. "Probably the best anybody else ever saw, I expect.

"Citation didn't have a fault. He could sprint, he could go two miles, he could go in the mud, and could go on a hard track. He could do it all."

Jones recently ranked Citation above 1970s superstar Secretariat, praising that horse, but claiming that "Secretariat couldn't run a bit in the mud."

Ben Jones went even further. "Man o' War? Citation is a better horse," he said.

Citation was a member of the fifth crop of foals sired by Calumet stallion Bull Lea. That crop also included the colt Coaltown, and a daughter, Bewitch, and is looked upon by many veteran pedigree experts as the strongest crop ever to represent an individual stallion. Coaltown, who finished second behind Citation in the 1948 Kentucky Derby, shared

Horse of the Year honors with Capot in 1949. Bewitch, who entered into the record books by being the first horse to beat Citation, was the champion two-year-old filly of 1947 and the year's leading money-earning juvenile among females and males.

Citation was racing's first millionaire, but he didn't get to that $1-million mark in a direct route. He raced at ages two and three, missed his four-year-old season after developing osselets, then came back to run at five and six.

Citation's record his first two years was absolutely extraordinary — twenty-seven wins from twenty-nine starts and those two losses, both runner-up efforts, came under questionable circumstances. His earnings as a three-year-old, during which he won nineteen of twenty races, were a seasonal record $709,470. As a five-year-old in 1950, Citation extended his win streak to a modern-day record sixteen (a mark equaled in 1996 by Cigar), and the following year he topped the $1-million mark.

Citation's loss to Bewitch came in the 1947 Washington Park Futurity in his sixth start. The Calumet colt Free America also was in the race, and the outfit set its sights on a one-two-three finish. "We told the riders before the race, we'd split the fees three ways between them, and whoever was in front was to be allowed to win the thing without anybody whipping anything to death," Jimmy Jones said. "Well, Bewitch got out there. She could go five-eighths in :58 any time, so Citation just sort of went along. Bewitch kind of eased up, though, in the stretch, and Citation picked up five lengths on her. She won by a neck (actually won by a length), Citation finishing a head in front of Free America.

"When the riders came back to us after the race, Doug Dodson, who was on Bewitch, says he could have gone on and pulled away any time he wanted, but Steve Brooks says, 'Naw, Citation, was just loafing.' About that time Jackie Westrope comes back with Free America and says, 'You guys are just kidding yourself, I coulda taken both of you without even going to the whip.' "

Citation went on to win his final three races of the year and was named champion two-year-old male.

Sent to Hialeah for the winter, Citation proved to be classics material right from the start. He won all four of his races, including the Seminole Handicap from older stablemate Armed. Armed was 1947 Horse of the Year, and Citation's triumph seemed to take on the appearance of a changing of the guard in the Calumet ranks.

Citation was ridden in his next start by Arcaro for the first time. Al Snider, who had ridden Citation at Hialeah, had disappeared in Florida and would never be heard from again. In Arcaro's first ride, Citation finished second to Saggy in the Chesapeake Trial Stakes over a muddy track, but the effort still pleased the eventual Hall of Fame rider. "I could have caught him," Arcaro said about Saggy, "but I wasn't about to burn up that horse for an $8,300 pot with all those $100,000 races ahead."

Five days later, Citation beat Saggy in the Chesapeake Stakes, and was on his way to Churchill Downs. Citation won the Derby Trial the week of the Kentucky Derby, but the talk of the town centered on another Calumet Derby contender, Coaltown, who had broken the track record in the Blue Grass Stakes at Keeneland the previous week. Churchill thought so highly of the two Bull Lea colts that it dropped place and show betting.

Citation and Coaltown ran as an entry against four others and finished in that exact order, the winner easing across the finish line in 2:05⅖ over a sloppy track. Ben Jones was listed as the official Derby-winning trainer, even though his son had been in charge of Citation's progress leading up to the race.

Citation next won the Preakness in the absence of Coaltown, then set a track mark of 2:03 for one and a quarter miles in the Jersey Stakes at Garden State Park. Two weeks later, it was Citation's chance to become racing's eighth Triple Crown winner. Seven challenged, but none got closer than eight lengths at the wire. His time of 2:28⅕ equaled Count Fleet's

BULL LEA, br, 1935	Bull Dog, 1927	Teddy, 1913	Ajax / Rondeau
		Plucky Liege, 1912	Spearmint / Concertina
	Rose Leaves, 1916	Ballot, 1904	Voter / Cerito
		Colonial, 1897	Trenton / Thankful Blossom
HYDROPLANE II (GB), ch, 1938	Hyperion, 1930	Gainsborough, 1915	Bayardo / Rosedrop
		Selene, 1919	Chaucer / Serenissima
	Toboggan, 1925	Hurry On, 1913	Marcovil / Tout Suite
		Glacier, 1907	St. Simon / Glasalt

CITATION, bay colt, 1945

stakes record set in 1943. It had been twenty-eight years since Man o' War's farewell race in Canada, and here at last might be the great one's successor.

"It was Citation, which I have watched grow in stature for almost a year, now, with the slowly crystallizing hope that here, at long last, was the horse we'd been looking for since a great golden chestnut roared to a stop at Kenilworth Park back in 1920," wrote Joe Palmer for *The Blood-Horse*. "I could not see Arcaro move. But with some slight dropping of the hands, he released the swelling energy of the great racer beneath him. Citation opened away. He was three-sixteenths away but he was home."

Citation spent the summer in Chicago before returning to New York for the fall. In a remarkable display of versatility at Belmont Park, he won the Sysonby Mile over First Flight and Coaltown on Sept. 29, then three days later won the two-mile Jockey Club Gold Cup over Phalanx. His victory in the Pimlico Special in late October was a walkover.

Citation ended his three-year-old season with fifteen consecutive victories. Following a year off, he won an allowance race at Santa Anita in January of 1950 in his first race back to set the modern-day record of sixteen straight. That year also marked a distinct rivalry between Citation and Noor in California. Noor won four stakes between the two, but received a great deal of weight in two of them.

Citation surpassed the $1-million mark in taking down the $100,000 winner's purse in the 1951 Hollywood Gold Cup in July, and was retired soon after. At year's end, he was co-champion handicap male with Hill Prince. Citation entered stud at Calumet in 1952, which at that time was owned by Mrs. Wright. Warren Wright had died before seeing Citation become racing's first millionaire.

Like many of the Turf's greatest horses, Citation failed to sire a horse of equal caliber, although he did get two good ones. His daughter Silver Spoon is a member of the Racing Hall of Fame, and son Fabius won the 1956 Preakness. Citation also was the sire of the dams of thirty-three stakes winners. Citation was elected to the Racing Hall of Fame in 1959, and died at age twenty-five on Aug. 8, 1970. — *D. S.*

RACE and (STAKES) RECORD

YEAR	AGE	STS	1ST	2ND	3RD	EARNED
1947	at 2	9	8(3)	1(1)	0	$155,680
1948	at 3	20	19(16)	1(1)	0	$709,470
1949	at 4	0	0	0	0	—
1950	at 5	9	2(1)	7(5)	0	$73,480
1951	at 6	7	3(2)	1(1)	2	$147,130
Lifetime		45	32(22)	10(8)	2	$1,085,760

Kelso

THE THOROUGHBRED INDUSTRY has two distinct but some-times inseparable facets: bloodlines and running lines. Although the breeding business is all about pedigree, the racing business isn't always. Good blood doesn't always produce a good runner. And a good runner — even a great one — doesn't always come from a royal family.

In 1957, at Claiborne Farm near Paris, Kentucky, the mare Maid of Flight, stakes-placed and a winner of only three of nineteen starts, produced her first foal, by Your Host, a top racehorse who didn't have a sterling reputation as a stallion. Owned and bred by Mrs. Richard du Pont, the colt became a gelding at two before his first start on the racetrack.

It was a nondescript beginning of a career that would be anything but mundane. Kelso, one of the most beloved geldings in racing history, would go on to win thirty-nine races, smash numerous records, and earn an unprecedented number of awards. Of course, he never would be a stallion. But he nevertheless would capture the hearts and imagination of the public, perhaps even define a generation of sport.

The year was 1959. Atlantic City Race Course at that time was one of the premier tracks in the country, but surely the 13,626 patrons in attendance the afternoon of Friday, Sept. 4, had no inkling an ordinary maiden event would produce a champion many times over. On that day, Kelso, owned by Mrs. du Pont's Bohemia Stables and trained by Dr. John Lee, won his debut under John Block.

Kelso was 6-1 that afternoon and, when he made his second start at Atlantic City ten days later, he was dismissed at 4-1 and finished second. Lee fired him right back at the same track Sept. 23, and Kelso, this time the 9-5 favorite, again finished second. He was defeated in those two races by Dress Up and Windy Sands, respectively. Those names would become footnotes, his the story.

Kelso didn't race again until his three-year-old season, and only after the Triple Crown races were history. He won his 1960 debut at Monmouth Park for new trainer Carl Hanford, then won a mile event at Aqueduct in 1:34⅕, believed to be a record for a three-year-old at that distance. Kelso then won the Choice Stakes, Jerome Handicap, the Discovery Handicap, the Lawrence Realization Stakes, the Hawthorne Gold Cup, and the Jockey Club Gold Cup, the latter two against older horses.

"There's no doubt about it. He's the best horse in America today," jockey Eddie Arcaro said after the Jockey Club Gold Cup at Aqueduct. "He can beat anything at any distance."

In the Lawrence Realization, Kelso defeated Kentucky Derby favorite Tompion in 2:40⅕ to equal the great Man o' War's time for a mile and five-eighths. With eight wins in nine starts, he was voted three-year-old champion male and Horse of the Year. And his remarkable run had just begun.

In 1961, Kelso won seven of nine starts, including the Metropolitan Handicap, which Hanford believed was the gelding's best effort of the year. Kelso lugged 130 pounds in the mile event and, despite a troubled trip, squeezed out a neck victory. Kelso also won the Whitney Stakes (on a disqualification), the Suburban Handicap, the Brooklyn Handicap, the Woodward Stakes, and the Jockey Club Gold Cup that year.

In the Brooklyn, he carried 136 pounds, eighteen more than Divine Comedy, but still had more than a length on that foe at the wire. Kelso tried the turf for the first time in the Washington, D.C., International but fell victim to the grass-loving T. V. Lark at equal weights. It didn't matter. After all the races had been run that year, Kelso was voted champion older horse and Horse of the Year.

At five, Kelso made twelve starts, but the defining moments came late in the season. It wasn't a great year by Kelso standards — only six wins — but he did decimate a Jockey Club Gold Cup field by ten lengths and, in the Washington, D.C., International, he finished second, ahead of all but Match II, who shipped in from France.

But this was a love affair, and Kelso returned to New Jersey, where it all began. On Dec. 1, before a throng of 29,661 at Garden State Park, Kelso won the first running of the Governor's Plate by five lengths in 2:30⅕, a track record for a mile and a half, under new regular rider Ismael Valenzuela. The win pushed Kelso's lifetime earnings to more than $1 million, a record at the time, and sealed his second consecutive champion older horse title and third Horse of the Year.

At six, when most top horses have either been retired or have lost their ability to compete in the upper echelon of the sport, Kelso authored an amazing season. He won nine of twelve starts, with two seconds, and banked $569,762, his largest single-year total.

Kelso took home the laurels in the Woodward Stakes, Whitney Stakes, Suburban Handicap, Seminole Handicap, Nassau County Handicap, John B. Campbell Handicap, Gulfstream Park Handicap, and the Aqueduct Stakes. He also won the Jockey Club Gold Cup, the grueling two-mile test, for the fourth year in a row.

One of Kelso's front ankles reportedly swelled only two days before the Oct. 19, 1963, Gold Cup, but he cruised home at Aqueduct before 50,131 fans, many of whom were there to see him, and him alone. "He gets better all the time," jockey Valenzuela said after the race. "He was galloping today. He could have beaten his own track record if we'd tried."

Later that year, Kelso returned to Laurel for the D.C., International, and again hooked a turf buzz saw in Mongo. He finished second again on the grass, but first in the hearts and minds of the public. He was voted champion older horse and Horse of the Year.

In 1964, Kelso won five of eleven starts, some of which featured battles with Gun Bow. At seven, Kelso understandably was expected to show the wear and tear of age. For good measure, he won his fifth Jockey Club Gold Cup, and in the process set the American standard of 3:19⅕ for two miles. And, though not a turf tiger, Kelso shipped to Laurel and won the D.C., International in a world record 2:23⅘ for one and a half miles on the grass.

He came away with his fourth consecutive title as champion older horse, and fifth consecutive Horse of the Year award. No horse has come close since.

The twilight of Kelso's career came later than most, but it had to come. He won three of six starts, including the Stymie Handicap and Whitney Stakes, in 1965, at the age of eight. He made one start at nine, at Hialeah Park to prep for the Donn Handicap at Gulfstream Park, but during a workout suffered a hairline fracture of the inside sesamoid of his right front foot.

Hanford, soon after the retirement of the great one was announced, was asked how he felt. "Well, not as good as I felt last week, but you have to come to the end of the line sometime."

Kelso fell $22,104 short of the $2-million mark in earnings, but to mention what he failed to accomplish really isn't fair. Here was a gelding who had won five Horse of the Year titles, was a divisional champion five times, set or equaled eight track records, and set three American standards. He met and often got the best of the best Thoroughbreds racing had to offer, on dirt and turf, under serious weight disadvantages. Kelso died on Oct. 16, 1983, at Mrs. du Pont's Woodstock Farm in Maryland.

Perhaps the last few lines in a retirement tribute that appeared in the *The Blood-Horse* of March 19, 1966, said it best: "Kelso demonstrated the durability of class. No horse in our time was so good, so long. His was mature greatness." — *T. L.*

YOUR HOST, ch, 1947	Alibhai, 1938	Hyperion, 1930	Gainsborough / Selene
		Teresina, 1920	Tracery / Blue Tit
	Boudoir II, 1938	Mahmoud, 1933	Blenheim II / Mah Mahal
		Kampala, 1933	Clarissimus / La Soupe II
KELSO, dark bay or brown gelding, April 4, 1957	Count Fleet, 1940	Reigh Count, 1925	Sunreigh / Contessina
		Quickly, 1930	Haste / Stephanie
MAID OF FLIGHT, br, 1951	Maidoduntreath, 1939	Man o' War, 1917	Fair Play / Mahubah
		Mid Victorian, 1932	Victorian / Black Betty

RACE and (STAKES) RECORD

YEAR	AGE	STS	1ST	2ND	3RD	EARNED
1959	at 2	3	1	2	0	$3,380
1960	at 3	9	8(6)	0	0	$293,310
1961	at 4	9	7(6)	1(1)	0	$425,565
1962	at 5	12	6(4)	4(4)	0	$289,685
1963	at 6	12	9(9)	2(2)	0	$569,762
1964	at 7	11	5(3)	3(3)	0	$311,660
1965	at 8	6	3(3)	0	2(1)	$84,034
1966	at 9	1	0	0	0	$500
Lifetime		63	39(31)	12(10)	2(1)	$1,977,896

Count Fleet

A COUPLE YEARS BEFORE Count Fleet's death at age thirty-three, the manager of Stoner Creek Stud described the 1943 Triple Crown champion as a "docile horse." Humph. Charles A. Kenney must not have known the stallion when he was young. Or maybe Count Fleet simply settled down after he had shown he had nothing left to prove. He did that in 1948, the year his first crop of babies turned two. Of fifteen runners, thirteen were winners.

The numbers just got better as his second career went along. He was leading sire in 1951 and leading broodmare sire in 1963. He ranked in the top twenty on the annual sires list seven times. It was a perfect match for his stellar racing career, in which he never finished off the board. He raced twenty-one times, won sixteen, finished second four times, and once was third. In his brief three-year-old season, he was six-for-six. His career purses totaled $250,300, a huge sum for the World War II era. Regardless of his brilliance, Count Fleet was not a docile horse when he was young. He was so rambunctious as a two-year-old that John Hertz, whose wife was Count Fleet's listed owner and breeder, was afraid contract rider Johnny Longden would get hurt riding him. As far as the taxicab magnate was concerned, it was just one more reason to leave the "For Sale" sign on the son of 1928 Kentucky Derby winner Reigh Count and a hard-knocking sprinter named Quickly. He had been priced at $4,500, but there were no takers.

Years later, Longden acknowledged the colt didn't look like much as a two-year-old. "He was medium size, about 15 hands, and though he was deep in the girth and had a good shoulder, he was weedy behind," Longden told *The Blood-Horse* in 1985. "As a two-year-old he looked more like a filly than a colt. And those rough, unpredictable manners didn't exactly endear him to anyone."

But Longden loved him anyway. "When that leggy brown colt wants to run, he can just about fly," he said in trying to convince Hertz to keep him.

Eventually, Longden got his way. Eventually, Hertz was glad he did.

It took the colt a while to put his speed to full use. He just couldn't get the hang of the starting gate. In his debut, on June 1, 1942, he was left at the gate some fifty yards but still managed to charge from behind fast enough to finish second.

Later, while training for the Futurity at Belmont Park, he ripped off a six-furlong work in 1:08⅕, a full second faster than the Widener track record. Unfortunately, the move left him a little tired for the race itself four days later. He thus suffered his only third-place finish, beaten by five lengths and another head by Occupation, his top rival for two-year-old honors. That proved to be the last defeat of his career.

Eddie Blind, an assistant starter in New York, thought that Count Fleet could benefit from another lesson in the gate. When he loaded the colt for the Champagne Stakes, Blind climbed up behind him and smacked him on the rear, then yelled when the gate opened. Count Fleet won the mile Champagne in world-record time for a two-year-old of 1:34⅕, starting a ten-race win streak that would take him through the rest of his career. The second victory of the string was by five lengths, over Occupation in the Pimlico Futurity, in a track-record-equaling 1:43⅗ for the one and one-sixteenth miles. He closed out his juvenile season in the Walden Stakes at Pimlico with a thirty-length margin of victory.

Racing secretary John Blanks Campbell was so impressed he assigned Count Fleet a then-record 132 pounds on the Experimental Free Handicap.

Count Fleet opened his sophomore season in a mile-and-seventy-yards allowance. He beat Bossuet by three and a half lengths. Next up was the Wood Memorial, then at one and one-sixteenth miles, in which he beat Blue Swords by three and a half lengths.

Unfortunately, the colt suffered an injury to the coronet band of his left rear hoof during the Wood, and his connections worried he would not be ready to race in the Kentucky Derby. Meanwhile, as word of the mishap circulated, other owners decided it would be a propitious time to get Derby Fever. By the time everyone assembled at Churchill Downs, Count Fleet had nine challengers.

Longden did double duty on the train trip to Louisville, sitting in the box car with the colt to ice the injury. The foot may still have been painful on Derby Day, but not enough to keep Count Fleet, the 2-5 favorite, from defeating Blue Swords by three lengths.

Afterward, *The Blood Horse* described the race: "It was as if the horses in the Derby had caught the military spirit of the times. They marched around the track almost exactly according to their rank, as indicated on the mutuel boards on the infield."

Only three horses took him on in the Preakness a week later, and they might as well have stayed home. Count Fleet led wire-to-wire and beat second-place Blue Swords eight lengths. His time for the one and three-sixteenth miles over a track labeled "good" was 1:57⅖ — just a second off the track record.

Both Triple Crown victories looked so easy, someone asked Hertz why Longden hadn't pressed him to get records. Hertz replied that the season was still young.

It wasn't, though, for Count Fleet. By then he had only two races left to go. Because the Preakness was about a month before the Belmont, Count Fleet got a tune-up in the Withers halfway between them. Bet down to 1-20, he easily won the mile stakes in 1:36.

		Sundridge, 1898	Amphion
	Sunreigh, 1919		Sierra
REIGH COUNT,		Sweet Briar II, 1908	St. Frusquin
ch, 1925			Presentation
		Count Schomberg, 1892	Aughrim
	Contessina, 1909		Clonavarn
COUNT FLEET,		Pitti, 1898	St. Frusquin
brown colt, 1940			Florence
		Maintenant, 1913	Maintenon
	Haste, 1923		Martha Gorman
QUICKLY,		Miss Malaprop, 1909	Meddler
blk, 1930			Correction
		Stefan the Great, 1916	The Tetrarch
	Stephanie, 1925		Perfect Peach
		Malachite, 1913	Rock Sand
			Miss Hanover

New York's racing secretary found only two horses to face Count Fleet in the Belmont. And, just as in the Preakness, they might as well have stayed in their barns. The colt soared off to a twenty-five-length victory, the longest in history until Secretariat came along and won by thirty-one in 1973. His time for the mile and a half also was a stakes record, 2:28⅕.

Count Fleet rapped an ankle during the Belmont, though, and Hertz retired him, saying he'd never allow the champion to "appear at a track as a patched-up horse." If he had not been so headstrong, however, the injury might not have been so serious. "I felt him bobble in the stretch and knew he had hurt himself," Longden said. "I started to pull him up, but he'd have none of it. He just grabbed the bit in that bull-headed way of his and took off again."

After his first crop showed themselves to be runners, Count Fleet's value began escalating rapidly. By the time he became leading sire in 1951, he was insured by Lloyd's of London for $550,000, a sum believed to be a record for those times. But he was worth it.

His runners in 1951 included Kentucky Derby winner Count Turf, creating the first three-generation list of Derby winners, Horse of the Year Counterpoint, and champion three-year-old filly Kiss Me Kate. During his years at stud — he was pensioned after the 1966 breeding season — he sired a total of thirty-eight stakes winners, including one other Horse of the Year, One Count.

His female offspring went on to produce 119 stakes winners, among them seven champions, including Quill, Lamb Chop, Furl Sail, and five-time Horse of the Year Kelso.

Count Fleet enjoyed seven years as a pensioner before dying at Stoner Creek in 1973 at the age of thirty-three.

"Always been a docile horse," Charles Kenney, Stoner Creek manager, said the year Count Fleet turned thirty. "Never gives us any trouble unless we try to leave him out at night. Mr. Hertz always was so afraid Count Fleet would be hit by lightning or have an accident that the horse has grown used to being in his stall at night. If we try to leave him out when it's pleasant in the summer, he raises a ruckus."

That sounds more like the horse Longden knew as a two- and three-year-old. — P. S.

RACE and (STAKES) RECORD

YEAR	AGE	STS	1ST	2ND	3RD	EARNED
1942	at 2	15	10(4)	4(2)	1(1)	$76,245
1943	at 3	6	6(5)	0	0	$174,055
Lifetime		**21**	**16(9)**	**4(2)**	**1(1)**	**$250,300**

Dr. Fager

IF THOROUGHBRED RACING could be portrayed as a fantasy, much like baseball is in *The Natural* and *Field of Dreams*, it would look something like this: The gates open, and the wild and tempestuous Dr. Fager comes charging out, his noble head held high. His Lilliputian rivals are of little significance. The camera zooms in on the big bay to reveal the flared nostrils and the fire in his eyes. His long mane is already blowing wildly in the breeze. As he passes each pole, the tote board lights displaying the fractional times burst into a fireworks display of luminous splendor.

Dr. Fager continues to hurtle past each pole, running with the reckless abandon of a wild mustang bounding across the Great Plains. He wants nothing in front of him but the wind, and when someone attempts to challenge his superiority, he attacks with all the ferocity pent up inside him. As he turns for home and surges down the stretch, he leaves a trail of scorched hoofprints on the sandy loam. As he crosses the finish line, the slow motion camera captures the poetry of his power and majesty. The fireworks from the tote board are now rocketing toward the sky as the Doc shatters another track record. The music of Beethoven's *Ode to Joy* builds to the thunderous crescendo. Then there is silence, as the crowd, still numb from the experience, tries to absorb all they have just witnessed.

This was Dr. Fager, an unharnessed force of energy who recorded what many believe to be the single greatest season by any racehorse in the history of the sport. By being named Horse of the Year, champion handicap horse, champion sprinter, and co-champion grass horse in 1968, Dr. Fager became the first and only horse ever to win four titles in a single year.

His world-record mile of 1:32⅕, under 134 pounds, lasted twenty-nine years. His seven-furlong track record of 1:20⅕ at Aqueduct, under a staggering 139 pounds, lasted thirty-one years. He also equaled the track record in the Suburban Handicap at Aqueduct for one and a quarter miles under 132 pounds, and set a track record at Rockingham as a three-year-old.

In "that championship season" of 1968, he captured seven of eight starts, never carried less than 130 pounds, and in his only defeat, was second to the great Damascus in the Brooklyn Handicap, carrying 135 pounds to Damascus' 130.

In Dr. Fager's world-record mile, set in the Washington Park Handicap, he ran his second quarter in :20$\frac{3}{5}$, believed to be the fastest quarter ever run within the body of a race. What made that race even more remarkable was the fact that he was eased up the entire length of the stretch, while winning by ten lengths. In the final furlong, the Doc had his ears pricked, while jockey Braulio Baeza was bent over with his head buried in the colt's flying mane. It was truly a sight to behold.

As he pulled up, Arlington track announcer Phil Georgeff's microphone went dead for several seconds. Then out of the silence came one word: "Wow!"

"I just said it to myself," Georgeff said. "And I didn't even know at the time he had broken the world record, because in those days it took a while before they posted the time. When I saw the time afterward, I was shocked, because he was running so effortlessly and was merely galloping through the stretch."

Trainer John Nerud always thought Dr. Fager had a chance to break a record every time he went out, and this race was no different. But in the paddock, he could see the fire building up inside the colt. Although a bully by nature, the Doc normally was relaxed in the paddock. On this occasion, however, he was showing the signs that something special was about to happen.

"If he took weight off one leg and his shoulder started to quiver a little I knew he was on edge," Nerud said. "His eyeballs would appear a half-size bigger, and by the time he got to the gate he had totally psyched himself."

In his seven-furlong record in Aqueduct's Vosburgh Handicap, he made 139 pounds look feathery, as he cut out fractions of :43$\frac{4}{5}$ and 1:07$\frac{4}{5}$ before drawing off to win by six lengths in 1:20$\frac{1}{5}$ over a track that had recently been made slower by winterization.

Dr. Fager was named after neurosurgeon Dr. Charles Fager, who saved Nerud's life after the trainer was thrown from a pony, suffering a blood clot on his brain. Several years ago, Fager wrote a manuscript about his relationship with Nerud and his experiences with his namesake that has never been published. It was titled, *A Hole in the Wind.*

Although his records finally have fallen, there is no doubt that the hole Dr. Fager ran in the wind never will be filled. But even with his incredible displays of speed, the Doc's greatest performance likely came in a race he won by only a neck. In the United Nations Handicap at Atlantic City, Dr. Fager was making his first and only start on the turf, a surface trainer John Nerud said the colt didn't care for. In the one and three-sixteenths-mile race, he faced just about every top grass horse in America, including future Horse of the Year Fort Marcy, to whom he was conceding sixteen pounds. The race turned out to be unforgettable, as Dr. Fager and the hard-knocking Advocator, in receipt of twenty-two pounds, hooked up on the backstretch. Dr. Fager, obviously uncomfortable over the slippery turf, lost the lead to Advocator three times, but battled back three times to outfinish his stubborn foe.

Each of Dr. Fager's races was a study in greatness, whether it was sprinting, racing a distance of ground, or racing on turf. Even after three decades, the images he provided remain burned in the mind. There was the Californian Stakes, when Baeza used all his strength to try to restrain him. Down the backstretch, Dr. Fager literally was jumping up in the air and Baeza finally had to let him go. He took off like a runaway train and ran the best horses in California into the ground. In the stretch, Baeza hit him with the whip, something the Doc detested, and he reacted by throwing his tail straight up in the air.

Then came the Suburban Handicap, in which Dr. Fager, carrying 132 pounds, and Damascus, under 133, hooked up after a half-mile and sizzled their next quarter in :22⅗. Every time Damascus made a run at his rival, the Doc's eyes and nostrils opened wide and he would turn back the challenge. Finally, like so many before him who dared to look the tiger in the eye, Damascus cracked and gave up the chase. Dr. Fager opened up and went on to a comfortable victory, equaling the track record of 1:59⅗.

There was the New Hampshire Sweepstakes at three, when In Reality came up the rail on the backstretch and tried to catch Dr. Fager napping. When the Doc spotted him, he reached over and attempted to savage his rival. Even early in his three-year-old campaign, the signs were there. Who could forget the sight of Baeza wrapped up on Dr. Fager after going head and head with the undefeated Tumiga in the Withers Stakes through fractions of :44⅕ and 1:08 flat? The way he coasted home in a common gallop to cover the mile in 1:33⅕ was evidence of what was to come.

As a stallion, Dr. Fager was expected to become a sire of precocious youngsters, but just the opposite was true. His horses took a while to come around. Syndicated for a then-hefty $3.2 million by Nerud and Tartan Farm owner William McKnight, Dr. Fager actually looked at first to be a bust as a sire. His first two crops produced only one restricted stakes winner: Rosemont winner Plastic Surgeon. Then, in 1974, in the span of six days, Tree of Knowledge won the Hollywood Gold Cup; Lady Love captured the Molly Pitcher Handicap; and Lie Low won the Open Fire Stakes. At the end of the year, Dr. Fager was a respectable ninth on the leading sires list.

In 1975, he was represented by the champion two-year-old filly Dearly Precious, and finished the year as the third leading sire in the country. In August of 1976, however, Dr. Fager died of a twisted intestine. His loss was felt the following year when he became the leading sire in the nation with earnings of almost $1.6 million. He was only the fourth stallion outside of Kentucky to top the list in this century. He was the sire of thirty-five stakes winners, which, in addition to Dearly Precious, included Canadian Horse of the Year L'Alezane and champion sprinter Dr. Patches. Dr. Fager sired the dams of ninety-five stakes winners.

Perhaps it is best to remember Dr. Fager the way he was seen the day he departed the racetrack on a cold, windy, November morning in 1968. As he left the barn and passed one of Nerud's grooms who was holding a sign which read, "Farewell Doc," a gust of wind blew his mane on end, just as it had on so many memorable Saturday afternoons. Dr. Fager arched his neck and flared his nostrils one last time as he pranced toward the awaiting van. On his way to his new home, as a publicity stunt, the van was stopped by a state trooper after arriving in Florida. The officer went inside the van and issued Dr. Fager a summons for — what else — speeding. — S. H.

RACE and (STAKES) RECORD

YEAR	AGE	STS	1ST	2ND	3RD	EARNED
1966	at 2	5	4(2)	1(1)	0	$112,338
1967	at 3	9	7(7)	0	1(1)	$484,194
1968	at 4	8	7(7)	1(1)	0	$406,110
Lifetime		22	18(16)	2(2)	1(1)	$1,002,642

Native Dancer

THE 1953 KENTUCKY DERBY held great anticipation, much of it centered around Alfred Vanderbilt's big gray colt, Native Dancer. Undefeated in eleven races previous to the season's first classic, Native Dancer had been the 1952 champion two-year-old male after winning all nine starts.

Coupled with Social Outcast as a 2-3 favored entry, Native Dancer was widely expected to emerge from the Derby with his unblemished record intact. But as the race unfolded, the worst fears of trainer Bill Winfrey and jockey Eric Guerin materialized.

Rounding the first turn, Native Dancer was bumped soundly by longshot Money Broker. The colt recovered and began to move on the leaders, Dark Star and Correspondent. Once clear of traffic, Native Dancer began his pursuit of Dark Star that many believed would have a predictable result: another win for the "Gray Ghost." But at the wire, Native Dancer's run came up a head short.

Not only did the Derby outcome end one of racing's best winning streaks, it was also a bitter defeat for the thousands of Americans who had embraced the colt. "When he lost the Kentucky Derby by a head, thousands turned from their TV screens in sorrow, a few in tears," *Time* magazine later reported in a cover story about Native Dancer and his popularity. "Hundreds of people, old and young, have sent him letters and greeting cards. Little girls have organized fan clubs in his name."

In his first outing after the stunning Derby loss, Native Dancer began another winning streak that ended ten races and fifteen months later when he was retired.

Native Dancer's final tally sheet of twenty-one victories from twenty-two starts stands as one of the all-time best and placed him in elite company with Man o' War, Secretariat, and Citation. Not unlike those stars, Native Dancer also became a household name across the country as his exploits were chronicled on television, the new medium that was becoming increasingly popular in the early 1950s.

A son of Polynesian, Native Dancer was foaled March 27, 1950, at Dan W. Scott's Scott

Farm near Lexington, Kentucky, and sent to his owner's Sagamore Farm in Maryland not long afterward. Winner of the 1945 Preakness Stakes, Polynesian was known for his quickness. On the male side, Native Dancer traced back to Phalaris, one of the most successful male lines in American breeding. Geisha, the gray dam of Native Dancer, was a daughter of Discovery, among Vanderbilt's best horses before the "Gray Ghost." Through Discovery, Geisha traced back to Fair Play, the sire of Man o' War and a source of stamina.

Prepped at Santa Anita for his racing career, Native Dancer caught the attention of clockers when he worked a quarter-mile in :23 in company. The 7-5 favorite in his first career start at Jamaica on April 19, 1952, the colt won by four and a half lengths. Along with a non-betting exhibition in his final start two years later, the race was the only start in which Native Dancer did not go to post as a prohibitive odds-on favorite.

Four days after breaking his maiden, Native Dancer won the Youthful Stakes by six lengths before being sidelined for more than three months by bucked shins. He returned to competition at Saratoga with a two and a quarter-length victory in the Flash Stakes. That was the first of four victories in as many weeks that August. In the Saratoga Special, Native Dancer rallied over the sloppy track to win by three and a half lengths and he carried 126 pounds, highest impost of his juvenile season, to a three and a half-length win in the

Grand Union Hotel Stakes. The month ended with a two-length win in the Hopeful Stakes. Following a three-week hiatus from racing, Native Dancer won an allowance before facing his toughest competition to date in the Futurity Stakes. Blocked early before running down Tahitian King, Native Dancer posted a two and a quarter-length victory with a final time of 1:14⅖, equaling the world record for six and a half furlongs over a straight track.

With another stakes win concluding his undefeated season, Native Dancer was the unanimous champion juvenile male. He set a juvenile earnings record of $230,495 and shared the Horse of the Year title with One Count. He was assigned 130 pounds atop the Experimental Free Handicap.

After wintering in California, Native Dancer returned to action on April 18, 1953. Following a two-length triumph in a division of the Gotham Stakes, Native Dancer extended his unbeaten record to eleven when he took the Wood Memorial one week later. That set the stage for his unforgettable Kentucky Derby.

The sight of the 16.2-hand, 1,200-pound, Native Dancer on the newsreels rallying to win America's top races captivated both racing and non-racing fans. The extent to which the public responded to Native Dancer was seen by the reaction to his lone career loss. The New York *Times* wrote, "There hadn't been so much furor over a horse losing a race since Man o' War's defeat by Upset in the Sanford Stakes in 1919."

The setback did not last long as Vanderbilt's charge won the one-mile Withers Stakes by four lengths. A rematch between the Derby runner-up and Dark Star followed two weeks later, in the Preakness Stakes. Dark Star again took an early lead that he maintained until the stretch, but he faded to finish fifth. A post-race examination determined Dark Star had injured a tendon and he was retired. Native Dancer, meanwhile, was all out to hold off Jamie K. for a neck victory. As the 1-5 favorite in the seven-horse field, Native Dancer generated a minus show pool of $46,012, one of the then-largest in racing history.

With Dark Star retired, Native Dancer assumed leadership of his division with a neck win over Jamie K. in the Belmont Stakes as the 2-5 favorite. The colt's final time of 2:28⅗ for one and a half miles was the third-best time at that point in Belmont history.

In his fourth straight triumph after the Derby, Native Dancer was sent off at 1-20 to win the Dwyer Stakes at Aqueduct. Shipped to the Midwest for the Arlington Classic, the colt was a runaway nine-length winner, then returned to New York to post a five and a half-length romp in the Travers Stakes.

With Guerin suspended, Eddie Arcaro, who had ridden Jamie K. in the Derby and Preakness, rode Native Dancer in the American Derby at Washington Park. After the colt rallied from six lengths back nearing the stretch to post a two-length victory under 128 pounds, Arcaro was effusive in his praise of Native Dancer. "Sheer power is the only way to describe him."

POLYNESIAN, br, 1942	Unbreakable, 1935	Sickle, 1924	Phalaris / Selene
		Blue Glass, 1917	Prince Palatine / Hour Glass II
	Black Polly, 1936	Polymelian, 1914	Polymelus / Pasquita
NATIVE DANCER, gray colt, March 27, 1950		Black Queen, 1930	Pompey / Black Maria
GEISHA, ro, 1943	Discovery, 1931	Display, 1923	Fair Play / Cicuta
		Ariadne, 1926	Light Brigade / Adrienne
	Miyako, 1935	John P. Grier, 1917	Whisk Broom II / Wonder
		La Chica, 1930	Sweep / La Grisette

A late-season showdown with Tom Fool, the top older horse in the midst of an undefeated campaign, did not materialize after it was discovered that Native Dancer bruised his left forefoot in the American Derby and he was put up for the rest of the year. While Native Dancer was a cinch for three-year-old male championship honors, the Horse of the Year title went to Tom Fool, victorious in all ten of his outings.

Native Dancer won his four-year-old debut, an allowance race at Belmont Park. In the Metropolitan Handicap under 130 pounds, Native Dancer unleashed his customary late kick to make up seven lengths, catch leader Straight Face, and win by a neck. The colt was being readied for the Suburban Handicap when soreness was detected in his right foreleg. Rested for three months, Native Dancer made what was to be his final career start when he carried 137 pounds to a nine-length victory in the betless, seven-furlong Oneonta Handicap. Soreness recurred in the right foreleg, and Vanderbilt retired his star.

Honored with the Horse of the Year title that eluded him the previous year, Native Dancer retired with just one loss from twenty-two starts and earnings of $785,240. Despite his record, questions remained about Native Dancer's overall ability since he never faced older horses as a three-year-old and raced only three times after that.

Native Dancer entered stud at Sagamore and left an indelible mark on the breed. The sire of forty-four stakes winners, including 1966 Kentucky Derby winner Kauai King, he is also the grandsire of the great Mr. Prospector and broodmare sire of Northern Dancer. He sired dams of eighty-four stakes winners, and linked two of America's most important sire lines. Son Raise a Native sired Alydar, Exclusive Native (sire of Affirmed), and Majestic Prince (sire of Majestic Light). Native Dancer also sired Atan (sire of Sharpen Up) and Dan Cupid (sire of the great Sea-Bird). Native Dancer died on Nov. 16, 1967, of complications from colic. — R. M.

RACE and (STAKES) RECORD

YEAR	AGE	STS	1ST	2ND	3RD	EARNED
1952	at 2	9	9(7)	0	0	$230,495
1953	at 3	10	9(9)	1(1)	0	$513,425
1954	at 4	3	3(1)	0	0	$41,320
Lifetime		22	21(17)	1(1)	0	$785,240

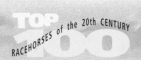

Forego

THE SAYING THAT WEIGHT WILL STOP A FREIGHT TRAIN didn't apply to Forego during his four seasons as the heavyweight champ. Forego carried 130 pounds or more in twenty-four stakes, all graded, and his relentless running style helped him to twenty-one top three finishes under those heavy imposts. Two of the unplaced efforts came over sloppy tracks and the other came in a fourth-place finish when he was beaten only by two and three-quarters lengths. There was no such thing as "too much weight" for Forego, and race fans loved him and owner Martha Gerry for taking that notion to the limit.

"A horse is supposed to carry weight and try to beat the best," said Mrs. Gerry, who bred and raced Forego in the name of Lazy F Ranch. "That's why they call it handicap racing."

Handicap racing meant that Forego carried more weight than the others and was fair game for an upset. Those upsets happened, but even when they did, his fans knew that he had given his best and greeted him with a round of applause.

Forego, who suffered from chronic leg problems throughout his career, first was associated with that 130-pound figure while finishing second in the 1974 Metropolitan Handicap under 134 pounds. His first win at the 130-pound level came later that year in the seven-furlong Vosburgh Handicap under 131 pounds. He closed out the year with an easy victory in the $100,000, weight-for-age Jockey Club Gold Cup at 124 pounds at two miles in November in his first and only appearance in that race.

The fact that Forego suffered from physical ailments meant that his races had to be planned carefully and sometimes that meant he didn't stay in training long enough for the Jockey Club Gold Cup. That weight-for-age race was tailor made for Forego, and served as a respite from the burdening handicaps. Forego ended his career some $40,000 behind then-all-time leader Kelso, and many thought that if he had had the opportunity of running in additional renewals of the Jockey Club Gold Cup, he would have surpassed Kelso's record. A gelding himself, Kelso dominated the Jockey Club Gold Cup, winning it five con-

secutive times in the 1960s. Forego was named Horse of the Year in 1974 for the first of three consecutive years. He also chalked up his first of four consecutive titles as champion older male and was voted champion sprinter.

Like Kelso with the Jockey Club Gold Cup and Exterminator with the Saratoga Cup following World War I, Forego owned the race named for William Woodward Sr. Forego took the Woodward four times (1974-77), the first two times under 126 pounds when it was a weight-for-age event and the last two under handicap conditions. Forego also matched Discovery's record in winning the historic Brooklyn Handicap three consecutive years.

Forego's victory in the 1975 Woodward went a long way in earning Horse of the Year honors over the late developing three-year-old Wajima. A record-priced son of Bold Ruler, Wajima had beaten Forego in their two earlier races while getting a big break in the weights. Forego gave Wajima nineteen pounds in the Governor Stakes and finished about two and three-quarters lengths behind him in fourth place. He gave him ten pounds in the Marlboro Cup Invitational Handicap and failed to catch him by a head. The Woodward spread was only seven pounds, and Forego decisively beat Wajima by one and three-quarters lengths. He was named Horse of the Year for the second consecutive year.

Forego had won five of his six earlier efforts in 1975, starting off the season with victories in the Seminole and Widener Handicaps in Florida. Returned to New York, he won the seven-furlong Carter Handicap under 134 pounds before trying the New York Handicap Triple. He missed winning the first race in the series, the mile Metropolitan Handicap, by a length under 136 pounds, then took the next two races, the Brooklyn and Suburban Handicaps. Both wins bordered on the extraordinary.

Forego bettered Whisk Broom's disputed track mark of 2:00 (set in 1913) in winning the one and a quarter-mile Brooklyn. The massive gelding got home under 132 pounds in track-record time of 1:59⅕ while giving the runner-up twenty-three pounds.

The Suburban for years had been contested at one and a quarter miles, but was lengthened to one and a half miles for the 1975 running. Under 134 pounds, Forego won by a head to become the first horse in modern U.S. history to win a major race at that kind of distance with that much weight. (In 1920, Exterminator had captured the two and a quarter-mile Ontario Jockey Club Cup under 134 pounds at old Woodbine.)

In 1976, Forego gave an even better account of himself in the Handicap Triple than he had given the previous year, starting off with a victory in the Met Mile under 130 pounds over Master Derby. After taking the Nassau County Handicap, Forego just missed Foolish Pleasure by a nose in the Suburban while giving that colt nine pounds (134 to 125). Next was the Brooklyn under another 134 pounds, and he cruised home by two lengths.

Third in the Amory L. Haskell Handicap at Monmouth in August, Forego got up to win his third Woodward, this time under 135 pounds for his new regular rider, Bill Shoemaker, who had taken over from Heliodoro Gustines. (Pete Anderson had ridden Forego early in the gelding's career, but gave way to Gustines. Forego was ridden by only one other jockey during his career, Jacinto Vasquez.)

Two weeks after the Woodward, Forego met Honest Pleasure in the Marlboro Cup and accomplished the seemingly impossible. Under 137 pounds over a sloppy track, Forego trailed by four lengths at the eighth pole, but managed to nip Honest Pleasure by a head. *Daily Racing Form* assigned Forego a record 140 pounds on its 1976 Free Handicap for older males. Only six other older horses shared the previous record weight of 136 pounds: Tom Fool, Native Dancer, Kelso, Gun Bow, Buckpasser, and Dr. Fager, plus Forego himself in 1975.

Forego came back in 1977 and the heavy weights continued to haunt him. He won the

Metropolitan under 133 pounds and the Nassau County under 136, but missed the winner by a neck in the one and a quarter-mile Suburban under 138 pounds. He then lost the Brooklyn under 137 and the Whitney under 136, but came through once again in the Woodward (under 133) for the fourth consecutive time. He lost out to Triple Crown winner Seattle Slew in Horse of the Year balloting, but was voted champion older male for the fourth consecutive year.

FORLI (Arg), ch, 1963			
	Aristophanes, 1948	Hyperion, 1930	Gainsborough / Selene
		Commotion, 1938	Mieuxce / Riot
	Trevisa, 1951	Advocate, 1940	Fair Trial / Guiding Star
		Veneta, 1940	Foxglove / Dogaresa
FOREGO, bay gelding, April 30, 1970			
LADY GOLCONDA, br, 1958	Hasty Road, 1951	Roman, 1937	Sir Gallahad III / Buckup
		Traffic Court, 1938	Discovery / Traffic
	Girlea, 1951	Bull Lea, 1935	Bull Dog / Rose Leaves
		Whirling Girl, 1945	Whirlaway / Nellie Flag

Forego competed twice as an eight-year-old in the summer of 1978 before Mrs. Gerry retired him. One ankle, in addition to being tender, was disfigured by ringbone. He had won thirty-four of fifty-seven races, run second nine times, and was third seven times. He had captured twenty-four stakes, placed in fourteen others, and earned $1,938,957.

Forego was trained the first part of his career by Eclipse Award-winning conditioner Sherrill Ward, then went to another Hall of Fame member, Frank Y. Whiteley. Ward was ill during part of the time he had Forego, and his assistant Eddie Hayward helped get the gelding ready for racing. Hayward, in fact, was the listed trainer for Forego when the gelding won the Roamer and Discovery Handicaps in his last two starts as a three-year-old in 1973. Whiteley took over the gelding's conditioning in 1976.

A member of the same foal crop as Secretariat and the great stallion Mr. Prospector, Forego met Secretariat once, in the 1973 Kentucky Derby, and finished fourth after being slammed into the rail on the far turn. Forego and Secretariat both raced on Belmont Stakes Day five weeks later. Forego won a one and a sixteenth-mile allowance race in 1:40⅘, one-fifth second off the track record, while Secretariat set the Belmont Stakes record.

The following year, Forego met and defeated the speedy Mr. Prospector in the seven-furlong Carter. That victory, along with his score in the Vosburgh that fall, earned him champion sprinter honors.

Forego, who was foaled at Claiborne Farm near Paris, Kentucky, was sent to John Ward's farm near Keeneland after his retirement, then was moved to the Kentucky Horse Park near Lexington in 1981. Forego was euthanized after fracturing his right hind leg pastern bone in his paddock on Aug. 27, 1997, and was buried nearby. He was elected to the Racing Hall of Fame in 1979. — D. S.

RACE and (STAKES) RECORD

YEAR	AGE	STS	1ST	2ND	3RD	EARNED
1973	at 3	18	9(2)	3(3)	3(1)	$188,909
1974	at 4	13	8(8)	2(2)	2(2)	$545,086
1975	at 5	9	6(6)	1(1)	1(1)	$429,521
1976	at 6	8	6(5)	1(1)	1(1)	$491,701
1977	at 7	7	4(3)	2(2)	0	$268,740
1978	at 8	2	1	0	0	$15,000
Lifetime		57	34(24)	9(9)	7(5)	$1,938,957

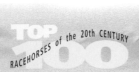

Seattle Slew

SEATTLE SLEW WILL ENTER the 21st Century as the only horse to win the Triple Crown while undefeated. Although Seattle Slew did not win all his career starts, he won all his races before the Kentucky Derby, Preakness, and Belmont Stakes. That took some doing, especially since the other ten Triple Crown winners didn't even make it past their two-year-old season without a loss. The 20th Century's greatest horse, Man o' War, whose owner withheld him from the Derby, didn't make it past the summer of his juvenile year without a blemish on his record.

Seattle Slew was bred by Central Kentucky horseman Ben Castleman and raised at his breeder's White Horse Acres near Lexington. Castleman had bred Seattle Slew by mating his homebred stakes-winning mare My Charmer (by Poker) to Bold Reasoning, who was standing his first year at stud at the Hancock family's Claiborne Farm near Paris. Castleman had planned to breed My Charmer to Jacinto, but the stallion's book was full, so Hancock suggested Bold Reasoning, whose fee was an affordable $5,000.

In the name of Pearson's Barn Inc., Karen and Mickey Taylor, in partnership with Jim and Sally Hill, bought Seattle Slew from Castleman for $17,500 at the 1975 Fasig-Tipton Kentucky July yearling sale. Jim Hill, a veterinarian, picked out the colt.

Seattle Slew was turned over to young trainer Billy Turner, whose wife, Paula, had broken the colt at Mrs. Henry Obre's farm near Monkton, Maryland. Campaigned in Karen Taylor's name, Seattle Slew scored by five lengths in 1:10⅕ under jockey Jean Cruguet at Belmont Park on Sept. 20 in his debut. Two weeks later, he led all the way in a seven-furlong allowance event at Belmont.

With no real divisional standout, the Taylors and Hills decided to try their colt in the mile Champagne Stakes on Oct. 16 off just those two starts. Seattle Slew scored by nine and three-quarters lengths in 1:34⅖, breaking Vitriolic's stakes record, set in 1967, by a fifth of a second.

Mickey Taylor, a fourth-generation logger, thought his dreams had come true. "I turned

to Karen after the race and said, 'If we can keep this horse in one piece, I'll never have to cut down another tree,'" Taylor recalled.

Seattle Slew won the juvenile male championship off that performance, but his assignment of the standard topweight of 126 pounds on the Experimental Free Handicap was viewed by some as a knock, especially since Count Fleet had been assigned 132 pounds.

Sent to Florida to prepare for the classics, Seattle Slew won by nine lengths in track-record time of 1:20⅗ for seven furlongs. Next up was the mile and an eighth Flamingo Stakes at Hialeah, which he won in 1:47⅖.

Slew was sent to Aqueduct for the Wood Memorial Stakes for his final Kentucky Derby prep and came home a winner in 1:49⅗ for the mile and an eighth. Sent off as the 1-2 favorite in the Derby, Seattle Slew provided a few anxious moments to his backers by nearly unseating jockey Jean Cruguet at the start. Cruguet soon regained his balance, and Seattle Slew caught pacesetter For The Moment near the first quarter mile. The two colts raced as a team until the top of the stretch, where Seattle Slew pulled away and won in the modest time of 2:02⅕.

Even with that Derby victory, horsemen were still griping that Seattle Slew hadn't beaten anything. "Just a good horse in a bad lot," many said. The Preakness and Belmont would change all that.

The 2-5 favorite in the Pimlico classic, Seattle Slew put away Cormorant around the far turn and scored by one and a half lengths over Iron Constitution. Cormorant faded to fourth, slightly in front of European champion J. O. Tobin. Time for the one and three-sixteenths-mile race, 1:54⅖, was only two-fifths of a second slower than the track mark.

All that was left was the one and a half-mile Belmont Stakes, and racing would have its first unbeaten Triple Crown winner. Sent off again at 2-5, Seattle Slew went right to the lead and made it look easy, scoring by four lengths over Run Dusty Run in 2.29⅗ over a muddy track.

Instead of a well-deserved rest, Seattle Slew was taken to Hollywood Park for the July 3 Swaps Stakes at one and a quarter miles. Seattle Slew finished fourth, sixteen lengths behind the winner, J. O. Tobin.

That was the last start of the year for Seattle Slew, who beat out the older Forego for 1977 Horse of the Year honors, and also was named champion three-year-old male.

Even with those two championship trophies, all was not right with the Slew Crew. Turner, who thought the colt needed an extended rest after the Triple Crown, was let go by the owners in December of 1977.

"It was tough, but we had to do the right thing," said Taylor.

With Turner out, Doug Peterson became Slew's new trainer. Peterson's quick action at Hialeah in January of 1978 helped save the colt from a life-threatening viral disease. The colt missed only a few weeks of training.

That winter, the Taylors and Hills, in the name of their equine firm Wooden Horse Investments, sold a half-interest in Seattle Slew for $6 million to a group of horsemen headed by Brownell Combs, general manager of his father's Spendthrift Farm near Lexington. Seattle Slew would continue to race in the name of Karen Taylor and would enter stud at Spendthrift.

Seattle Slew won a pair of allowance races in New York in May and August as a four-year-old, then was beaten a neck by Dr. Patches in the Paterson Handicap at Meadowlands. Cruguet at that point voiced his disapproval over the colt's training regimen, and he, too, was gone.

Jockey Angel Cordero Jr. came on board, and had the distinction of riding Seattle Slew in the Marlboro Cup Handicap in what was the first battle between Triple Crown winners. Affirmed, who had won the 1978 Triple Crown, was favored at 1-2, but it was Seattle Slew winning the race.

Seattle Slew next won the Woodward Stakes over Exceller in track-record time of 2:00. In the mile and a half Jockey Club Gold Cup, Seattle Slew and Affirmed locked horns from the beginning, but the real race was at the end, when Seattle Slew courageously battled Exceller through the stretch and just missed by a nose.

		Bold Ruler, 1954	**Nasrullah** / Miss Disco
	Boldnesian, 1963		
BOLD REASONING, dkb/br, 1968		Alanesian, 1954	Polynesian / Alablue
		Hail to Reason, 1958	Turn-to / Nothirdchance
	Reason to Earn, 1963		
SEATTLE SLEW, dark bay or brown, February 15, 1974		Sailing Home, 1948	Wait A Bit / Marching Home
		Round Table, 1954	Princequillo / Knight's Daughter
	Poker, 1963		
MY CHARMER, b, 1969		Glamour, 1953	**Nasrullah** / Striking
		Jet Action, 1951	Jet Pilot / Busher
	Fair Charmer, 1959		
		Myrtle Charm, 1946	Alsab / Crepe Myrtle

"The Jockey Club speaks for itself," said Taylor. "Plus, that race shows what he throws in his foals — the heart of a racehorse."

Seattle Slew ended his racing career with an easy victory in the Stuyvesant Handicap in November and was retired with fourteen wins from seventeen races and earnings of $1,208,726. He was voted champion older male, and entered stud at Spendthrift in 1979.

Just as he had on the racetrack, Seattle Slew got off to a quick start at stud. His first crop included Landaluce, who reached star status by winning the 1982 Hollywood Lassie Stakes by twenty-one lengths in 1:08, the fastest time ever recorded by a two-year-old at Hollywood Park. Landaluce died that fall of a bacterial infection. Her star status had reached such proportion that her death was reported on CBS by Dan Rather. That first crop also included grade I winners Adored, Slewpy, and Slew o' Gold, who is a member of the Racing Hall of Fame.

Other stars followed. Swale, from the next crop, won the 1984 Kentucky Derby and Belmont Stakes, but died unexpectedly eight days after the latter classic. Around that time, a share in Seattle Slew was sold for a reported $3 million. In 1985, a half-brother to Seattle Slew, Seattle Dancer, was sold for a still-standing world record price of $13.1 million at the Keeneland July yearling sale. The Seattle Slew colt A.P. Indy, whose $2.9 million price tag was the highest of 1990 for a yearling, was Horse of the Year two years later. He commands a six-figure fee at stud in Central Kentucky.

Seattle Slew was moved prior to the 1986 season to Mr. and Mrs. Robert N. Clay's Three Chimneys Farm near Midway, Kentucky, where he currently stands for $125,000. He has sired more than eighty-five stakes winners, and his daughters have produced more than seventy stakes winners. Seattle Slew was elected to the Racing Hall of Fame in 1981. — D. S.

RACE and (STAKES) RECORD

YEAR	AGE	STS	1ST	2ND	3RD	EARNED
1976	at 2	3	3(1)	0	0	$94,350
1977	at 3	7	6(5)	0	0	$641,370
1978	at 4	7	5(3)	2(2)	0	$473,006
Lifetime		17	14(9)	2(2)	0	$1,208,726

Spectacular Bid

THE 1970s WERE COMING TO AN END, and the racing gods still weren't satisfied. First, they had created Secretariat, with the physical beauty of Adonis and the strength of Hercules. Then came Seattle Slew, to whom they bestowed the powers of Aeolus, god of the wind. The following year, they came up with Affirmed, with the courage and determination of Odysseus.

But even with some of their finest work behind them, the gods made one final attempt to create the perfect racehorse. What they came up with was Spectacular Bid, and although others are generally placed before him in the rankings of the all-time greats, there is no doubt he was as close to the perfect racing machine as any of those before or after him.

He wasn't the best-looking horse. He wasn't the best-moving horse. He wasn't the best-bred horse. But he had one quality that separated him from other horses: He could do everything.

He could win on the lead or coming from ten lengths back. He could run seven furlongs in 1:20, and he could run one and a quarter miles in 1:57⅖, a time which has not been equaled on dirt in nineteen years. He could run track-record times as a two-year-old, three-year-old, and four-year-old, all over dead surfaces.

It was that versatile speed that enabled him to break seven track records and equal another at five different distances from five and a half furlongs to one and a quarter miles.

The son of Bold Bidder, who cost only $37,000 as a yearling, won twenty-six of thirty starts and twenty-four of his last twenty-six starts. His only two losses during that time came at one and a half miles, once to the older Affirmed, and once after he stepped on a safety pin the morning of the race, causing an infection that could have cost him his life.

A champion at the ages of two, three, and four, he won at fifteen different racetracks in nine different states, and carried 130 pounds or more to victory five times. He was held in

such high esteem, he was sent off at odds of 1-20 an incredible eight times and 1-10 six times. He was made the odds-on favorite in twenty-two of his last twenty-three races, even in the face of grade I winners such as Flying Paster, General Assembly, Coastal, Glorious Song, Cox's Ridge, and Golden Act. The only exception was the Jockey Club Gold Cup, in which he met Triple Crown winner Affirmed.

When his outspoken trainer Grover (Bud) Delp proclaimed him, "The greatest horse ever to look through a bridle," most people paid little attention. After all, they had recently seen some pretty good horses peering through bridles. But as the years went on and Spectacular Bid began to distance himself from his illustrious predecessors, his feats grew more and more impressive. Now there are many who feel Delp's comment is not quite as outrageous as they first thought.

When Delp got his hands on Spectacular Bid, the trainer was already a veteran of the Maryland wars. And there is no tougher breed of horseman than a Maryland hardboot. These are the guys who come out every day and pay little heed to the winter's fury that used to put old Bowie Racetrack in a perpetual state of frostbite. Babying a horse is not in their vocabulary, and when they come up with a good one, you can bet it won't take long for that horse to be toughened and battle tested. Delp found himself with a great one, but wasn't about to change what he knew best. All he had to do was give Spectacular Bid the morning donut the colt demanded, then send him out to battle.

The Bid, as he became known, ran his first race on June 30, 1978. His reputation had not exactly preceded him, as he was sent off at 6-1 in the five and a half-furlong race, with apprentice rider Ronnie Franklin aboard. An easy wire-to-wire victory was followed by a track-record-equaling allowance score at the same distance, in which he aired by eight lengths. Delp threw him into stakes company only eleven days later in the Tyro Stakes at Monmouth and he closed for fourth after being sixteen lengths back early and wide all the way. That was followed by another fast-closing second in Delaware's Dover Stakes.

Losing then became an extreme rarity for Bid, as he twice put together winning streaks of ten races or more.

Following the Dover, Spectacular Bid turned in one of the most awesome performances ever by a two-year-old. Over a dead Atlantic City strip, he romped by fifteen lengths in the World's Playground Stakes, covering the seven furlongs in a mind-boggling 1:20⅖. Two weeks later, he put himself on the map by beating General Assembly in Belmont's one-mile Champagne Stakes, in which he ran in a near-stakes-record 1:34⅘.

Instead of putting him away for the year with the two-year-old championship all but locked up, Delp ran Bid back eleven days later in the rich Young America Stakes at Meadowlands, which he won by a neck after having to check at the top of the stretch.

Through for the year? Not on your life. Back he came nine days later to win the Laurel Futurity by eight and a half lengths. And he wasn't through yet. Two weeks later, he cruised by six lengths in the Heritage Stakes at Keystone, concluding one of the most successful and demanding two-year-old campaigns seen in quite a while.

After a three-month freshening, Bid was back better than ever, rattling off victories in the seven-furlong Hutcheson Stakes in 1:21⅗, Fountain of Youth, Florida Derby, Flamingo, and Blue Grass Stakes. His average margin of victory in those five races was almost seven and a quarter lengths. And it would have been even higher had Franklin not given him one of the worst rides in history in the Florida Derby, in which Bid had to check and steady sharply on four separate occasions, yet still won by four and a half lengths. He won his next two — the Flamingo and Blue Grass — by a combined nineteen lengths, while being eased up both times.

The expected epic showdown between Bid and California sensation Flying Paster in the Kentucky Derby never materialized, as Flying Paster wilted badly while Bid cruised home by two and three-quarter lengths. It was the same scenario in the Preakness. Bid returned home to Maryland and put on a show, winning by five and a half lengths, missing the track record by a fifth of a second. It looked as if nothing could prevent Spectacular Bid from becoming

BOLD BIDDER, b, 1962	Bold Ruler, 1954	Nasrullah, 1940	Nearco / Mumtaz Begum
		Miss Disco, 1944	Discovery / Outdone
	High Bid, 1956	**To Market**, 1948	**Market Wise / Pretty Does**
		Stepping Stone, 1950	Princequillo / Step Across
SPECTACULAR, ro, 1970	Promised Land, 1954	Palestinian, 1946	Sun Again / Dolly Whisk
		Mahmoudess, 1942	Mahmoud / Forever Yours
	Stop on Red, 1959	**To Market**, 1948	**Market Wise / Pretty Does**
		Danger Ahead, 1946	Head Play / Lady Beware

SPECTACULAR BID, gray colt, February 17, 1976

the third consecutive Triple Crown winner and fourth of the decade. Nothing except a loose safety pin in his stall.

Delp contemplated scratching, but Bid seemed fine after the pin was removed. In a move he still regrets to this day, Delp told Franklin about the pin, and as a result, the young rider lost his cool, going after a 90-1 shot early. Bid struggled home in third, without changing leads, and it was obvious this wasn't the same horse. A deep infection in his hoof was caught by veterinarian Alex Harthill, who had to use a special drill to locate its source.

With a new rider in Bill Shoemaker, Bid returned to the races in late August, winning an allowance race at Delaware by seventeen lengths in track-record time. One incredible performance after another followed, highlighted by a brilliant five-length score over older horses in the Marlboro Cup. He was off for a month, during which time he came down with a brief fever. Stretching out to a mile and a half for the Jockey Club Gold Cup, he gallantly came again in the stretch, but fell three-quarters of a length short of Affirmed, costing him Horse of the Year honors. That accolade would come the following year.

Owner Harry Meyerhoff decided to keep Bid in training at four, sending him to Santa Anita. What followed was one of the greatest campaigns ever, as Bid won all nine of his starts, including an American-record performance on dirt in the Charles H. Strub Stakes, in which he knocked off his rival Flying Paster in 1:57⅖ for one and a quarter miles. Following a rare walkover in the Woodward Stakes, an old sesamoid injury started flaring up and the Bid was retired to Claiborne Farm in Kentucky.

Spectacular Bid has been considered a disappointment at stud, although he has sired forty-four stakes winners. He also is the sire of the dams of forty-six stakes winners. He eventually was moved to Milfer Farm in Unadilla, New York, where he is pampered and treated like a king, just as the racing gods intended. — S. H.

RACE and (STAKES) RECORD

YEAR	AGE	STS	1ST	2ND	3RD	EARNED
1978	at 2	9	7(5)	1(1)	0	$384,484
1979	at 3	12	10(9)	1(1)	1(1)	$1,279,334
1980	at 4	9	9(9)	0	0	$1,117,790
Lifetime		30	26(23)	2(2)	1(1)	$2,781,608

Tom Fool

AS ONE OF THE PRE-EMINENT RACING and breeding establishments in American racing, the Greentree Stable of John Hay Whitney and his sister, Mrs. Charles Payson, was noted for the top-class horses it bred and raced.

Tom Fool, the 1953 Horse of the Year campaigned by Greentree under the guidance of trainer John Gaver, represented a deviation from the nursery's program. Bred in Kentucky by Duval A. Headley at his Manchester Farm and foaled on March 31, 1949, Tom Fool was purchased privately as a yearling by Greentree for $20,000. A half-brother to champion two-year-old filly Aunt Jinny, Tom Fool was a son of Menow, the same sire of Greentree's Horse of the Year Capot, a selling point to Gaver and the Whitneys when Headley offered the colt to them.

The sale almost did not take place after Tom Fool injured himself in a paddock accident, sustaining a one-inch gash in his leg after becoming caught in a fence. Headley called Gaver and told him not to bother inspecting the colt, since it was unlikely Whitney would be interested because of the injury. But Whitney was undeterred.

That purchase price looked a real bargain after Tom Fool retired at the end of 1953 with earnings of $570,165 gleaned from twenty-one victories, seven seconds, and one third in thirty starts. In addition to being accorded racing's highest honor, Tom Fool was champion sprinter in 1953 and earlier honored as champion two-year-old male of 1951. During his best season, Tom Fool became one of racing's all-time top weight carriers.

Tom Fool did not make his first start until the second week of August 1951 at Saratoga. After breaking his maiden by four lengths, Tom Fool won the Sanford Stakes a week later at 4-5 odds. Facing the season's top two-year-old, Cousin, in the Grand Union Hotel Stakes, Tom Fool held off his rival for a one-length triumph. Cousin, who stumbled at the start of the race while conceding four pounds to Tom Fool, avenged the loss a week later when the two carried the same weight of 122 pounds in the Hopeful Stakes.

In a prep for the Futurity, Tom Fool encountered traffic problems in the sixteen-horse

field and finished second, four lengths behind Calumet's Hill Gail, the eventual 1952 Kentucky Derby winner. Five days later, the colt won the Futurity at nearly 6-1 odds as 19-10 favorite Hill Gail was fourth. In his final juvenile start, Tom Fool was all out over a sloppy track at Jamaica Park for a neck victory in the East View Stakes. The difficulty of the race convinced Gaver that Tom Fool had a disdain for sloppy tracks.

While he was at the top of his generation as a juvenile, Tom Fool was inconsistent at three, with a record of six wins and six placings in thirteen starts. Following Gaver's carefully scripted route to the Derby, Tom Fool won an allowance race in his 1952 debut but was caught in the final strides to finish second in the Wood Memorial. Following that upset, Tom Fool was diagnosed with a cough and fever, resulting in a nine and a half-week layoff.

Upon his return, Tom Fool was winless in two starts — a second and a fourth — before getting to the winner's circle when he carried 106 pounds against older horses in the Wilson Stakes at Saratoga. Second in a purse race, Tom Fool conceded twelve pounds to One Count before finishing third in the eventual three-year-old champion's Travers Stakes. After a one-month break from racing, Tom Fool rolled to a seven-length tally over Mark-Ye-Well in the one-mile Jerome. In five additional starts that year, Tom Fool had three wins and two seconds, all in stakes. His additional successes included a victory over older horses while carrying 126 pounds in the one-mile Sysonby Handicap, a game nose victory over

Battlefield (the 1950 champion juvenile male), and a triumph in the Empire City Handicap while carrying 128 pounds over one and three-sixteenths miles. After wintering with the rest of Greentree's stable in Aiken, South Carolina, Tom Fool regained his juvenile form as a four-year-old of 1953, a year in which he was asked to carry some sizable imposts.

Tom Fool started his season with a sprint victory. Next, he carried 130 pounds to win the Joe H. Palmer Handicap and was pointed toward the handicap triple consisting of the Metropolitan, Suburban, and Brooklyn Handicaps. He would pick up weight as the victories mounted.

Four days later, Tom Fool went to post in the Metropolitan, despite the track's being labeled "muddy." By race time, the Belmont oval was rated "good." Tom Fool engaged Royal Vale in a stretch duel that resulted in the Greentree color-bearer, carrying 130 pounds, winning by a half-length in near-record time. Despite the game victory, jockey Ted Atkinson said Tom Fool's running ability "was not quite so good as it would be on a completely dry track, but it was good enough."

A week later, Tom Fool met Royal Vale again in the Suburban, held on Memorial Day. Contested before a Belmont crowd of 42,000 under threatening weather conditions, the Suburban marked the only time in 1953 that Tom Fool was not odds-on, although he was the slight favorite. Giving Royal Vale four pounds (128 to 124), Tom Fool at one point held a three-length lead that diminished as the race grew longer, finally eking out a nose victory after another stretch duel with Royal Vale and running the second-fastest time in Suburban history. "Not that he's ever run a bad race, but today's was his best," Atkinson said. "He was so full of run for the first seven-eighths, he could have beaten all track records. I asked him to run just before we entered the straightaway and he responded."

With six weeks between the second and third legs of the handicap triple, Tom Fool met top sprinters in the seven-furlong Carter Handicap one month after his Metropolitan score. Tom Fool came from off the pace to win by two lengths while carrying 135 pounds. Weighted at 136 pounds and conceding twenty-six to thirty-one pounds to his four opponents in the Brooklyn Handicap, Tom Fool held a four-length advantage at one point before Atkinson backed off for the final one and a half-length margin. The *Daily Racing Form* chart noted Tom Fool "continued on gamely to win with speed in reserve."

In becoming the first winner of the handicap triple since Whisk Broom II in 1913, Tom

			Phalaris, 1913	Polymelus / Bromus
		Pharamond II, 1925		
			Selene, 1919	Chaucer / Serenissima
	MENOW, dk b, 1935			
			Supremus, 1922	Ultimus / Mandy Hamilton
		Alcibiades, 1927		
TOM FOOL, bay colt, 1949			Regal Roman, 1921	Roi Herode / Lady Cicero
			Teddy, 1913	Ajax / Rondeau
		Bull Dog, 1927		
			Plucky Liege, 1912	Spearmint / Concertina
	GAGA, b, 1942			
			Equipoise, 1928	Pennant / Swinging
		Alpoise, 1937		
			Laughing Queen, 1929	Sun Briar / Cleopatra

Fool had no rival as America's top handicapper. That was evident in his final four outings, all weight-for-age tests. None drew more than two other runners and each was contested as a non-betting event. In the Wilson Stakes at one mile, Tom Fool rolled to an eight-length victory over one challenger, Indian Land. Four days later, the champ again faced only one other runner and won the Whitney Handicap by three and a half lengths over Combat Boots.

As Belmont's fall meet began, Tom Fool was assigned a huge 148 pounds in the Fall Highweight Handicap, with the next-highest impost at 135. Atkinson was recovering from injuries sustained in a fall, and Tom Fool did not participate. In an effort to set up a race between Tom Fool and eventual champion three-year-old Native Dancer, the date for the Sysonby Mile was changed and the purse increased from $20,000 to $50,000. Native Dancer was withdrawn due to an injury, and Tom Fool rolled to a three-length victory over Alerted and the filly Grecian Queen as Atkinson eased up on his mount in the stretch.

In his career finale, Tom Fool rolled to an eight-length triumph over two other runners to win the Pimlico Special by eight lengths, getting the one and three-sixteenths miles in track record time of 1:55⅘.

Tom Fool, who stood 15.3 hands at the beginning of his career and grew to 16 hands, entered stud at Greentree in 1954, standing initially for $5,000. While plans to breed him were postponed that first season due to undisclosed problems, Tom Fool went on to a successful stud career. Syndicated by Greentree in 1958, with thirty shares selling for $50,000 each and the farm retaining fifteen, Tom Fool was represented by progeny that earned more than $8 million. He sired thirty-six stakes winners, including Horse of the Year Buckpasser, champion Tim Tam, and foundation broodmare Dinner Partner. Tom Fool also was the sire of the dams of eighty-nine stakes winners, including champions Foolish Pleasure, Late Bloomer, Rash Move, Meadow Court, and Madelia.

Pensioned from breeding in 1972, Tom Fool died on Aug. 20, 1976, and was buried in the Greentree cemetery. He was inducted into the Racing Hall of Fame in 1960, the same year the National Turf Writers Association voted Tom Fool the "horse of the decade." — R. M.

RACE and (STAKES) RECORD

YEAR	AGE	STS	1ST	2ND	3RD	EARNED
1951	at 2	7	5(4)	2(1)	0	$155,960
1952	at 3	13	6(4)	5(3)	1(1)	$157,850
1953	at 4	10	10(8)	0	0	$256,355
Lifetime		30	21(16)	7(4)	1(1)	**$570,165**

Affirmed

HOW HIGH WERE THE STANDARDS for greatness set by Louis Wolfson, who with his wife, Patrice, bred and owned three-time champion Affirmed in the name of their Harbor View Farm?

Minutes after Affirmed defeated his arch rival, Alydar, in the 110th running of the Belmont Stakes to become racing's eleventh Triple Crown winner, Wolfson declined to call the son of Exclusive Native a "great" horse.

"Yes, a great three-year-old, and so is Alydar," Wolfson said. "But I want to see him run at four before I call him great overall."

Fortunately for racing, Wolfson had that chance. Affirmed, a champion at two, was champion three-year-old and Horse of the Year in 1978. The following season, he continued to dominate his opposition, winning grade I races from coast to coast under burdensome weights at classic distances. The Horse of the Year title came his way again, and, by anyone's standards, so did greatness.

Foaled near Ocala, Florida, and produced from the Crafty Admiral mare Won't Tell You, Affirmed made his racing debut at Belmont Park on May 24, 1977, going wire to wire to win a five and a half-furlong maiden special weight race by four and a half lengths.

Trainer Lazaro S. Barrera, who the previous year had taken the Kentucky Derby and Belmont Stakes with Bold Forbes, wheeled Affirmed back three weeks later, in the Youthful Stakes, also at Belmont. He came from off the pace to win by a neck.

Affirmed wasn't favored in the Youthful. That distinction went to a Calumet Farm home-bred colt named Alydar, bet down to 9-5. Alydar never threatened while finishing fifth, but it was the first meeting in what would become one of racing's greatest rivalries.

After Alydar turned the tables on Affirmed in the Great American Stakes at Belmont on July 6, Barrera then sent Affirmed to California, where the chestnut colt won a division of the July 23 Hollywood Juvenile Championship by seven lengths. When he returned to New York for the Aug. 17 Sanford Stakes at Saratoga, Affirmed teamed up for the first time with Steve Cauthen, the sensational young jockey who that year was named Sportsman of the Year by

Sports Illustrated magazine. Affirmed won the Sanford going away.

Ten days later Affirmed resumed his rivalry with Alydar, beating him by a half-length in the Hopeful Stakes at Saratoga. The Futurity Stakes in September was an even tighter duel, with Affirmed and Alydar volleying for the lead the final three furlongs. Affirmed finally thrust his nose in front at the wire in a race that foreshadowed an even greater match over the Belmont oval the following spring.

When Alydar got a measure of revenge on Affirmed in the one-mile Champagne Stakes on Oct. 15, winning by a length and a quarter on a muddy Belmont track, the score was three-to-two, in favor of Affirmed. With the Eclipse Award hanging in the balance, the two colts traveled to Maryland two weeks later for the Laurel Futurity. After another stirring battle, Affirmed triumphed by a neck and received the year-end honors.

Affirmed arrived at Churchill Downs the next spring with a record of eleven wins in thirteen starts, and a four-to-two advantage against Alydar. The fans favored Alydar in the Kentucky Derby at odds of 6-5. Affirmed was the close second choice at 9-5 in a field of eleven three-year-olds going a mile and a quarter for the first time in their lives.

The early pace in the Derby was sizzling, and Cauthen allowed Affirmed to settle more than five lengths back. As the pacesetters faltered, he moved to the lead on the final turn and opened up by two lengths with a furlong remaining. Alydar, meanwhile, had only two horses beat going past the wire for the first time. Jorge Velasquez swung him wide for the stretch run, and the Calumet runner gained ground late but fell a length and a half shy of Affirmed.

The margin was narrower in the Preakness Stakes. Affirmed assumed command before leaving the first turn and controlled a moderate pace. Alydar made another strong run at Affirmed, but fell a neck short at the wire. Then came the Belmont Stakes, which stands out as one of the greatest classic races in history. Frustrated that Alydar was unable to get past Affirmed with his late rallies in the Derby and Preakness, trainer John Veitch switched tactics for the mile and a half Belmont, instructing Velasquez to go after Affirmed early.

As expected, Affirmed secured the early lead in the five-horse field, setting slow fractions

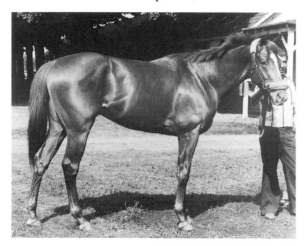

of :25 for the opening quarter-mile and :50 for the half. Alydar ranged up alongside Affirmed in the run down the backstretch, and the pace quickened, the six furlongs in 1:14 and the mile in 1:37⅖. The two warriors were locked on each other around the turn and into the stretch, neither one giving an inch. Affirmed cut the corner with a narrow advantage, but in mid-stretch it appeared that Alydar had him headed.

Cauthen sensed the Triple Crown could be slipping away, and knew he had to try something different to get the last ounce of energy from his mount. He had never used the whip left-handed on Affirmed, and Velasquez had him pinned so tight he was unable to use it in his right hand. Cauthen, who had turned eighteen the week of the Kentucky Derby, went to his left hand with the savvy of a veteran. Affirmed responded, inching away from Alydar and winning by a head.

The second half of 1978 was anticlimactic for Affirmed, who won the Jim Dandy Stakes at Saratoga, then finished first in the Travers Stakes but was disqualified and placed second behind Alydar for causing interference down the backstretch.

With autumn comes new challenges for any top three-year-old, and no challenge was greater than the Marlboro Cup Handicap at Belmont Park, where Affirmed took on Seattle Slew in the first meeting of Triple Crown winners. Affirmed was the odds-on favorite, but Seattle Slew got away to an easy lead and never looked back, winning by three lengths. A second crack at Seattle Slew in the Jockey Club Gold Cup also failed, when Affirmed's saddle slipped and he was beaten nineteen lengths. Exceller nosed out Seattle Slew for the win.

Winter in Southern California began dismally for Cauthen, who was mired in a slump that reached 110 consecutive losses. Two came on Affirmed, and Barrera replaced Cauthen for the Charles H. Strub Stakes in February, giving the call to Laffit Pincay Jr. Affirmed responded with a ten-length victory, the first of seven consecutive triumphs that would

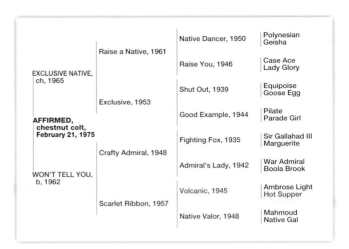

close out Affirmed's brilliant career.

Next came the Santa Anita Handicap. Affirmed carried high weight of 128 pounds and crushed the opposition, winning by four and a half lengths in track-record time of 1:58⅗ for the mile and a quarter. Under the allowance conditions of his next race, the May 20 Californian Stakes at Hollywood Park, Affirmed was forced to carry 130 pounds, but he cruised to the wire with five lengths to spare.

Hollywood Park racing secretary Eual Wyatt Jr. gave the Harbor View Farm runner a 132-pound impost for his next start, the Hollywood Gold Cup Handicap on June 24. Affirmed conceded from twelve to twenty pounds to his nine rivals and turned in perhaps the guttiest performance of his final year of racing. Forced through fast fractions by the Italian champion Sirlad, Affirmed refused to crack, winning by three parts of a length in 1:58⅖, just one-fifth of a second slower than the American record for a mile and a quarter.

After a two-month freshening, Affirmed returned to New York, winning a three-horse exhibition race at Belmont Park. An angry Barrera skipped the Marlboro Cup when Affirmed was assigned 133 pounds, seven more than that year's Kentucky Derby and Preakness winner, Spectacular Bid. A match-up with Spectacular Bid would come in the Jockey Club Gold Cup, also under weight-for-age conditions. Affirmed carried 126 to Spectacular Bid's 121. Bill Shoemaker, riding Spectacular Bid, made several runs at Affirmed throughout the mile and a half Gold Cup, but the Harbor View Farm runner won by three-quarters of a length and sealed his second consecutive Horse of the Year title.

Affirmed retired to Spendthrift Farm (he currently stands at Jonabell Farm, also in Kentucky) as the richest horse in racing history. He won twenty-two of twenty-nine starts, finishing off the board just once, and earned $2,393,818. He became racing's youngest millionaire and its first $2-million earner — records that have since been broken. At stud, Affirmed has been a very good sire, with seventy-one stakes winners from his first seventeen crops to race. Interestingly, his most accomplished runner, Harbor View Farm's Flawlessly, was twice voted an Eclipse Award as outstanding female on turf, a surface that Affirmed never tried.

His election to the Racing Hall of Fame came in 1980. — R. P.

RACE and (STAKES) RECORD

YEAR	AGE	STS	1ST	2ND	3RD	EARNED
1977	at 2	9	7(6)	2(2)	0	$343,477
1978	at 3	11	8(7)	2(2)	0	$901,541
1979	at 4	9	7(6)	1(1)	1(1)	$1,148,800
Lifetime		29	22(19)	5(5)	1(1)	$2,393,818

War Admiral

ONLY ONE SON OF THE IMMORTAL MAN O' WAR approached his sire in greatness — War Admiral. Not only was War Admiral his sire's most successful offspring on the racetrack, being named champion three-year-old and Horse of the Year in 1937, but was Man o' War's best son at stud, siring Horse of the Year Busher and thirty-nine other stakes winners.

Interesting to Turf historians is that War Admiral was bred and owned by Samuel Riddle, who had raced Man o' War. Riddle had considered the one and a quarter miles of the Kentucky Derby too much to ask of a young three-year-old, and had refused to let Man o' War participate in the spring classic.

War Admiral won only one stakes out of six races at two, the Eastern Shore Handicap by five lengths in front-running style. He also finished second in two stakes — the Richard Johnson Handicap at Laurel and the Great American Stakes at Aqueduct — and was third in Pompoon's National Stallion Stakes at Belmont. (Pompoon would become champion two-year-old of that year.) He was away from the races for eleven weeks due to a cough that swept through the East Coast that year.

He was weighted at 121 pounds on the very first Experimental Free Handicap, seventh below Brooklyn, Pompoon, Reaping Reward, Case Ace, Bottle Cap, and Privileged.

In his first two outings at three, War Admiral posted strong victories in an overnight race on April 14 and in the Chesapeake Stakes ten days after that. In the latter, he dashed to the lead and won by an easy six lengths.

Riddle decided the Derby wasn't such a risk after all, and instructed trainer George Conway to enter War Admiral.

The record crowd sent the 15.2-hand brown colt away the favorite in the 1937 Kentucky Derby field of twenty. True to form, jockey Charlie Kurtsinger took War Admiral right to the front from the first post position. War Admiral raced under restraint and was never headed, gradually increasing his lead in the long Churchill Downs stretch to score by one

and three-quarters lengths. Pompoon finished second, eight lengths in front of Reaping Reward. War Admiral's time of 2:03⅕ was the second-fastest recorded in the Derby to that date. (The record had been set by Twenty Grand under Kurtsinger six years earlier.)

In the Preakness a week later, War Admiral again drew the No. 1 post position and again was sent away the overwhelming favorite in the field of eight. War Admiral was known for his antics at the starting gate, and in the Preakness, he held true to form. Nevertheless, he broke well and was sent right to the front. War Admiral had a length on his nearest rival for the first mile, but in the stretch turn, Pompoon ranged up inside and hooked up with the leader. The two fought a furious battle down the stretch, eight lengths in front of their nearest rival. The comparison of the two rides showed both ends of the spectrum — Pompoon's rider was whipping his mount furiously in an effort to draw ahead, while Kurtsinger sat chilly and never touched his colt.

War Admiral won by a head. Time for the Preakness was only two ticks off the track record on a surface labeled good.

In the Belmont, the stakes were high as War Admiral attempted to accomplish the feat his sire was denied — sweep the Triple Crown. Perhaps because of his nature, or perhaps because he sensed the heightened tension of those around him, War Admiral was worse than ever at the start of the Belmont. He held up the start of the final leg of the Triple

Crown for eight minutes, dragging an unfortunate assistant starter through the starting gate several times before he could be contained.

Perhaps because of his wrought-up state, War Admiral stumbled when the gate flew open to release him. Worse, he grabbed a quarter when his hind foot slashed an inch-square chunk out of his right forefoot. As he scrambled to gather himself and race for the lead, War Admiral splattered blood over his belly and legs from his injury. Having expended a tremendous amount of energy before the race, and suffering from a horrific gash in his foot, War Admiral had every excuse to spit the bit and not run at all. Instead, he ran the race of his life.

War Admiral fought his way to the lead, and he still was three lengths in front at the end of the one and a half-mile race. He stopped the timer in 2:28⅗, which not only broke the Belmont track record set by his sire seventeen years earlier, but equaled the American record for the distance.

War Admiral was kept away from the races until the fall to allow his foot to heal. He raced three more times that year, scoring in the Washington Handicap and Pimlico Special while giving weight to good horses in both races. The Triple Crown winner was awarded Horse of the Year honors and named champion three-year-old. Riddle turned down an offer of $250,000 for the diminutive colt — a price that was considered astronomical at the time.

At four, War Admiral continued his form, both before and in his races. He took a seven-furlong overnight race in Florida on Feb. 19, and two weeks later was assigned top weight of 130 pounds in the Widener Handicap, conceding from thirteen to twenty-nine pounds to his dozen rivals. He refused to be loaded into the starting gate and finally was sent away from outside the gate. He galloped home one and a half lengths in front.

A $100,000, winner-take-all match race with Seabiscuit was proposed, but Seabiscuit was withdrawn shortly before the planned match at Belmont on Memorial Day. So, Conway entered the colt in the mile Queens County Handicap, which War Admiral easily won for his eleventh consecutive victory.

Some three weeks later, War Admiral suffered a stunning upset. While carrying 130 pounds, he finished fourth to Menow (under 107 pounds) in the one and an eighth-mile Massachusetts Handicap.

At Saratoga a month later, War Admiral took his usual early lead and romped to an eight-

		Hastings, 1893	Spendthrift / Cinderella
	Fair Play, 1905		
MAN O' WAR, ch, 1917		Fairy Gold, 1896	Bend Or / Dame Masham
		Rock Sand, 1900	Sainfoin / Roquebrune
	Mahubah, 1910		
WAR ADMIRAL, brown colt, 1934		Merry Token, 1891	Merry Hampton / Mizpah
		Ben Brush, 1893	Bramble / Roseville
	Sweep, 1907		
BRUSHUP, b, 1929		Pink Domino, 1897	Domino / Belle Rose
		Harry of Hereford, 1910	John o' Gaunt / Canterbury Pilgrim
	Annette K., 1921		
		Bathing Girl, 1915	Spearmint / Summer Girl

length victory in the mile Wilson Stakes, then took the one and a quarter-mile Saratoga Handicap and Whitney Stakes, and scored in the one and three-quarters-mile Saratoga Cup, all in front-running fashion. He rounded out his skein with a score in the two-mile Jockey Club Gold Cup.

Rumor had it that War Admiral would meet Seabiscuit, at last, in the Pimlico Special on Nov. 1.

War Admiral probably lost the Horse of the Year title for a second consecutive year when he lost to Seabiscuit in the one and three-sixteenths-mile Pimlico Special. In that race, five-year-old Seabiscuit was uncharacteristically booted away from the gate to an early lead. War Admiral fought gamely to range alongside Seabiscuit by the half-mile pole, racing to the outside of his rival. Seabiscuit, however, was able to draw away slowly and score by four lengths in track-record time.

War Admiral finished the year with a score in the Rhode Island Handicap.

War Admiral won his only race at five, being forced to miss the Widener because of a fever. He then was retired in May after injuring his ankle. The horse was sent to Riddle's Faraway Farm in Kentucky to enter stud.

War Admiral's female line was not distinguished. His dam, Brushup, earned $300 while a non-winner in three starts. His second dam, Annette K., was unplaced in one start. His third dam, Bathing Girl, was unraced. However, the cross of Man o' War and the Sweep mare Brushup did bring together three great male lines: Fair Play through Man o' War, and Ben Brush and Domino through Sweep.

War Admiral was the leading sire of 1945, the year his daughter Busher earned Horse of the Year honors. Eleven times during his career he ranked in the top twenty sires. He was leading sire of two-year-olds in 1948 and leading broodmare sire in 1962 and 1964.

In addition to Busher, he sired thirty-nine other stakes winners, including Busanda, Blue Peter, Searching, and Mr. Busher. War Admiral also was the sire of the dams of 113 stakes winners and eight champions.

The great War Admiral died in 1959 at the advanced age of twenty-five. He was buried next to Man o' War and Brushup at Faraway Farm. — *K. H.*

RACE and (STAKES) RECORD

YEAR	AGE	STS	1ST	2ND	3RD	EARNED
1936	at 2	6	3(1)	2(2)	1(1)	$14,800
1937	at 3	8	8(6)	0	0	$166,500
1938	at 4	11	9(8)	1(1)	0	$90,840
1939	at 5	1	1	0	0	$1,100
Lifetime		26	21(15)	3(3)	1(1)	$273,240

Buckpasser

BUCKPASSER WAS A CHAMPION in looks, in pedigree, and in racing ability, but like many champions, he had a mind of his own. One Turf writer of the time said after watching two or three races, there was no doubt that Buckpasser could run, but there always remained some doubt if Buckpasser *would* run, especially if there were no competition and no cheering fans. He was called an "impossible" work horse.

He was not interested in exerting himself unnecessarily, and rarely would if there were nothing to beat. A stablemate had to be sent out with him in the mornings to get any conditioning into him, and that didn't always work. While at Rockingham Park, training for the rich New Hampshire Sweepstakes at two, his final prep workout was so unsatisfactory that his breeder-owner Ogden Phipps and trainer W. C. (Bill) Winfrey declared him out of a race in which he would have been sent away 1-5.

In twenty-five career victories, Buckpasser's average win margin was one and one-third lengths. Thirteen of his wins came by margins of less than a length, and he once finished in a dead heat. His riders had to time his run perfectly because if Buckpasser got to the lead before the race was over, he pulled himself up. That was true whether he was running against other champions of his time, or against ordinary runners. However, he proved himself to be a fierce competitor. Twice — in the Flamingo as a three-year-old and in the Suburban at four — he seemed beaten with only twenty yards to go, yet managed to surge to victory in the final strides through pure determination and power.

Buckpasser was part of an exceptional crop of two-year-olds, and even though he was unanimously named champion juvenile colt of 1965, some doubted that he was the best that year. But his championship form continued as he was named Horse of the Year at three, when he set a world mark for the mile, and continued to compete as one of the best older horses at four.

The impeccably bred son of Tom Fool, out of the War Admiral mare Busanda, finished an inauspicious fourth in his debut. Two weeks later, Buckpasser broke his maiden by run-

ning five-eighths in a minute flat, then took an overnighter as a prep for the National Stallion Stakes. In that race, he came from nine lengths out of it to catch pacesetter Hospitality on the wire, finishing in a dead heat.

The following week in the Tremont Stakes, Buckpasser came from last to beat Spring Double by a neck, with Hospitality third. In his prep for the Sapling Stakes, Buckpasser won by seven lengths. He must have considered that margin wasteful, for he never again drew off for a victory. The Sapling, however, was the first race that showed Buckpasser was not just another good runner, but something special.

Buckpasser was left at the gate in the Sapling, giving the field five lengths at the start. He wore down horses relentlessly, overtaking pacesetter and favorite Our Michael to win by a half-length.

He then scored in the Hopeful before being shipped to Chicago for the Arlington-Washington Futurity. He almost lost that one after he pulled himself up with a four-length lead at the eighth pole, and just managed to hold off Fathers Image by a half-length.

Two weeks later, the Futurity victory was already considered to be Buckpasser's before the gates were sprung. A filly named Priceless Gem, a half-sister to champion Affectionately, would not give up when Buckpasser ranged up beside her leaving the back-stretch. Buckpasser got within a neck of victory, but could not (or would not) go by the filly, who won by a half-length. He didn't let that chivalrous moment last, however, for in his next race he charged through to win the mile Champagne Stakes by four lengths as Priceless Gem finished seventh. The purse from that rich race pushed Buckpasser's seasonal earnings to a record $568,096.

Winfrey resigned as trainer for the Phipps stable at that point, and Buckpasser was turned over to another conditioner who was to go on to greatness. Eddie Neloy that year established a new money record for trainers when he saddled the earners of $2,456,250. Buckpasser lost his first outing at three, a betless exhibition in which stablemate Impressive took the victory. That also was the first race that Bill Shoemaker rode Buckpasser.

The Phipps runner scored easily in the Everglades, and in the Flamingo, he was such a favorite that the betting windows were shut even though there were eight other horses in the race. Buckpasser got the lead at the three-sixteenths pole, then pulled himself up. In a heart-stopping finish, Abe's Hope rushed past and took a two-length lead at the sixteenth pole. Shoemaker rallied his mount and with an incredible closing rush, Buckpasser won by a nose.

Buckpasser missed the classics when two weeks after the Flamingo he suffered a quarter crack on the inside of his right front hoof. Infection set in, and Buckpasser was away from the races for three months. He made his comeback on the day Kauai King failed in his Triple Crown bid (Amberoid won the Belmont Stakes). On that day, Buckpasser won a six-furlong race against older horses in the fastest six furlongs run at that New York meeting. Two weeks later, Buckpasser won the Leonard Richards Stakes.

That set Buckpasser up to run a mighty race in the Arlington Classic. Kauai King was assigned top weight of 126, with Buckpasser at 125 and Creme dela Creme toting 123. Buckpasser's stablemate Impressive blazed away on the lead, setting fractions of :22⅕, :43⅗, and three-quarters in 1:06⅘. Buckpasser was next to last under Braulio Baeza until the final turn. At that point, the rider set the horse down for his run on the outside. Kauai King broke down in the race, but Buckpasser surged ahead to beat Creme dela Creme by one and three-quarter lengths. The time for the mile — 1:32⅗ — was a new world record.

		Pharamond II, 1925	Phalaris / Selene
	Menow, 1935		
TOM FOOL, b, 1949		Alcibiades, 1927	Supremus / Regal Roman
		Bull Dog, 1927	**Teddy** / Plucky Liege
BUCKPASSER, bay colt, April 28, 1963	Gaga, 1942		
		Alpoise, 1937	Equipoise / Laughing Queen
		Man o' War, 1917	Fair Play / Mahubah
	War Admiral, 1934		
BUSANDA, blk, 1947		Brushup, 1929	Sweep / Annette K.
		Blue Larkspur, 1926	Black Servant / Blossom Time
	Businesslike, 1939		
		La Troienne, 1926	**Teddy** / Helene de Troie

To finish out his three-year-old season, Buckpasser won the Chicagoan, Brooklyn, set a track record of 1:47 for one and an eighth miles in the American Derby, and equaled a twenty-year-old track record in taking the Travers. His prowess extended to the distances, beating all comers in the one and a quarter mile Woodward, one and five-eighths mile Lawrence Realization, and two-mile Jockey Club Gold Cup. He finished his three-year-old campaign (and really started his four-year-old one) with a win in the Dec. 31 Malibu Stakes.

While not named champion at four, Buckpasser was one of the top older runners of the year. His first victory of 1967 came in the San Fernando in preparation for the Charles H. Strub Stakes. A week before the Strub, Buckpasser again suffered a quarter crack in his right front foot. He did not race again for four and a half months. While the foot was healing, thoughts turned to shipping Buckpasser to France for the Grand Prix de Saint-Cloud on grass in July. So, after he healed, he was tried on grass in the one and five-eighths mile Bowling Green Handicap. Packing 135 pounds, he finished third to Poker and Assagai. The decision was made to stay home.

In perhaps his most spectacular finish, Buckpasser won the Suburban by a half-length. He carried top weight of 133 pounds, giving Widener winner Ring Twice twenty-two pounds and a two-length lead eighty yards from the finish. In typical fashion, Buckpasser came charging at the end for the victory. It was his last career win.

Buckpasser tried to take the Brooklyn for the second time, but failed to close and was second by eight lengths to Handsome Boy. In his last race, the memorable 1967 Woodward Stakes, Buckpasser could not beat champion Damascus and was beaten ten lengths by that rival, with Dr. Fager third.

The champion was syndicated for a record $4.8 million and retired to Claiborne Farm with career earnings of $1,462,014. Buckpasser sired thirty-six stakes winners, including champions La Prevoyante, Numbered Account, and Relaxing. He was the broodmare sire of 142 stakes winners, including eleven champions. Buckpasser died in 1978. — *K. H.*

RACE and (STAKES) RECORD						
YEAR	AGE	STS	1ST	2ND	3RD	EARNED
1965	at 2	11	9(6)	1(1)	0	$568,096
1966	at 3	14	13(12)	1	0	$669,078
1967	at 4	6	3(3)	2(2)	1(1)	$224,840
Lifetime		31	25(21)	4(3)	1(1)	$1,462,014

Colin

DISTANCE IN TIME, with its hazy distinctions between fact and legend, lends several rather bizarre elements to the oft-told tale of Colin. Among these was the possibility that he won the Belmont Stakes on a bowed tendon, and that he was raced once more because his arrogant owner sought to prove his star could fill the stands even in the absence of betting. More factually proven, but still slightly bizarre, was the aftermath in which a stallion of limited fertility managed to found a sire line that continues nearly a century later.

From the standpoint of expected realities of the Turf, however, the most bizarre aspect of Colin's career may be the one least in doubt: He was that least expected of phenomena, i.e., an undefeated racehorse!

Colin was bred and raced by James R. Keene, the London-born, American will o' the wisp of finance. Keene attained, lost, and re-built fortunes on Wall Street and, when times permitted, indulged his interest in breeding and racing a series of the world's best Thoroughbreds. This interest was apparently lacking in sentimental connection to the animal itself, for he was said to have visited his wonderful Castleton Stud in Kentucky only twice during the nineteen years he owned it.

Keene was lucky as well as efficient. He initially disliked Colin's prospects because of a curb, or thoroughpin, on a hock. This was consistent with his earlier judgment of the colt's grandsire, with whom he was so unimpressed that he would not have acquired him but for the action of son Foxhall Keene bidding on the colt. Named Domino, this one became a champion and a legend in his own time.

Colin was foaled in 1905 and was by Domino's son Commando and out of the English mare Pastorella, by Springfield. The mare had won the Zetland and Ascot Biennial Stakes at two. Colin was her only stakes winner from eleven named foals.

Keene's friend, De Courcey Forbes, routinely named the Castleton foals. Connecting the names of the mare, Pastorella, and Keene's trainer, James Rowe Sr., Forbes invoked a

pastoral poem about Poor Colin, written by English poet laureate Nicholas Rowe.

Colin won all his dozen races at two and added three more at three. He was sent to England with a view of resuming racing at four, but went wrong and was retired with fifteen wins in fifteen starts.

A seeming anomaly about Colin's reputation is that he often was cited as one of the commonly selected greatest horses by generations of horsemen intimate with the first half of the century. Sysonby, Man o' War, and Citation are frequently regarded as the others most commonly named at the highest planes.

What is curious about this status in Colin's case is that it was conferred by horsemen from eras when stamina and maturity were prized above early excellence, perhaps even more so than today. Colin had but three races after his juvenile season, and while he won all three he was not dominant in each. One is left to assume that the impression he left at two was such that it took but a few races afterward to ratify his suggested greatness.

Trainer Rowe brought Colin out at two in late May, and he raced away from twenty-two rivals in one of the breathtaking dashes accommodated by the old straight course angling across the Belmont Park oval. Next he set a record on this track of :58 for five fur-longs in the National Stallion Stakes.

In his third start, Colin was said to have bucked his shins, a common rite of passage. One of the rich races of the time, the $25,000 Great Trial Stakes, loomed just twenty-four days later, and Rowe had him back in time. Colin won without being extended.

The remainder of his campaign solidified his position. While he did come from slight-ly off the pace a time or two, he left such an impression of superiority that his image was later garnished unnecessarily by the claim that he was never headed in any race. His tri-umphs included the Brighton Junior, Saratoga Special, Grand Union Hotel, Futurity, and Matron. In the Matron, which only later became a filly race, Colin carried 129 pounds and won by four lengths while giving seven to runner-up Fair Play.

Colin's record of twelve wins in twelve starts at two in 1907 became a reference point sixty-five years later when the juvenile filly La Prevoyante duplicated those numbers.

Under the landscape of the time, the champion was pointed primarily for the Belmont Stakes as his major spring objective. To prep, he was entered in the one-mile Withers Stakes, which he won easily in his return. Two very nice colts, Fair Play and King James, tried him, but could not get closer than two lengths away.

The Belmont Stakes was run in natural fog and has been surrounded by fog of anoth-er kind ever since. Supposedly, Colin had suffered an injury, reported variously as being a pair of bowed tendons, one slight bow, or an unspecified soreness. Rowe and Keene appar-

				Alarm
			Himyar, 1875	Hira
		Domino, 1891		
			Mannie Gray, 1874	Enquirer
	COMMANDO,			Lizzie G.
	b, 1898		Darebin, 1878	The Peer
				Lurline
		Emma C., 1892		
COLIN,			Guenn, 1883	Flood
brown colt,				Glendew
1905			St. Albans, 1857	Stockwell
				Bribery
		Springfield, 1873		
			Viridis, 1864	Marsyas
	PASTORELLA (GB),			Maid of Palmyra
	ch, 1892		Strathconan, 1863	Newminster
				Souvenir
		Griselda, 1878		
			Perseverance, 1865	Voltigeur
				Spinster

ently had decided he could not make the Belmont, but, under procedures of the day, they decided late to make him an added starter.

In heavy going, over one and three-eighths miles, under 126 pounds, Colin thus was sent out to defend his unbeaten status as best he could against Fair Play, King James, and Robert Cooper. Chart callers were silent as to the first portions of the race as they peered through rain and fog, and no time was recorded for the event. In the final quarter-mile, the field finally came within view. Colin had a five-length lead, but it dwindled in the face of furious rally by Fair Play. It was the reverse of the 1998 Belmont, for Colin (the Real Quiet) just held off Fair Play (Victory Gallop) to win by a short head.

An interpretation immediately promulgated was that Colin's jockey, Joe Notter, had misjudged the placement of the finish and eased up, nearly blowing the race and the unbeaten record. Notter insisted that he knew Fair Play was coming and tried to shake up Colin, but the colt was laboring. Given the distance, condition, weight — and with an ill-defined bit of lameness in the mix — Notter's explanation is certainly plausible.

About that time, a shuffle of New York law rendered betting on races a crime. Keene had Colin run, despite the colt's injury, in the one and a quarter-mile Tidal Stakes some three weeks later. He boasted that Colin would attract a capacity crowd at Sheepshead Bay for a betless exhibition. He was wrong by about half a crowd, but Colin did win, preserving his unbeaten status. He had won fifteen of fifteen and earned $178,110.

Because he was in England when next injured, Colin initially stood abroad. He later was returned to America after Keene's death. While his rival Fair Play became a major stallion and sired the great Man o' War, Colin sired only eighty-one foals in twenty-three crops. Nevertheless, Colin sired eleven stakes winners. His link in the Domino sire line survived and in recent decades has been represented by Ack Ack, Youth, Teenoso, leading sire Broad Brush, and 1994 Breeders' Cup Classic winner Concern. Colin also was the broodmare sire of twenty stakes winners, including 1935 champion handicap mare Late Date. Colin died at twenty-seven in 1932 at Capt. Raymond Belmont's Belray Farm in Virginia.

— E. L. B.

RACE and (STAKES) RECORD

YEAR	AGE	STS	1ST	2ND	3RD	EARNED
1907	at 2	12	12(11)	0	0	$129,205
1908	at 3	3	3(3)			$48,905
Lifetime		15	15(14)	0	0	$178,110

Damascus

DAMASCUS WON THE RACE that many Turf historians and racing fans consider the Race of the Century. The 1967 Woodward Stakes brought together three of the era's superstars, and Damascus defeated Dr. Fager and Buckpasser, clinching Horse of the Year honors in the process.

The Woodward's status as the century's best race is reflected in the fact that Damascus, Dr. Fager, and Buckpasser are ranked in the top sixteen horses of the 20th Century. There wasn't another race this century in which three horses of that ranking competed against each other. As good as the race looked on paper, it looked better at the end, with three-year-old Damascus putting plenty of distance between himself and his rivals through the stretch. Under Bill Shoemaker, Damascus crushed the field by ten lengths before a crowd of 55,259 for his fifth consecutive stakes victory. The older Buckpasser finished second, a half-length in front of three-year-old Dr. Fager, with Handsome Boy, Hedevar, and Great Power farther back.

Those in the Buckpasser camp felt that the colt's problem foot hurt his chances. Those in the Dr. Fager camp thought the result inconclusive because of the use of Damascus' stablemate Hedevar in softening up their hero in the early going. Years later, Damascus' Hall of Fame trainer Frank Whiteley Jr. said, "I got more kick out of that, I guess, than any other race I ever did win."

Damascus next won the Jockey Club Gold Cup at two miles, thus emulating his sire, Sword Dancer, in winning both the Woodward and Jockey Club Gold Cup in the same year. Whiteley then tried Damascus in the nation's premier turf event, the Washington, D.C., International at Laurel on Armistice Day. It was Damascus' first grass start, and he came within a nose of beating subsequent grass champion Fort Marcy. The International was his last start of 1967, and his tally sheet showed a dozen wins from sixteen starts, with victories in the Preakness and Belmont Stakes highlighting his spring campaign.

Damascus earned a slew of honors that year and praise for his versatility and iron-horse ability from prominent Turf historian Charles Hatton.

"He danced all the dances and ran all the distances from a mile to two miles," Hatton wrote in the *American Racing Manual*. "Never did we see him spit out the bit, as the homely expression goes, and he was confronted with such defiant tasks as carrying topweight of 128 pounds in the Dwyer, giving Ring Twice and Straight Deal actual weight in the Aqueduct, and running smooth-shod in unaccustomed going in the grassy Laurel International. Fort Marcy won the money that day, but Damascus won the crowd's heart."

Damascus was named Horse of the Year and champion three-year-old colt, and he shared champion handicap male honors with Buckpasser. The voting at that time was conducted by members of several organizations, including representatives of *Daily Racing Form* and Morning *Telegraph*. The *Form* and *Telegraph* in their combined poll awarded Damascus four championships. They gave Damascus all forty votes for both Horse of the Year and best three-year-old regardless of gender. They also named Damascus the top three-year-old male and top handicap male, and voted him the third-best grass performer.

Damascus also set an earnings record, breaking Nashua's mark set in 1955. Damascus' earnings of $817,941 for the year were the most earned by a horse in a single season until Secretariat came along several years later. On *The Blood-Horse* Free Handicap for three-year-old males of 1967, Damascus was weighted at 133 pounds, four pounds above Dr. Fager.

Although he won the race that counted most for Horse of the Year honors, Damascus lost a big one that many thought he would have won if he had been himself that afternoon. The humid weather and noise on Kentucky Derby Day contributed to Damascus' third-place finish as the favorite at Churchill Downs the first Saturday in May. Whiteley got Damascus a stable pony, hoping that the little fella might help Damascus relax on the way to the post. Damascus was his old self and favored for the Preakness, and his trademark burst of speed that carried him from seventh to first around the far turn was too much for Derby winner Proud Clarion and eight others at Pimlico.

Damascus next won the Belmont Stakes as the 4-5 favorite over a field that included

Proud Clarion, and the "What if?" question soon started. Damascus would have been racing's first Triple Crown winner since Citation in 1948 and would have stolen much of the thunder that accompanied Secretariat's Triple Crown in 1973.

The Belmont win also focused attention on Damascus' owner-breeder, Mrs. Thomas Bancroft, whose father, William Woodward Sr., won five Belmonts in the 1930s. (The Woodward Stakes was named in his honor.) Mrs. Bancroft's brother, William Woodward Jr., won the 1955 Belmont with Nashua in the family's silks of white with red dots. For jockey Bill Shoemaker, Damascus' Belmont win brought back memories of his 1959 Belmont victory aboard Damascus' sire, Sword Dancer.

Following the Belmont, Damascus won the Leonard Richards, then ran second in the William du Pont Jr. Handicap before reeling off wins in the Dwyer Handicap, American Derby, Travers Stakes, and Aqueduct Stakes prior to the Woodward. His victory in the Travers at one and a quarter miles proved historic in itself. Some fifteen lengths behind after the first half-mile, Damascus stormed home by twenty-two lengths, equaling the track record of 2:01⅗ shared by Buckpasser.

Damascus took his act to California for the winter of 1968, winning the Malibu and San Fernando Stakes and running second in the Charles H. Strub Stakes. He was named the top older horse and sprinter at the Santa Anita winter meeting. Dr. Fager also spent time in California, and the expected matchup between the two stars upon their return East was awaited eagerly. The racing world, it seemed, was divided into Damascus fans or Dr. Fager fans.

Dr. Fager fans celebrated first, as their hero equaled the one and a quarter-mile track

SWORD DANCER, ch, 1956	Sunglow, 1947	Sun Again, 1939	Sun Teddy / Hug Again
		Rosern, 1927	Mad Hatter / Rosedrop
	Highland Fling, 1950	By Jimminy, 1941	Pharamond II / Buginarug
		Swing Time, 1935	Royal Minstrel / Speed Boat
KERALA, b, 1958	My Babu, 1945	Djebel, 1937	Tourbillon / Loika
		Perfume II, 1938	Badruddin / Lavendula
	Blade of Time, 1938	Sickle, 1924	Phalaris / Selene
		Bar Nothing, 1933	Blue Larkspur / Beaming Beauty

DAMASCUS, bay colt, April 14, 1964

mark of 1:59⅗ in the Suburban Handicap while in receipt of a pound from 133-pound topweight Damascus, who ran third. Two weeks later, Damascus lowered the track record to 1:59⅕ in winning the Brooklyn Handicap while in receipt of five pounds from 135-pound topweight Dr. Fager. Damascus, who had run third in the Amory L. Haskell Handicap between the two encounters with Dr. Fager, became racing's eighth millionaire in winning the Brooklyn.

Following the Brooklyn, Damascus then took the William du Pont Jr. Handicap and Aqueduct Stakes under 134 pounds and ran second in the Michigan Mile and One-Eighth Handicap and Woodward Stakes. In what would be his final start, Damascus bowed a tendon in the Jockey Club Gold Cup and came home last in what was his only off-the-board finish. Damascus, whose lone stakes win as a two-year-old had come in the Remsen Stakes, was retired with twenty-one wins from thirty-two races and earnings of $1,176,781.

Damascus entered stud at Arthur B. (Bull) Hancock Jr.'s Claiborne Farm near Paris, Kentucky, in 1969. Hancock had bought Damascus' dam, Kerala (by My Babu), for Mrs. Bancroft for $9,600 at the 1959 Keeneland July yearling sale. Damascus, who was foaled at John A. Bell III's Jonabell Farm near Lexington, was syndicated into thirty-two shares at $80,000 per share, the total package coming to $2,560,000.

Damascus, who was elected to the Racing Hall of Fame in 1974, revitalized the Teddy male line and provided a prominent outcross for stallions and mares with Northern Dancer, Raise a Native, or Nasrullah blood. His seventy-one stakes winners include successful stallions Private Account, Time for a Change, Timeless Moment, Ogygian, Zen, and Crusader Sword.

Private Account, who is pensioned at Claiborne, is represented by unbeaten champion Personal Ensign among his fifty-nine stakes winners. Time for a Change sired champion Fly So Free, and Timeless Moment sired champion Gilded Time, who also has developed into a fine stallion. Damascus' daughters have produced more than 125 stakes winners.

Damascus died of natural causes at age thirty-one in his paddock on Aug. 8, 1995, at Claiborne. He had been pensioned in March of 1989 because of infertility stemming from his advanced age. He was buried at the nursery. — D. S.

RACE and (STAKES) RECORD

YEAR	AGE	STS	1ST	2ND	3RD	EARNED
1966	at 2	4	3(1)	1	0	$25,865
1967	at 3	16	12(11)	3(3)	1(1)	$817,941
1968	at 4	12	6(5)	3(3)	2(2)	$332,975
Lifetime		32	21(17)	7(6)	3(3)	$1,176,781

Round Table

ROUND TABLE WAS A HORSE OF THE YEAR, handicap champion, grass champion three successive years, and the all-time leading money earner at the time of his retirement. He was a marvel of consistency, a weight-bearer of the old school, and part of the traveling troupe of his era. Round Table was all of these things. Not only that, he literally saved the farm. The sale of a majority interest in the Claiborne Farm colt to Travis M. Kerr early in his three-year-old season "more or less held the farm together, paid the estate taxes, and so on," said A. B. (Bull) Hancock after the death of his father, A. B. Hancock Sr.

Round Table's success prompted Hancock to figure out a way to have the best of both worlds — annual cash income and a piece of the breeding action. From that time of hardship bloomed an idea that for years brought success to the Paris, Kentucky farm. Hancock decided to sell a half-interest in his entire foal crop each year, with Claiborne later sharing the breeding qualities of the animals with its racing partners.

The majority interest in Round Table was sold to Kerr for $145,000 on Feb. 9, 1957, with Hancock retaining twenty percent interest in the horse's future breeding qualities (probably worth about $500,000). It was in Kerr's colors that the champion raced from that date forward. The smallish son of Princequillo—Knight's Daughter, by Sir Cosmo, had won the Breeders' Futurity, Lafayette Stakes, and three other races as a two-year-old for Claiborne.

Kerr's trainer, William Molter, took over the colt's education in 1957. On the day of the sale, Round Table finished sixth in a seven-horse field as Iron Liege won an allowance race in record time. In his next outing, the Kerr runner won by six lengths in an allowance race.

Round Table was sent to California, where he was supplemented for the Santa Anita Derby and beaten a head and a nose. In the San Bernardino (on an off track), Round Table finished fifth. He then took the Bay Meadows Derby the first Saturday in April, and Kerr wanted to go to Churchill Downs the first Saturday in May. Molter didn't think much of the colt's chances, but he had been wrong three years earlier when Andrew Crevolin had

wanted to send Determine to the Derby, and that colt won. So, Round Table was shipped to Keeneland, where he romped by six lengths in track-record time winning the Blue Grass Stakes. In the Derby, he finished a credible third, three lengths behind Iron Liege and Gallant Man and an equal distance ahead of Bold Ruler.

Molter took the colt back to California. Against top older horses, Round Table finished second in the Californian Stakes, his last loss for eleven consecutive races. Round Table won five stakes at Hollywood Park, including the Hollywood Gold Cup. Against tough veterans in the Gold Cup, he raced ten furlongs in 1:58⅗, matching Swaps' track record and claiming the fastest time for the distance ever recorded by a three-year-old.

Round Table was given a prep race in Chicago before the American Derby. He won both easily. In fact, in the American Derby on turf, he finished four lengths clear of Derby winner Iron Liege. That race gave just a hint of Round Table's turf prowess. He next won the United Nations Handicap on grass, then took an exhibition prep race prior to winning the Hawthorne Gold Cup

While Round Table had been running off his eleven-race win skein, Gallant Man and

Bold Ruler had been terrorizing all comers in their parts of the world. The three met in the one and a quarter-mile Trenton Handicap at Garden State Park. The legendary Bill Shoemaker regularly rode Round Table, but he chose to take the mount on Gallant Man in the Trenton. Bill Harmatz chose Round Table, who was hindered by a heavy track and never threatened. Shoemaker, afraid to make Gallant Man match early speed with Bold Ruler, did not challenge early. Therefore, Eddie Arcaro and Bold Ruler turned the race into a runaway and took the victory, and co-Horse of the Year honors.

Molter decided to give Round Table one last outing at three. The colt took the Dec. 28 Malibu Sequel Stakes at Santa Anita under 130 pounds. That victory, his fifteenth in twenty-two starts in 1957, raised his three-year-old earnings to $600,383. That amount was topped only by Nashua and Citation in a single year.

At four, Round Table was handicap champion on dirt and turf, and Horse of the Year. He won fourteen of twenty starts, setting five records at four tracks and matching two others. At Santa Anita, he won the San Fernando and Santa Anita Maturity. Then under 130 pounds he matched the world record of 1:46⅕ in the nine-furlong San Antonio. In the Santa Anita Handicap, Round Table won by two and a half lengths and pushed the one and a quarter-mile track record to 1:59⅖.

Molter shipped the colt to Florida to win a prep race and the Gulfstream Park Handicap, where he matched Coaltown's ten-furlong track mark of 1:59⅕.

Kerr sought for Round Table to pass the $1-million mark as a four-year-old, then surpass Nashua as the world's leading earner. After the Gulfstream victories, Round Table was less than $30,000 away from the first goal. Caliente put together a $50,000 pot to revive the Caliente Handicap and give the colt his shot at going over the mark. Round Table obliged. At that point, Round Table had won his first seven races of 1958, and an incredible nineteen of his last twenty starts over two years. He then lost to Seaneen in the Californian.

At Hollywood Park, Round Table toted 132 pounds for the Argonaut Handicap and struggled to win. He then shipped back to Chicago, and won four of seven races. Round Table got past Nashua's earnings record when defeating Swoon's Son in the Hawthorne Gold Cup.

At five, Round Table won nine of his fourteen outings. He carried 132 pounds eight times that year, and twice carried more. Round Table won six times under 132 pounds and once under 136.

		Rose Prince, 1919	Prince Palatine / Eglantine
	Prince Rose, 1928		
PRINCEQUILLO (GB), b, 1940		Indolence, 1920	Gay Crusader / Barrier
		Papyrus, 1920	Tracery / Miss Matty
	Cosquilla, 1933		
ROUND TABLE, bay colt, April 6, 1954		Quick Thought, 1918	White Eagle / Mindful
		The Boss, 1910	Orby / Southern Cross II
	Sir Cosmo, 1926		
KNIGHT'S DAUGHTER (GB), b, 1941		Ayn Hali, 1913	Desmond / Lalla Rookh
		Friar Marcus, 1912	Cicero / Prim Nun
	Feola, 1933		
		Aloe, 1926	Son-in-Law / Alope

In the first week of 1959, Hillsdale beat Round Table by a head while receiving seventeen pounds in the San Carlos. Round Table next led all the way to win the San Marcos by five. In that one and a quarter-mile grass race under 132 pounds, Round Table was clocked in 1:58⅖, the fastest time ever at that distance on grass, and only one-fifth of a second slower than the world record. That score earned Round Table 134 pounds for the Washington's Birthday Handicap, but he fell out of contention and finished last of sixteen. A quarter crack was found and he did not race again for almost four months.

Molter trained Round Table up to the Citation Handicap, and the horse carried 130 pounds to a neck score. He then won an overnight race, and carried 132 pounds to a course-record time of 1:47⅕ for nine furlongs on grass in Washington Park's Stars and Stripes Handicap. He lost the Equipoise Mile over an off track, then won the Clem McCarthy and the Arlington Handicap (setting an American grass record of 1:53⅖ for one and three-sixteenths miles). He won the Washington Park Handicap in track-record time.

In the Woodward at the new Aqueduct, Round Table forced Hillsdale's pace, but fell back and was a well-beaten third as Sword Dancer won by a head. Round Table trounced Bald Eagle under 132 pounds in the one and five-eighths-mile Manhattan Handicap (considered no mean feat even in those days). In his last race, the Jockey Club Gold Cup, he was beaten seven lengths by Sword Dancer. He was named champion older horse and was grass champion for the third year, retiring with record earnings of $1,749,869.

Round Table entered stud at Claiborne Farm late in 1959. Of the 401 foals he sired, eighty-three (twenty-one percent) were stakes winners. Among his best offspring were Apalachee, Advocator, King Pellinore, King's Bishop, Poker (broodmare sire of Seattle Slew and Silver Charm), Royal Glint, and Upper Case. His daughters foaled 124 stakes winners.

RACE and (STAKES) RECORD

YEAR	AGE	STS	1ST	2ND	3RD	EARNED
1956	at 2	10	5(2)	1(1)	0	$73,326
1957	at 3	22	15(11)	1(1)	3(3)	$600,383
1958	at 4	20	14(11)	4(4)	0	$662,780
1959	at 5	14	9(7)	2(2)	2(2)	$413,380
Lifetime		66	43(31)	8(8)	5(5)	$1,749,869

Even after being pensioned from stud duty for five years, Round Table still retained his aura as a champion. During a tour of Central Kentucky farms in 1984, Queen Elizabeth rearranged her schedule to see the great horse when she learned he was still alive. Round Table died on June 13, 1987, at the age of thirty-three. — *K. H.*

Cigar

FEW HORSES GET THE KIND OF OVATION afforded Cigar on the occasion of his sixteenth consecutive victory, at Arlington International Racecourse in suburban Chicago, on July 13, 1996. Fans stood and cheered for twenty minutes when Jerry Bailey brought him back to the winner's circle that day.

No Thoroughbred ever got the send-off that Cigar received when he was retired from racing later that year. Riding a special van with his name emblazoned on the side, Cigar was paraded down the streets of New York and onto the world's most famous stage, Madison Square Garden, where 16,000 fans bid a tearful farewell.

Cigar left the racetrack with earnings of $9,999,815 — more than any other North American horse of the 20th Century. He won back-to-back titles as Horse of the Year, and almost single-handedly put the tiny emirate of Dubai on the world's racing map when he scored an electrifying victory in the inaugural Dubai World Cup in March of 1996.

Breeders from throughout the world wanted to obtain the stallion services of Cigar, who combined speed and power on the racetrack with an eye-catching physique and a pedigree rich in family lore. Allen Paulson, the aviation magnate who bred and raced Cigar sold a seventy-five percent interest in the horse to the Irish-based Coolmore operation of John Magnier. The deal put a value of $25 million on Cigar as a stallion prospect, and he entered stud at Coolmore's North American operation, Ashford Stud in Versailles, Kentucky, just down the road from Paulson's Brookside Farm, where Cigar was raised.

The partners recruited one of the best book of mares that any young stallion had ever seen. Seemingly, all that stood between Cigar and a new generation of potential champions was the wonder of nature. Incredibly, Cigar was not able to impregnate a single mare. He was sterile.

Wisely, Cigar's owners had purchased fertility insurance, and a settlement was paid, effectively transferring ownership of the horse to an insurance company. Over the next two years, fertility specialists from around the world were called in, but Cigar's condition

remained the same. After prolonged negotiations among various parties, Cigar was moved in early May of 1999 to the Hall of Champions at the Kentucky Horse Park in Lexington, where his many fans will have the opportunity to see him again and again.

Cigar was conceived in Kentucky at Brookside but foaled in 1990 at Country Life Farm in Maryland, where Paulson had an interest in two stallions. Cigar's sire, Palace Music, was a grandson of Northern Dancer who was a group/grade I winner in Europe and the United States. His dam, Solar Slew, was a daughter of Seattle Slew purchased by Paulson for $510,000 as a two-year-old in training. She failed to win in seven starts.

Cigar did not race until February of his three-year-old season, and his first win did not come until May of that year, in a six-furlong maiden special weight race on the dirt track at Hollywood Park. Alex Hassinger trained the colt as a three-year-old, and he expected him to follow in the footsteps of his sire, who excelled on turf. Cigar won just once in seven tries on grass in 1993. After his final race of the year, veterinarians discovered small chips in each of Cigar's knees, and arthroscopic surgery was performed. When he returned to training the next year, Cigar was sent to the East Coast stable of Bill Mott.

Mott had no more success with Cigar than Hassinger had had, until, after four frustrating losses on turf, he was switched back to the dirt track for an Oct. 28 allowance race at Aqueduct. Under Mike Smith, Cigar cruised to an eight-length victory, signaling better things to come. Less than a month later, Mott jumped Cigar back into stakes competition, in the NYRA Mile Handicap, a grade I event that since has been renamed the Cigar Mile. Carrying a feathery 111 pounds, the big bay colt overpowered a good field that included grade I winners Devil His Due, Brunswick, and Bertrando. Jerry Bailey was in the irons, replacing Smith, who opted for the more seasoned Devil His Due.

Cigar next won a Gulfstream Park allowance race in January. The win, his third in a row, was largely overshadowed by a stakes victory by the reigning Horse of the Year, Holy Bull, just thirty minutes earlier. Cigar faced Holy Bull at Gulfstream three weeks later in the Donn Handicap, where Holy Bull was the 3-10 favorite. Cigar jumped out to an early lead in the nine-furlong Donn and was going easily down the backstretch when Holy Bull took a bad step and suffered a career-ending injury. Cigar won by five and a half lengths, though many thought he won by default.

Those same critics said Cigar beat a weak field when he ran his winning streak to five in the Gulfstream Park Handicap on March 5, but they were mostly silenced after he scored a decisive victory over Silver Goblin, Concern, and Best Pal in the Oaklawn Handicap in April. In May, Cigar easily won the Pimlico Special Handicap — his fifth grade I triumph.

Cigar's next win, in the June 3 Massachusetts Handicap at Suffolk Downs, was little more than a walkover, but victory number nine (in a row), in the Hollywood Gold Cup Handicap, came at the expense of a top-class field vying for a $1-million purse. If there were skeptics in California, where Cigar began his career so ignominiously, they were gone after his three and a half-length Gold Cup win as the 126-pound highweight.

With that year's Breeders' Cup at Belmont Park, Mott shipped Cigar to New York in anticipation of a fall campaign. Cigar rolled to consecutive victories in the Woodward Stakes and Jockey Club Gold Cup, then braced for his biggest challenge of the year in the Breeders' Cup Classic on Oct. 28 — one year to the day that his winning streak began. Cigar unleashed a powerful move going into the final turn, took command with a quarter-mile to run, then stretched his margin of victory to two and a half lengths over a stubborn L'Carriere.

The streak reached twelve, and Cigar's 1995 season was a perfect ten-for-ten — including eight grade I events. Eclipse Awards as the older male champion and Horse of the Year were a mere formality.

Looking for new worlds to conquer, Paulson and Mott took aim at the $4-million Dubai

World Cup, a race created by Dubai's ruling family. Cigar prepped for the March 27 race by winning his second consecutive Donn Handicap, this time under 128 pounds, thirteen pounds more than he carried a year earlier.

					Northern Dancer, 1961	Nearctic / Natalma
			The Minstrel, 1974			
	PALACE MUSIC, ch, 1981				Fleur, 1964	Victoria Park / Flaming Page
					Prince John, 1953	Princequillo / Not Afraid
			Come My Prince, 1972			
CIGAR, bay colt, April 18, 1990					Come Hither Look, 1962	Turn-to / Mumtaz
					Bold Reasoning, 1968	Boldnesian / Reason to Earn
			Seattle Slew, 1974			
	SOLAR SLEW, dkb/br, 1982				My Charmer, 1969	Poker / Fair Charmer
					Solazo, 1959	Beau Max / Solar System II
			Gold Sun, 1974			
					Jungle Queen, 1956	Claro / Agrippine

He demonstrated his superiority over the world's best horses by taking the World Cup in impressive fashion, winning by a hard-fought half-length. Soul of the Matter and L'Carriere completed a one-two-three American sweep under the lights of the Nad Al Sheba racecourse in Dubai.

The win gave racing's biggest star of the 1990s a new, unofficial title of the Horse of the World. His winning streak had reached fourteen, and sights were set on the record sixteen straight won by Citation nearly a half-century earlier.

A repeat in the June 1 Massachusetts Handicap made it fifteen in a row, and a specially created race, the July 13 Arlington Citation Challenge, provided Cigar with the vehicle for his sixteenth consecutive win. A national television audience witnessed the explosive three and a half-length triumph, as did an enthusiastic crowd at Arlington. In both races, Cigar carried 130 pounds to victory.

The streak came to an end one month later, in the Pacific Classic at Del Mar, where a Richard Mandella-trained upstart named Dare and Go stunned Cigar and his growing legion of fans by three and a half lengths. Critics said Bailey had Cigar too close to a fast pace that day.

Cigar bounced back with a victory in the Woodward Stakes in September. Then he was beaten again, this time by an up-and-coming three-year-old named Skip Away, in the Jockey Club Gold Cup. In Cigar's final start, the Oct. 26 Breeders' Cup Classic at Woodbine in Canada, he finished third behind Alphabet Soup and Louis Quatorze. Although he was beaten only a nose and a head for all the money, Cigar was beginning to show the signs of a horse who had given everything he had over an incredible two-year run.

Cigar bid farewell to racing as a hero. As expected, Eclipse Award voters bestowed a second Horse of the Year title on the charismatic bay after his retirement. — R. P.

RACE and (STAKES) RECORD

YEAR	AGE	STS	1ST	2ND	3RD	EARNED
1993	at 3 in NA	9	2	2(1)	2(1)	$89,175
1994	at 4 in NA	6	2(1)	0	2	$180,840
1995	at 5 in NA	10	10(9)	0	0	$4,819,800
1996	at 6 in NA,UAE	8	5(5)	2(2)	1(1)	$4,910,000
Lifetime		**33**	**19(15)**	**4(3)**	**5(2)**	**$9,999,815**

Bold Ruler

A CHAMPION AT THREE in 1957, competing against a crop of colts that would define future generations of runners and sires, Bold Ruler was a standout. Bred and owned by Mrs. Henry Carnegie Phipps' Wheatley Stable, Bold Ruler was born at Claiborne Farm near Paris, Kentucky, on the same spring night as Round Table. Notwithstanding his championship racing form, Bold Ruler truly made his mark on Thoroughbred history as a sire. He led the sire list for eight years, seven of them consecutive, and counted eleven champions among his offspring.

Bold Ruler was a son of Nasrullah and one of eight classic winners of his sire's ninety-nine stakes winners. He was out of the stakes-winning Discovery mare Miss Disco. Bold Ruler in the 1970s had seven of the ten Kentucky Derby winners as his male line descendants, including Secretariat, Seattle Slew, Spectacular Bid, and Foolish Pleasure.

A series of nagging ills plagued Bold Ruler throughout his life. During his racing career, he was hampered by a chronic rheumatic condition, and it was said he was never completely sound. His refusal to be rated early in his racing career was attributed to a tongue injury he suffered as a yearling. Bold Ruler twice was injured in starting gate incidents, and a pulled back muscle and a hock injury interrupted his juvenile campaign.

Despite his problems, Bold Ruler won his first five outings at two and was considered the leading two-year-old of 1956. His wins included a score in the Youthful Stakes. Nashville then beat him in an allowance race, ending Bold Ruler's unbeaten skein. The dark bay colt bounced back to win the Futurity on the same afternoon that Nashua won his final outing, the Jockey Club Gold Cup. In his last two races of the year, Bold Ruler ran up against some tough racing luck in the Garden State Stakes and Remsen Stakes. Garden State winner Barbizon was awarded champion juvenile status, an honor that many thought belonged to Bold Ruler.

At three, Bold Ruler had an up and down campaign. Early on, he won the Bahamas, Flamingo (in track-record time), and Wood Memorial (in track-record time). The latter was considered the New York springboard for the Kentucky Derby. His loss in the Florida Derby to Gen. Duke required the latter to race the fastest one mile and an eighth ever recorded by a three-year-old to that date, 1:46⅕, which equaled the world record.

Trained by Jim Fitzsimmons, who also trained the great Nashua, Bold Ruler unfortunately followed in his predecessor's footsteps in losing the Kentucky Derby. Eddie Arcaro (who also rode Nashua in the Derby) and Fitzsimmons considered Gallant Man to be their main competition in the Derby. Bold Ruler, favored for the Derby, already had beaten Iron Liege, and they felt that Federal Hill could be taken at any time in the race. They opted to hold Bold Ruler out of a duel with the speedy Federal Hill unless Bold Ruler chose to take the lead on his own.

In hindsight, Arcaro acknowledged that he held Bold Ruler too much, for too long, when the colt tried to race to the lead with Federal Hill. "He was so full of run that he could have gone right on past Federal Hill, and I should have let him do that, but it wasn't until then that I realized I was fighting him too hard. Then he was empty. I had discouraged and confused him by fighting him when he wanted to run."

Iron Liege won from Gallant Man, with Round Table third and Bold Ruler fourth. In the Preakness, Bold Ruler was allowed to run his own race, and he trounced Iron Liege. Then

he failed to hold up against the torrid pace set by the double team of Bold Nero and Gallant Man in the Belmont, where Gallant Man won in 2:26⅗, a new American record. After a rest, Bold Ruler had a remarkable fall campaign that earned him three-year-old colt and Horse of the Year honors in 1957. He beat Gallant Man and Round Table in the Trenton, set a track record over a sloppy strip in winning the Vosburgh, easily carried 136 pounds and won by a dozen lengths in the Benjamin Franklin, and toted 130 pounds or more in a total of four added-money events that fall.

At four, Bold Ruler won five of seven starts and finished second once. He had 134 pounds piled on him for the one and a quarter-mile Suburban Handicap. Repeatedly challenged in the race by Clem, who carried only 109 pounds, Bold Ruler fought back each time until he reached the wire first through sheer heart and determination. Next, under 134 pounds, Bold Ruler held off Sharpsburg to win the Monmouth Handicap. That was his last victory of the year.

In the Brooklyn Handicap, Bold Ruler packed 136 pounds, but was pulled up lame. An ankle injury forced his retirement to stud at Claiborne in 1959.

Bold Ruler proved a tremendous success at stud, much to the benefit of Wheatley Stable, Claiborne, and their connections. The stallion's champions were Lamb Chop, bred by A. B. (Bull) Hancock Jr. and raced in partnership with William Haggin Perry, the leading three-year-old filly in 1963; Queen Empress, bred and raced by Wheatley, top two-year-old filly of 1964; Bold Lad, a Wheatley homebred, champion two-year-old colt of 1964; an Irish Bold Lad, bred and raced by the Countess of Granard, champion at two in England and Ireland in 1966; Successor, Bold Lad's full brother, bred and owned by Mrs. Phipps, champion two-year-old colt of 1966; Bold Bidder, bred by Wheatley and later raced by John Gaines, champion older horse in 1966; Queen of the Stage, bred and owned by Ogden Phipps, champion juvenile filly in 1967; Vitriolic, bred and raced by Ogden Phipps, champion juvenile colt of 1967; Gamely, bred by Hancock and raced in partnership with Perry,

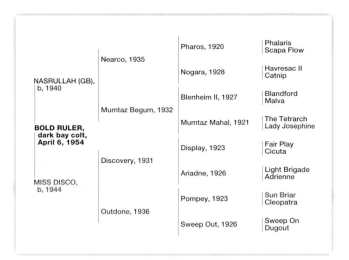

				Pharos, 1920	Phalaris Scapa Flow
NASRULLAH (GB), b, 1940		Nearco, 1935		Nogara, 1928	Havresac II Catnip
		Mumtaz Begum, 1932		Blenheim II, 1927	Blandford Malva
BOLD RULER, dark bay colt, April 6, 1954				Mumtaz Mahal, 1921	The Tetrarch Lady Josephine
		Discovery, 1931		Display, 1923	Fair Play Cicuta
MISS DISCO, b, 1944				Ariadne, 1926	Light Brigade Adrienne
		Outdone, 1936		Pompey, 1923	Sun Briar Cleopatra
				Sweep Out, 1926	Sweep On Dugout

co-champion three-year-old filly of 1967 and champion older female in 1968 and 1969; Secretariat, bred and owned by Meadow Stable, Horse of the Year in 1972 and 1973, champion at two and three, grass champion at three; Wajima, bred by Claiborne and raced by East-West Stable, champion three-year-old colt of 1975.

The tenacity and heart Bold Ruler showed on the racetrack and as a sire stood him in good stead for the greatest battle of his life, and one he was destined to lose — cancer. In July of 1970, Bold Ruler first showed signs of illness, which soon progressed. Specialists were called in from the University of Pennsylvania, but Bold Ruler continued to lose weight. A malignant mass was discovered.

Mrs. Phipps, ailing mistress of Wheatley, and her son, Ogden Phipps (then-chairman of The Jockey Club), were adamant that Bold Ruler should not be permitted to suffer. Convinced that his only chance of recovery lay in cobalt treatment, they agreed to send him to the veterinary school at Auburn University in late August.

As a racehorse, Bold Ruler could be headstrong, but he always was willing, even anxious, to run his best. Bold Ruler at sixteen fell back on that pattern and proved to be a good patient. When the treatments were completed, there was no claim that the stallion had been cured. However, regression of the tumor was evident.

Mrs. Phipps died at her home in New York a week after Bold Ruler was returned to Claiborne Farm in October. Bold Ruler had been given a new lease on life. He regained some of the weight he had lost. He was bred to thirty-seven mares during the 1971 breeding season, with twenty-seven reported to be in foal.

In June of 1971, his weight again began to decline, even though he was cleaning his feed tub every day. By the end of the month, he was showing more and more signs that he was not well. On July 2, a biopsy revealed that the malignancy had surfaced again. Bold Ruler was euthanized on July 12, 1971, and buried in the Claiborne cemetery with the other great ones who had lived, and died, as champions. He sired eighty-two stakes winners, and is the broodmare sire of six champions and 121 stakes winners. — *K. H.*

RACE and (STAKES) RECORD

YEAR	AGE	STS	1ST	2ND	3RD	EARNED
1956	at 2	10	7(3)	1	0	$139,050
1957	at 3	16	11(9)	2(2)	2(2)	$415,160
1958	at 4	7	5(5)	1(1)	0	$209,994
Lifetime		33	23(17)	4(3)	2(2)	$764,204

Swaps

RECORDS WERE MADE TO BE BROKEN. At least that is what Swaps set about doing while he was racing. The son of Khaled out of the Beau Pere mare Iron Reward broke track records all over the country, at various distances, under heavy weight assignments, and sometimes broke records on the way to breaking records. All in all, he set or equaled six world marks during his career, at one point lowering his own one and a sixteenth world record by one and two-fifths seconds.

Swaps was bred and raced by Rex Ellsworth, who with his brother entered the Thoroughbred business in 1933 with $850 saved from their $50 a month wages earned as cowhands. Rex Ellsworth eventually bred more than 100 stakes winners after that inauspicious start.

Ellsworth operated a ranch near Ontario, California, where Swaps was foaled on March 1, 1952. At two, under the tutelage of Mesh Tenney, he was a good racehorse, but not one who would wow the stopwatch crew in clocker's corner. He won half of his six starts, including the June Juvenile Stakes. His three-year-old campaign actually began on Dec. 30, when he won an overnighter that would mark the start of a nine-race win skein.

In his first start of 1955, Swaps easily won the San Vicente Stakes in the mud, but water was forced into the sole of his thin, shelly right front foot, causing an infection about the size of a dime. Tenney opened, drained, and treated the abscess, and twelve days after the San Vicente the colt was galloping again. A week after his first gallop, Swaps won the Santa Anita Derby even after drifting out and back in during the stretch run.

Shipped to Louisville by rail for the Kentucky Derby, the gleaming chestnut colt scored an eight and a half-length win on Churchill's opening day in time one-fifth of a second slower than the track record for six furlongs. His flash was hardly noticed in the frenzy of anticipation pending the rematch of Nashua and Summer Tan.

When Bill Shoemaker sent Swaps into the lead soon after the start of the Derby, no one paid much attention. When Eddie Arcaro began his move with Nashua entering the last

turn, Summer Tan could not match him. Nashua pulled even with Shoemaker's boot, but that was as close as it got. Swaps pulled away in the last eighth to win by one and a half lengths. That was the first night in two weeks Tenney did not sleep in Swaps' stall...instead he slept in his car parked next to the barn.

Swaps returned to California, leaving the Preakness and Belmont to Nashua. He won the Will Rogers Stakes by twelve lengths, then on June 11, he was sent against good older horses (including the previous year's Derby winner Determine) in the Californian. Swaps set a world record for one and a sixteenth miles of 1:40⅖ "almost casually." He then took the Westerner Stakes by six, and was shipped off to Chicago and a planned $100,000 match race with Nashua.

Swaps raced in the American Derby on grass before the match, and he won the one and three-sixteenths-mile event in 1:54⅗, which was a new course record and equaled the American record on the grass.

The day before the match, Swaps worked a mile in 1:35 on a track washed by a hard rain, and re-injured his foot. Ellsworth and Tenney decided to risk taking on Nashua, but Swaps swerved leaving the gate and raced badly, giving up in the stretch to lose by six and a half lengths. Swaps went into the match the favorite; Nashua came out Horse of the Year.

The soft spot was cut out of Swaps' foot, and he was out of training the rest of the year.

At four, Swaps often was bothered by his bad foot, which was complicated by a quarter crack early in the year. But when he was sound, he ran the hands off the stopwatches.

He prepped for the Santa Anita Handicap, but skipped it and was shipped to Florida. At Gulfstream Park, he raced in an overnighter carrying 130 pounds for the first time. He clipped a full second from the track record and lowered the world mark for a mile and seventy yards to 1:39⅗. Returned to Hollywood, he suffered a defeat when Shoemaker quit driving him in the last furlong of the Californian and could not get him going again to hold off Porterhouse, who got nine pounds and a head victory.

In the Argonaut under 128 pounds, he broke the track record by one and three-fifths seconds and lowered Citation's world mark for the mile to 1:33⅕. Next came the Inglewood, in which he ran the first mile in a record-breaking 1:32⅗, then lowered the world mark for one and a sixteenth miles to 1:39. In the American Handicap, Swaps equaled Noor's world record of 1:46⅘ for one and an eighth miles. In the Hollywood Gold Cup, he dropped the track mark for one and a quarter miles by a full second, running it in 1:58⅗. In the one and five-eighths-mile Sunset Handicap, he lowered the track record by two and two-fifths seconds, establishing another world record at 2:38⅕.

Shipped to Chicago, Swaps packed his customary 130 pounds in the Arch Ward Memorial over a soft course. He managed to work his way to the lead on the final turn, then faded to finish next to last. Nine days later, he raced his final time. In the Washington Park Handicap, Summer Tan (carrying fifteen pounds less than Swaps) sped the first half-mile in :44⅕. Swaps passed him on the turn and was clocked in 1:07⅘, two-fifths of a second faster than the world record for six furlongs. Swaps finished out the mile in track-record time of 1:33⅖, the fourth time that year he had beaten Citation's former world mark.

Two days later, it was announced that John W. Galbreath had purchased a half-interest in the colt for $1 million. Shipped to Atlantic City for the United Nations, Swaps came back

		Gainsborough, 1915	Bayardo Rosedrop
	Hyperion, 1930		
		Selene, 1919	Chaucer Serenissima
KHALED, br, 1943			
		Ethnarch, 1922	The Tetrarch Karenza
	Eclair, 1930		
SWAPS, chestnut colt, March 1, 1952		Black Ray, 1919	Black Jester Lady Brilliant
		Son-in-Law, 1911	Dark Ronald Mother-in-Law
	Beau Pere, 1927		
IRON REWARD, b, 1946		Cinna, 1917	Polymelus Baroness La Fleche
		War Admiral, 1934	Man o' War Brushup
	Iron Maiden, 1941		
		Betty Derr, 1928	Sir Gallahad III Uncle's Lassie

from a morning work showing soreness in his right forefoot. He was a late scratch from the race, and the abscess was drained. Ten days later, he was in training again for the Washington, D. C., International. Shipped to Garden State, he was in the midst of a seven-furlong work-out on Oct. 9 when a pony boy heard something "like the snap of a pistol."

Swaps had suffered two linear fractures of the cannon bone in his right hind leg. Five days later, he banged the injured leg in his stall, breaking the cast and extending the fracture all the way into the pastern joint. The leg was set in a stronger cast that was re-enforced by metal rods looped under the foot. Most of Swaps' 1,170 pounds was rested on a belly sling. The great horse tolerated his treatment, no complications arose, and on Nov. 27, 1956, he walked away from his sling.

He was retired with career earnings of $848,900, below only the totals of Nashua, Citation, and Stymie.

Swaps stood his first season at Ellsworth's ranch in California. Mrs. Galbreath purchased the other half-interest for another $1 million, and Swaps was moved to the Galbreaths' Darby Dan Farm near Lexington, Kentucky, where he stood his next ten seasons. He re-injured his hind leg in his paddock, and although he was in a cast for a week, he seemed to mend well. In later years, the leg would bother him when it was stretched forward, but did not hamper his breeding abilities.

At the age of fifteen, Swaps was syndicated for $20,000 a share and moved to Spendthrift Farm, where he stood his last five seasons alongside his rival Nashua.

Swaps got off to a good start as a sire, although he failed to maintain his early success in later years. His first crop included Primonetta, champion handicap filly of 1962. In his third crop was Affectionately, champion at two and five, and Kentucky Derby winner Chateaugay. In all, Swaps sired thirty-five stakes winners, including other good runners No Robbery, Eurasian, Irish County, and Fix the Date. His daughters produced such notable runners and producers as Horse of the Year Personality, champion Numbered Account, and Alma North.

Swaps was euthanized at the age of twenty in late 1972 at Spendthrift. — *K. H.*

RACE and (STAKES) RECORD

YEAR	AGE	STS	1ST	2ND	3RD	EARNED
1954	at 2	6	3(1)	0	2(2)	$20,950
1955	at 3	9	8(7)	1(1)	0	$418,550
1956	at 4	10	8(6)	1(1)	0	$409,400
Lifetime		25	19(14)	2(2)	2(2)	$848,900

Equipoise

EQUIPOISE EMBODIED THE BEST QUALITIES of the Thoroughbred in his determination to succeed, often under adverse conditions. In so many ways, "The Chocolate Soldier" did just that. Had he not suffered from unsoundness, there's no telling what Equipoise might have achieved. Equipoise was plagued with thin, shelly feet and quarter cracks that undermined him on the racetrack.

Born just before the Great Depression, the small son of Pennant, out of the good Broomstick mare Swinging, greeted the world in 1928. Equipoise was bred by H. P. Whitney, who sent the colt as a yearling to Freddy Hopkins. That trainer had galloped Upset and other good Whitney horses.

At two, Equipoise won half of his sixteen starts, placing second in five others and finishing third once. Equipoise took his first two outings in April of 1930 within eight days, then finished third in Vander Pool's Aberdeen Stakes. In the Pimlico Nursery Stakes, jockey Sonny Workman was assigned the mount for the first time, but the relationship that was to last several years got off to a rocky start. Equipoise stumbled at the start, tossing the rider. A week later, the two managed to stay connected in the Youthful at old Jamaica, but suffered from early interference. Equipoise bullied his way through the pack to catch unbeaten Vander Pool and win by four lengths, but he was taken down and placed last. "Ekky" then developed quite a following after taking the Keene Memorial, Juvenile, National Stallion (by six lengths), and Great American.

In early August, Equipoise met Jamestown for the first time, in the Saratoga Special. Equipoise was odds-on, but got off behind a wall of horses, and couldn't reach Jamestown and finished second. In the Champagne at Belmont in September, he was beaten a head

		Commando, 1898	Domino / Emma C.
	Peter Pan, 1904	Cinderella, 1888r	Hermit / Mazurka
PENNANT, ch, 1911	Royal Rose, 1894	Royal Hampton, 1882	Hampton / Princess
EQUIPOISE, chestnut colt, 1928		Belle Rose, 1889	Beaudesert / Monte Rosa
	Broomstick, 1901	Ben Brush, 1893	Bramble / Roseville
		Elf, 1893	Galliard / Sylvabelle
SWINGING, ch, 1922	Balancoire II, 1911	Meddler, 1890	St. Gatien / Busybody
		Ballantrae, 1889	Ayrshire / Abeyance

while giving thirteen pounds to Mate. A week later, he lost the Futurity to Jamestown by the same margin. Equipoise next won the Eastern Shore Handicap at Havre de Grace by five, then finished second to Twenty Grand in Aqueduct's Junior Champion Stakes. Shipped to Churchill Downs, Equipoise hooked up with Twenty Grand in the Kentucky Jockey Club Stakes, losing by just a neck in the fastest mile (1:36) ever run by a two-year-old to that point.

Ten days later, H. P. Whitney died and his son, Cornelius Vanderbilt Whitney, assumed the mantle. The first horse C. V. Whitney raced in his name was Equipoise in the Pimlico Futurity on Nov. 5, 1930. It was a race, Workman said, that was Equipoise's finest. Equipoise got turned sideways in the gate and was left at the post, then grabbed a quarter trying to right himself. In an effort that was ranked with some of the greatest in Turf history, Equipoise ran out of his shoes, literally, in defeating Twenty Grand by a half-length.

Equipoise was named co-champion two-year-old male. At three, he only raced three times. He won easily at Havre de Grace, then finished last and was pulled up in distress in the Chesapeake because of his feet. Nevertheless, he was sent back two weeks later for the Preakness (run then before the Kentucky Derby), but could finish no better than fourth.

He returned to be Horse of the Year and champion older male at four and five, as well as champion older male in 1934 as a six-year-old. At four, Equipoise set a world mark of 1:34⅖ in the one-mile Delavan Handicap at Arlington. At seven, Equipoise was sent West for the opening of Santa Anita. Second in the San Diego Exposition Handicap, Equipoise then defeated Twenty Grand in the Oakwood Handicap, but was disqualified to second. In his last race, the $100,000-added Santa Anita Handicap, Equipoise packed 130 pounds, but never threatened and finished seventh.

In Equipoise's abbreviated stud career (he sired only four crops before he died in 1938), he was represented by nine stakes winners, including 1942 Kentucky Derby winner Shut Out. That year, Equipoise topped the sire list when his progeny earned $437,141. — K. H.

RACE and (STAKES) RECORD

YEAR	AGE	STS	1ST	2ND	3RD	EARNED
1930	at 2	16	8(6)	5(5)	1(1)	$156,835
1931	at 3	3	1	0	0	$3,000
1932	at 4	14	10(8)	2(2)	1(1)	$107,375
1933	at 5	9	7(7)	1(1)	1(1)	$55,760
1934	at 6	6	3(3)	1(1)	1(1)	$15,490
1935	at 7	3	0	1	0	$150
Lifetime		51	29(24)	10(9)	4(4)	$338,610

Phar Lap

THE LATE HALL OF FAME TRAINER Charlie Whittingham was too young to see Man o' War race. However, he did witness the spectacular performance of Phar Lap in the Agua Caliente Handicap in 1932. "I never got to see Man o' War," Whittingham said in his biography of the same name. "But he'd have to be a helluva horse to be better than Phar Lap."

The winner of thirty-seven of fifty-one starts, Phar Lap was an international legend whose racing exploits and storied life were chronicled in the world's leading newspapers. Several books and a movie documented the gelding's life and his mysterious death.

Foaled Oct. 28, 1926, at Seadown Stud in New Zealand, Phar Lap was purchased by trainer Harry Telford on behalf of himself and American businessman David J. Davis for 160 Australian guineas, the equivalent of about 800 U.S. dollars. The source of the gelding's name is open to question, as the words mean "lightning strike" in the Javanese language. Davis reportedly said he named the son of Night Raid after being told by a friend that "phar lap" was a medical term for lightning.

A chestnut gelding with a distinctive white star, Phar Lap stood at 17.1 hands and had a girth measuring seventy-nine inches. Phar Lap's success could be attributed in part to his long stride, once measured at twenty-three feet and seven inches in a winning performance.

Phar Lap was not an instant success, with four unplaced efforts before breaking his maiden on April 27, 1929, in the final start of the season. Phar Lap's 1929-30 campaign also began slowly, but he finally came around to win thirteen of twenty starts, including nine in a row. Second in his 1930-31 debut, Phar Lap unleashed another lengthy unbeaten skein, winning fourteen in a row before another second-place finish at the end of the season. Included in his victories at age four was a three-length triumph in the two-mile Melbourne

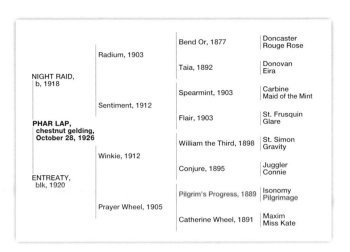

NIGHT RAID, b, 1918	Radium, 1903	Bend Or, 1877	Doncaster Rouge Rose
		Taia, 1892	Donovan Eira
	Sentiment, 1912	Spearmint, 1903	Carbine Maid of the Mint
		Flair, 1903	St. Frusquin Glare
ENTREATY, blk, 1920	Winkie, 1912	William the Third, 1898	St. Simon Gravity
		Conjure, 1895	Juggler Connie
	Prayer Wheel, 1905	Pilgrim's Progress, 1889	Isonomy Pilgrimage
		Catherine Wheel, 1891	Maxim Miss Kate

(PHAR LAP, chestnut gelding, October 28, 1926)

Cup while carrying 138 pounds.

Nicknamed the "Red Terror," Phar Lap continued to excel at age five, losing just once while eighth in the Melbourne Cup under a huge impost of 150 pounds, giving some fifty pounds to the winner.

As the gelding continued to pile up victories, the off-track stories began to multiply. Due to concerns over Phar Lap's safety, armed security guards and a police dog were enlisted to protect him. Even with those precautions, assistant trainer Tommy Woodcock reported gunshots were fired at Phar Lap one morning after a workout.

With his international reputation growing, Phar Lap was pointed toward a North American invasion in the $50,000 Agua Caliente Handicap. Housed in a twelve-by-twelve-foot stall, the gelding made a 10,000-mile, three-week journey aboard ship from New Zealand to San Francisco. At Caliente, he carried high weight of 129 pounds and rolled to a two-length victory while setting a track record of 2:02⅖ for one and a quarter miles.

Plans for Phar Lap to embark on a U.S. campaign were postponed after the gelding pulled a tendon and was sent to the Edward Perry ranch near San Francisco to recuperate. However, the gelding stunned the racing world with his death on April 5, 1932. The official cause was listed as colic, but tests revealed the presence of arsenic in the horse's system and a controversy ensued. The arsenic's source was later traced to insecticide sprayed on plants by a farm employee. The insecticide was apparently spread by wind to the grassy area where Phar Lap grazed. Many Australians were not satisfied with those explanations of their hero's death, preferring to speculate that Phar Lap was done in by organized crime.

In *The Phar Lap Story*, author Michael Williams noted that American writer Damon Runyon addressed the gelding's death in a letter to a U.S. soldier during World War II. "Phar Lap was a mighty runner from Down Under," the novelist wrote. "He won his only race on these shores…and American turfmen who saw the race gaped and said that Phar Lap was something out of the equine world. No, sonny, no one in this country would dream of murdering a horse like that." A taxidermist stuffed Phar Lap's body and it was placed on display at the Museum of Victoria in Melbourne. — *R. M.*

RACE and (STAKES) RECORD

YEAR	AGE	STS	1ST	2ND	3RD	EARNED
1929	at 2-3 in Aust	15	5(4)	1(1)	1(1)	$77,397
1930	at 3-4 in Aust	21	19(19)	1(1)	1(1)	$141,240
1931	at 4-5 in Aust	14	12(12)	1(1)	0	$32,715
1932	at 6 in NA	1	1(1)	0	0	$50,050
Lifetime		**51**	**37(36)**	**3(3)**	**2(2)**	**$301,402**

John Henry

ON A LATE SUMMER AFTERNOON at Arlington Park, a pint-sized, plain brown gelding took center stage in the racing world with an impossible victory in the inaugural Arlington Million. On that day in August of 1981, John Henry came charging down the stretch after The Bart and looked to have no hope of beating the wire. Somehow, John Henry managed to get his nose in front just in time.

For most horses, such a victory would be the pinnacle of a career, but for John Henry, who was already six years old, it merely measured the halfway point. He still had more to do. But just getting to that point — the Million — had not been easy, much less beyond it.

Foaled in 1975 at Golden Chance Farm in Kentucky, John Henry was the horse no one wanted. Gelded, thanks to his less-than-winning personality, he was sold at auction for a mere $1,100 as a yearling, then $2,200 as a juvenile. Finally, Sam Rubin acquired the three-year-old sight unseen for $25,000 in May of 1978. In a fortuitous move, Rubin sent John Henry to California in the fall of 1979 to trainer Ron McAnally.

Before that, John Henry already had started thirty-eight times and won twelve races. Three of those wins were stakes. With McAnally, the gelding took his game to another level. Kept mainly on the grass, John Henry began his rise to the top in 1980, with six consecutive stakes triumphs, including the San Luis Rey, and the San Juan Capistrano and Hollywood Invitationals. That year, John Henry collected his first championship for top turf horse.

In 1981, John Henry became one of racing's stars, winning eight of ten starts and earnings of $1,798,030. The son of Ole Bob Bowers started with a victory in the San Luis Obispo Handicap on the grass. He next won the Santa Anita Handicap on the dirt. Returned to the turf, John Henry posted back-to-back victories in the San Luis Rey Stakes and the Hollywood Invitational Handicap. After a fourth on the main track in the Hollywood Gold Cup in June, John Henry was shipped East to Belmont Park where he easily won the Sword Dancer Stakes on the grass by three and a half lengths.

JOHN HENRY, bay gelding, March 9, 1975			
OLE BOB BOWERS, b, 1963	Prince Blessed, 1957	Princequillo, 1940	Prince Rose / Cosquilla
		Dog Blessed, 1941	**Bull Dog** / Blessed Again
	Blue Jeans, 1950	Bull Lea, 1935	**Bull Dog** / Rose Leaves
		Blue Grass, 1944	Blue Larkspur / Camelot
ONCE DOUBLE, dkb/br, 1967	Double Jay, 1944	Balladier, 1932	Black Toney / Blue Warbler
		Broomshot, 1926	Whisk Broom II / Centre Shot
	Intent One, 1955	Intent, 1948	War Relic / Liz F.
		Dusty Legs, 1945	Mahmoud / Dustemall

Ridden for the first time by Bill Shoemaker in the Sword Dancer, John Henry and the legendary jockey teamed up again to win the Arlington Million. Afterwards, John Henry continued with victories in the Jockey Club Gold Cup on Belmont's main track and the Oak Tree Invitational on the lawn at Santa Anita. He took home Eclipse Awards that year for champion older and grass horse and was named Horse of the Year. He also moved to the top of the all-time leading money earner's list with $3,022,810 in career earnings.

Nagging injuries hampered John Henry throughout 1982 and 1983, although triumphs in the Hollywood Turf Cup and American Handicap and places in the Budweiser Million and Oak Tree Invitational were enough to earn champion grass horse honors in 1983.

In 1984, John Henry finally reached the pinnacle of his career. Nine years old by that time, he put together an astonishing season, winning six of nine races for earnings of $2,336,650. He won the Golden Gate Handicap in course-record time of 2:13 for eleven furlongs, then took his second Hollywood Invitational. He also added victories in the Sunset Handicap, a second Arlington Million, the Turf Classic, and the Ballantine's Scotch Classic. He received his second Horse of the Year Eclipse, plus champion turf horse.

John Henry was retired to the Kentucky Horse Park in Lexington in 1985. He tried a comeback in 1986, but was retired for good that year after tearing the suspensory ligament in his left foreleg. He still resides at the Horse Park, where fans from across the country can come and visit him. McAnally also visits the venerable gelding when in town.

"The grand old man" retired with thirty-nine victories and twenty-four placings in eighty-three starts, and was the all-time leading money earner with $6,591,860. He and McAnally were both elected to the Racing Hall of Fame in 1990.

—J. L. M.

RACE and (STAKES) RECORD

YEAR	AGE	STS	1ST	2ND	3RD	EARNED
1977	at 2 in NA	11	3(1)	2	2	$49,380
1978	at 3 in NA	19	6(2)	2(2)	3(2)	$120,319
1979	at 4 in NA	11	4(1)	5(4)	0	$129,864
1980	at 5 in NA	12	8(8)	3(3)	1(1)	$925,217
1981	at 6 in NA	10	8(8)	0	0	$1,798,030
1982	at 7 in JPN, NA	6	2(2)	0	2(2)	$580,300
1983	at 8 in NA	5	2(2)	2(2)	0	$652,100
1984	at 9 in NA	9	6(6)	1(1)	1(1)	$2,336,650
Lifetime		83	39(30)	15(12)	9(6)	$6,591,860

Nashua

A CONFLUENCE OF CIRCUMSTANCES entrenched Nashua deeper into public consciousness than is true of most champion horses. Not the least of his appeal was his own prowess as a racehorse, but it took more than that to establish the degree of fame that settled upon him.

Nashua represented the historic Belair Stud and, by the time he came along, his trainer, Sunny Jim Fitzsimmons, was a stooped and aging figure. The sympathy that "Mr. Fitz" engendered was a comfortable type, combined with admiration that the trainer of Triple Crown winners of the 1930s was still at his craft in the middle 1950s. Nashua's personality also accounted for some of his exceptional fame. Goofing around and seeming to win by as small a margin as possible might not have amused Fitzsimmons and the great rider Eddie Arcaro, but it had a quirky charm to a television audience which had been enthralled only two years earlier by its first hero, Native Dancer.

Nashua's rivalry with Swaps took horse racing off the sports pages and into front-page status and, then, only weeks after his greatest glory, Nashua became a silent figure in one of the top social scandals of the century. His owner, William Woodward Jr., was shot fatally by his wife in a high society tragedy that reverberated into the 1980s and beyond, being given new life by Dominick Dunne's fictionalized version, *The Two Mrs. Grenvilles*. There followed a sealed-bid auction that gave Nashua more headlines as the most expensive horse of all time, and the next year he completed his climb to be the all-time leading earner. Finally, in a long stud career, Nashua remained a magnet of tourism in Kentucky.

The athletic ability that made most of this notoriety possible was flashed early. The handsome bay by Nasrullah—Segula, by Johnstown, emerged early in 1954 as a top two-

				Phalaris
			Pharos, 1920	Scapa Flow
	Nearco, 1935			Havresac II
NASRULLAH (GB), b, 1940			Nogara, 1928	Catnip
			Blenheim II, 1927	Blandford Malva
	Mumtaz Begum, 1932			The Tetrarch
NASHUA, bay colt, 1952			Mumtaz Mahal, 1921	Lady Josephine
			Jamestown, 1928	St. James Mlle. Dazie
	Johnstown, 1936			
SEGULA, dk b, 1942			La France, 1928	Sir Gallahad III Flambette
			Sardanapale, 1911	Prestige Gemma
	Sekhmet, 1929			Sans Souci
			Prosopopee, 1916	Peroraison

year-old. The colt's breeder, William Woodward Sr., had intended Nashua for an English campaign, but after the elder Woodward's death, William Jr. figured an American stable was all he could handle so he jettisoned the English division.

Nashua's main rival at two was Summer Tan. The Belair colt held sway in the Juvenile, Hopeful, and Futurity, but Summer Tan beat him in the Cowdin. Nashua was voted the juvenile championship, winning six of eight at two to earn $192,865, although Summer Tan was given top weight of 128 on the Experimental Free Handicap.

In Florida the next winter, Nashua won his three races, including the Flamingo and Florida Derby. The rematch with Summer Tan came in the Wood Memorial. Arcaro was sitting out a suspension, and Ted Atkinson rode Nashua, who seemed unable to catch Summer Tan until a desperate surge in the final yards. Nashua paraded on to the Kentucky Derby, but his colors were lowered by the flashy California-bred Swaps. The winner returned West, and Nashua swept the Preakness, Belmont, Dwyer, and Arlington Classic.

National television took notice of the Nashua-Swaps match race arranged for Chicago that summer. Nashua dominated, winning by six and a half lengths, but questions about Swaps' soundness distracted, and detracted. Nashua concluded his Horse-of-the-Year campaign by winning the two-mile Jockey Club Gold Cup. He had won ten of twelve at three to set a one-year record of $752,550.

In the auction after young Woodward's death, Leslie Combs II's syndicate bid a record $1,251,200. Remaining in Fitzsimmons' stable, Nashua reappeared to score in a four-horse finish in the Widener Handicap. Nashua won six major stakes in ten starts at four, concluding his racing career with a second Jockey Club Gold Cup, in record time. He had won twenty-two of thirty races and topped Citation's former record, earning $1,288,565.

Nashua lived to thirty, standing his entire career at Combs' Spendthrift Farm in Kentucky. He sired seventy-seven stakes winners, including champion Shuvee. As a broodmare sire, Nashua sired the dams of 122 stakes winners, including one champion, but his enduring imprint could rest alone on his status as grandsire of Mr. Prospector. — E. L. B.

RACE and (STAKES) RECORD

YEAR	AGE	STS	1ST	2ND	3RD	EARNED
1954	at 2	8	6(4)	2(2)	0	$192,865
1955	at 3	12	10(9)	1(1)	1(1)	$752,550
1956	at 4	10	6(6)	1(1)	0	$343,150
Lifetime		30	22(19)	4(4)	1(1)	**$1,288,565**

Seabiscuit

SEABISCUIT LOST THE FIRST SEVENTEEN RACES of his career. During that ignominious streak, he four times raced with a price tag figuratively dangling from his bridle, for $2,500 on three occasions and for $4,000 once, and nobody considered him worth an investment. And yet this same diminutive colt whose career began so inauspiciously in 1935 became the hero of one of the sport's most dramatic moments and retired in 1940 as its all-time leading money winner.

As a two-year-old Seabiscuit had thirty-five races, a busy schedule even for those days and which encourages two assumptions: First, Seabiscuit was even then remarkably resilient and tough; second, his trainer, eventual Hall of Famer Sunny Jim Fitzsimmons,

thought it prudent to get as much as possible from the colt early, as if immediate prospects were more attractive than future potential.

Four days after breaking his maiden and equaling the track record at Narragansett Park, Seabiscuit broke the track's five-furlong standard by four-fifths of a second in the Watch Hill Claiming Stakes. (He was entered for $5,500.) He won three more races during the season and earned $12,510. The campaign hardly dazzled, but it paid the bills.

In the celebrated stable of Mr. Fitz, Seabiscuit, who was bred and owned by Wheatley Stable, did not command much attention. The star was Granville, who lost his rider in the Kentucky Derby, finished second in the Preakness, then won the Belmont Stakes en route to Horse of the Year honors. Seabiscuit, on the other hand, soon headed elsewhere.

Charles Stuart Howard, a Georgia native who became wealthy selling Buicks in California, was eager to purchase a good allowance horse for his stable. For such a role, Seabiscuit was a prospect. The son of Hard Tack out of the Whisk Broom II mare Swing On had raced forty-seven times, with nine victories and earnings of $18,465. Fitzsimmons sold him for $7,500.

With "Silent" Tom Smith as his new trainer and John "Red" Pollard his new rider, Seabiscuit underwent a remarkable transformation. By 1937, the former claimer became the best older horse in the land, winning seven consecutive stakes races and setting four track records. At season's end, with a record of eleven victories in fifteen starts, he was named the champion handicap horse.

In 1938, he won six of eleven starts, including an eventful match race with Bing Crosby's Ligaroti. All the while there naturally arose a popular clamor for Seabiscuit to face War Admiral, the Triple Crown winner of 1937. A $100,000 match race between the two was agreed upon for Belmont Park, but it had to be canceled when Seabiscuit became ill.

When the two finally met, on Nov. 1, 1938, in a $15,000 winner-take-all match race arranged by Alfred Vanderbilt, War Admiral was the overwhelming favorite at 1-4, with Seabiscuit at 2-1. The quicker horse always has an advantage in a match race, and War Admiral was reputed to be a lightning bolt. But jockey George Woolf immediately urged Seabiscuit to the lead, and as the horses passed the Pimlico grandstand for the first time, the grinning rider, as popular lore has it, looked back at Charley Kurtsinger on War Admiral and laughed. Seabiscuit won by four lengths with his ears pricked and set a track record of 1:56⅗ for the one and three-sixteenths miles. Seabiscuit gathered up honors for champion handicap horse and Horse of the Year for 1938.

Seabiscuit ran only once in 1939, pulling up lame, about $36,000 short of Sun Beau's earnings record, after an overnight handicap. Seabiscuit was bred to seven mares, then in 1940 brought back to the races for a run at the record. Pollard also returned to ride him, joking that together they had four good legs between them. And four sufficed. In one of the sport's eternally shining moments, Seabiscuit easily won the 1940 Santa Anita Handicap, setting a track record and becoming the first ever to earn more than $400,000. After eighty-nine races and thirty-three victories, Seabiscuit was retired with earnings of $437,730. — G. W.

Pedigree of SEABISCUIT, bay colt, 1933

HARD TACK, ch, 1926	Man o' War, 1917	Fair Play, 1905	Hastings / Fairy Gold
		Mahubah, 1910	**Rock Sand** / Merry Token
	Tea Biscuit, 1912	**Rock Sand**, 1900	Sainfoin / Roquebrune
		Tea's Over, 1893	Hanover / Tea Rose
SWING ON, b, 1926	Whisk Broom II, 1907	Broomstick, 1901	Ben Brush / Elf
		Audience, 1901	Sir Dixon / Sallie McClelland
	Balance, 1919	Rabelais, 1900	St. Simon / Satirical
		Balancoire II, 1911	Meddler / Ballantrae

RACE and (STAKES) RECORD

YEAR	AGE	STS	1ST	2ND	3RD	EARNED
1935	at 2	35	5(3)	7(1)	5(1)	$12,510
1936	at 3	23	9(6)	1	5(3)	$28,995
1937	at 4	15	11(10)	2(2)	1(1)	$168,580
1938	at 5	11	6(4)	4(4)	1(1)	$130,395
1939	at 6	1	0	1	0	$400
1940	at 7	4	2(2)	0	1	$96,850
Lifetime		89	33(25)	15(7)	13(5)	$437,730

Whirlaway

THE NAMES OF SOME HORSES RESONATE, transcending the decades — and even, in some cases, their own actual performances. No one would quibble with the adulation accorded Man o' War or Citation in years when racing was fashionable. Few would begrudge Cigar the attention he brought back to the sport when he reeled off his sixteenth straight victory, in 1996 at Arlington International Racecourse.

But the public didn't always require perfection, or even near-perfection from the horses it chose to put upon a pedestal. And so the name Whirlaway also echoes through the years, evoking an image of greatness that even those closest to him would not have claimed.

Whirlaway certainly was surrounded by greatness. He was foaled in 1938 at Calumet Farm. He was from the first U.S. crop of English Derby winner Blenheim II. And, when he was put into training in the fall of 1939, Whirlaway was given over to the care of Ben A. Jones, who was taking on his first group of yearlings for Calumet. And certainly Whirlaway did great things. His sweep of the 1941 Triple Crown races was one of the most convincing. He won the Kentucky Derby by eight lengths, setting a track record of 2:01⅖ that stood for twenty-one years. He followed that by winning the Preakness by five and a half lengths and the Belmont by two and a half. At age four, he won five races under 130 pounds.

Nevertheless, H. A. (Jimmy) Jones later was reported to have said that the horse known fondly by his fans as Mr. Longtail "wouldn't be compared in any way with a lot of good horses that we had or that a lot of other people had."

There might be several reasons. For one, Whirlaway had a habit of heading for the outside rail at the crucial juncture in many of his races. The trait first manifested itself in his

WHIRLAWAY, chestnut colt, 1938

- **BLENHEIM II, br, 1927**
  - Blandford, 1919
    - Swynford, 1907 — John o' Gaunt / Canterbury Pilgrim
    - Blanche, 1912 — White Eagle / Black Cherry
  - Malva, 1919
    - Charles O'Malley, 1907 — Desmond / Goody Two-Shoes
    - Wild Arum, 1911 — Robert le Diable / Marlicacea
- **DUSTWHIRL, b, 1926**
  - Sweep, 1907
    - Ben Brush, 1893 — Bramble / Roseville
    - Pink Domino, 1897 — Domino / Belle Rose
  - Ormonda, 1916
    - Superman, 1904 — Commando / Anomaly
    - Princess Ormonde, 1912 — Ormondale / Ophirdale

debut on June 3, 1940, at Lincoln Fields near Chicago. Ben Jones tried all kinds of cures — blinkers with one eye completely covered and training his colt to run through minute openings along the inside rail at the top of the stretch. The regimen didn't always make a lot of difference. Occasionally, even in winning, Whirlaway would be so far on the outside that it was difficult for the photo finish camera to discern his proper placing.

His running style was coupled with inconsistency. His longest winning streak was five races, which included the Triple Crown victories. The result was a record that sometimes surprises fans who recognize the name but weren't around to watch the horse run.

As a two-year-old, Whirlaway won two of his first three starts. He struggled through the Chicago summer and by the time he arrived at Saratoga, he made his first East Coast start in the United States Hotel Stakes at odds of 14-1 and managed to finish second. He added a triumph in the Saratoga Special, then won the Hopeful Stakes in the mud. However, he was shipped south to failure in both the Futurity Trial and the Futurity. By year's end, his juvenile record was seven wins from sixteen starts. His year's earnings of $77,275 were tops among two-year-olds, and in one year-end poll, he was voted juvenile champion, an honor he shared with rival Our Boots, who received the accord in another poll.

At age three, before his Triple Crown success, Whirlaway posed problems for his trainer. In the Blue Grass Stakes at Keeneland, he bore out so sharply in the stretch run that he finished six lengths behind Our Boots, after seemingly having that rival's measure. Whirlaway had his ups and downs the rest of the year, finishing with a mark of thirteen wins from twenty starts. He was never off the board, adding five seconds and two thirds.

At age four, often giving much weight to his rivals, Whirlaway again was on the tote board after each of his starts, winning twelve of twenty-two races, with eight seconds and two thirds and pushing his earnings to record levels beyond $500,000. Whirlaway raced twice at age five, then was retired to Calumet. He had moderate success, siring eighteen stakes winners, including Scattered, winner of the 1948 Coaching Club American Oaks. He was sent to stand in France in 1950 and died there in 1953. — B. K.

RACE and (STAKES) RECORD

YEAR	AGE	STS	1ST	2ND	3RD	EARNED
1940	at 2	16	7(4)	2(2)	4(3)	$77,275
1941	at 3	20	13(8)	5(5)	2	$272,386
1942	at 4	22	12(10)	8(6)	2(2)	$211,250
1943	at 5	2	0	0	1	$250
Lifetime		60	32(22)	15(13)	9(5)	$561,161

Alydar

NEVER HAS A HORSE BEEN SO BELOVED for not winning a race. Or three races, in the case of Alydar. The gallant chestnut's runner-up finishes in all three Triple Crown events — the Kentucky Derby, Preakness, and Belmont Stakes — of 1978 made him as popular as the winner, Affirmed, and forever linked his name with his rival's.

The rivalry of the 1978 Triple Crown was one for the ages. In the 104th Derby, Alydar, who was a slight favorite, seemed to have trouble handling the Churchill Downs surface and dropped well off the pace, while Affirmed shadowed the leaders all the way. The final margin in the Derby was the widest of the three races at one and a half lengths after Alydar

came charging late. But Affirmed was well in hand at the finish.

In the Preakness, Alydar again was second, but this time only by a neck as the two chestnut colts vied down the stretch. Alydar battled his rival in the turn and through the stretch of the Belmont Stakes and again fell just short, this time by a head. Alydar's trainer, John Veitch, best summed up the Triple Crown: "We didn't have any bad luck in any of the Triple Crown races. The only bad luck was that Alydar came along in the same year as Affirmed."

Alydar did help keep the venerable Calumet Farm in the spotlight for a little longer. Calumet, which bred and raced the son of Raise a Native out of the On-and-On mare Sweet Tooth, was owned at the time by the aging Admiral and Mrs. Gene Markey, and the Lexington farm was well past its glory days of Citation, Whirlaway, and Coaltown.

As a two-year-old, Alydar began his career in the Youthful Stakes at Belmont Park, closing well for fifth. The winner was Affirmed. After winning a maiden event at Belmont, Alydar defeated Affirmed in the Great American Stakes. Alydar then added the Tremont at

Belmont and the Sapling at Monmouth Park. In the fall, Alydar and Affirmed met four times, with Alydar getting the better of his rival only once, in the Champagne.

At three, Alydar and Affirmed took separate paths to the Triple Crown, and Alydar finally had a chance to shine on his own. At Hialeah, he warmed up with an allowance victory, then easily took the Flamingo. At Gulfstream Park, Alydar won the Florida Derby, then romped by thirteen lengths in the Blue Grass Stakes at Keeneland. Next came his runner-up Triple Crown.

Alydar, however, rebounded to win his last three outings as a sophomore. He easily won both the Arlington Classic and the Whitney, the latter over older horses. In his final start, Alydar achieved a weak revenge against Affirmed when the Calumet colt was awarded first in the Travers upon the disqualification of the latter. Alydar was sidelined the rest of the year with a fractured coffin bone in his left front foot. He returned at four but was not at the same level, although he managed to win the Nassau County Handicap.

Alydar was retired to Calumet with fourteen wins and ten placings in twenty-six starts and earnings of $957,195. At stud Alydar was a sensation, siring seventy-seven stakes winners, including dual classic winner and Horse of the Year Alysheba; champions Easy Goer, Turkoman, Althea, and Lindo Shaver; 1990 Horse of the Year Criminal Type; and 1991 Derby winner Strike the Gold. Alydar led the national sire list in 1990, the year he died.

Late that year, Alydar was found to have suffered a fractured cannon bone, allegedly by kicking his stall door. As of 1999, the horse's death was still surrounded by questions and being investigated in the courts. His death also sounded the death knell for the old guard at Calumet, which was run at that time by J. T. Lundy, who had married the granddaughter of the farm's founder, Warren Wright Sr. The farm fell into bankruptcy, and was sold in 1992 at public auction to Henryk de Kwiatkowski.

A year before his tragic death, Alydar joined his old racetrack rival Affirmed in the Racing Hall of Fame. Fittingly, despite their accomplishments separately on and off the track, the two mighty chestnuts are remembered forever together.

— J. L. M.

Pedigree of ALYDAR, chestnut colt, March 23, 1975

RAISE A NATIVE, ch, 1961	Native Dancer, 1950	Polynesian, 1942	Unbreakable / Black Polly
		Geisha, 1943	Discovery / Miyako
	Raise You, 1946	Case Ace, 1934	Teddy / Sweetheart
		Lady Glory, 1934	American Flag / Beloved
SWEET TOOTH, b, 1965	On-and-On, 1956	Nasrullah, 1940	Nearco / Mumtaz Begum
		Two Lea, 1946	Bull Lea / Two Bob
	Plum Cake, 1958	Ponder, 1946	Pensive / Miss Rushin
		Real Delight, 1949	Bull Lea / Blue Delight

RACE and (STAKES) RECORD

YEAR	AGE	STS	1ST	2ND	3RD	EARNED
1977	at 2	10	5(4)	4(4)	0	$285,026
1978	at 3	10	7(6)	3(3)	0	$565,071
1979	at 4	6	2(1)	2(2)	1(1)	$107,098
Lifetime		26	14(11)	9(9)	1(1)	$957,195

Gallant Fox

IT IS REPORTED THAT BELAIR STUD OWNER William Woodward preferred a good horse to a bag of gold. As the owner of Gallant Fox, he could have said a trunk of gold, for the colt was much better than a good horse.

Woodward did not believe in over-racing two-year-olds. He preferred that a horse be capable of reaching its true worth and that too much racing while young sapped that potential. As a result, Gallant Fox started only seven times at two. At Saratoga the juvenile

won the Flash Stakes and at Aqueduct the Junior Championship Stakes before being rested for the remainder of the year.

Woodward's decision, made in conjunction with trainer Sunny Jim Fitzsimmons, proved beneficial. At three, Gallant Fox fulfilled the promise of his brief and bright two-year-old season. He also lived up to the potential of his pedigree, as a son of Sir Gallahad III and the Celt mare Marguerite.

Gallant Fox commenced his march toward the classics in the Wood Memorial Stakes. Using this race as a prep race, he defeated a field of classic hopefuls by four lengths. In 1930 the Preakness Stakes preceded the Kentucky Derby, and the colt ventured to Pimlico for its thirty-ninth running. Ridden by Earl Sande, the Belair colorbearer overcame a troubled running and won going away.

The Kentucky Derby had escalated in importance and was becoming one of the big events of American racing. Gallant Fox faced fourteen rivals. In a drizzling rain over a good track, he pressed the pace for the first half-mile and assumed the lead after six furlongs. At the wire, Gallant Fox was two lengths ahead of his nearest competitor. With this victory, he became the second horse in history to capture both the Preakness and the Derby; the other was Sir Barton, the first winner of the Triple Crown.

On June 7, 1930, Gallant Fox became the second winner of the Triple Crown when he crossed the finish line three lengths ahead in the Belmont Stakes.

SIR GALLAHAD III (Fr), b, 1920	Teddy, 1913	Ajax, 1901	Flying Fox / Amie
		Rondeau, 1900	Bay Ronald / Doremi
	Plucky Liege, 1912	Spearmint, 1903	Carbine / Maid of the Mint
		Concertina, 1896	St. Simon / Comic Song
GALLANT FOX, bay colt, 1927			
MARGUERITE, ch, 1920	Celt, 1905	Commando, 1898	Domino / Emma C.
		Maid of Erin, 1895	Amphion / Mavourneen
	Fairy Ray, 1911	Radium, 1903	Bend Or / Taia
		Seraph, 1906	St. Frusquin / St. Marina

Fitzsimmons did not hesitate to keep his charge from competition. In the Dwyer Stakes Gallant Fox extended his unbeaten streak at age three to five. There is no better advertisement than success, and Gallant Fox's success had given the colt quite a reputation. A crowd of 60,000 people poured into Arlington Park to witness the Classic Stakes, the colt's sixth start over six different tracks. He did not disappoint, winning by a neck. Seven is usually thought to be a lucky number, but not for Gallant Fox. In the seventh start of his sophomore season, he battled main rival Whichone in the Travers Stakes at Saratoga, but both colts were passed by Chaffee Earl's Jim Dandy, who won by eight lengths over Gallant Fox. It was the biggest upset at Saratoga since Upset upset Man o' War.

As if to prove that his loss was a mere fluke, Gallant Fox returned two weeks later in the Saratoga Cup, and beat older horses for the first time. The Lawrence Realization at Belmont Park marked another milestone when he became America's leading money-winning horse.

Gallant Fox's final start was the two-mile Jockey Club Gold Cup in which only two others were bold enough to meet the test. They might as well have stayed in the barn, for the race was for second money. At year's end Gallant Fox was voted champion three-year-old colt, hardly a surprise given the breadth of his accomplishments.

Woodward retired Gallant Fox to the place of his birth, Claiborne Farm near Paris, Kentucky. The colt retired with eleven wins in seventeen starts, three seconds, two thirds, and earnings of $328,165. Gallant Fox was a success at stud as well if for no other reason than he is to date the only winner of the Triple Crown to sire a winner of the Triple Crown. His first crop contained Woodward's 1935 Triple Crown winner Omaha. Thus, Woodward's Belair Stud and Warren Wright's Calumet Farm are the only breeders and owners of two Triple Crown winners apiece. Gallant Fox died at age twenty-seven and was buried at Claiborne Farm alongside his sire and his dam. — T. H.

RACE and (STAKES) RECORD

YEAR	AGE	STS	1ST	2ND	3RD	EARNED
1929	at 2	7	2(2)	2(1)	2(2)	$19,890
1930	at 3	10	9(9)	1(1)	0	$308,275
Lifetime		17	11(11)	3(2)	2(2)	$328,165

Exterminator

CALLED "OLD BONES" because of his angular appearance, Exterminator's nickname reflected the lack of respect he received early in his racing career. As time wore on, though, the grand gelding outran his pedigree, appearance, and every expectation that can be burdened on a horse. His reputation eventually became so great that Colonel Matt J.

Winn, father of the Kentucky Derby, ranked Old Bones "the greatest all-around Thoroughbred in American racing history."

Born in 1915 outside of Lexington, Exterminator was officially listed as bred by F. D. (Dixie) Knight, although it was actually Knight's mother, Mrs. M. J. Mizner, who owned and had bred Old Bones.

Consigned to the 1916 Saratoga August yearling sale, Exterminator brought $1,500 from J. Calvin Milam. Both a trainer and owner, Milam grudgingly gelded his new purchase as a two-year-old, feeling the procedure necessary for Exterminator's health. A brief, albeit winning, juvenile campaign ended with a muscle strain.

In the spring of 1918, Exterminator was preparing for his sophomore season when trainer Henry McDaniel laid eyes on him. He recommended to a client, Willis Sharpe Kilmer, that Exterminator be purchased as a work mate for their stable star and intended Kentucky Derby horse, the imported colt Sun Briar. The deal was made, and the gelding was relocated to McDaniel's barn for $9,000 in cash and two maiden fillies, each valued at $500.

In two workouts before the Derby, Sun Briar beat Exterminator by several lengths. However, Sun Briar failed to train forwardly, and Exterminator was entered in his place. "All right. All right," Kilmer reportedly consented. "Against my better judgment I'll send him to the post instead of to a livery stable."

In his first start in nearly ten months, Exterminator captured the Kentucky Derby at nearly 30-1, in what was just the beginning of a storied career. The iron horse would continue to race to the age of nine, often against the top horses of the current generation, and he would carry more weight than any modern horse before him. He once carried 138 pounds to victory at one and a quarter miles and won nineteen other races under imposts of 130 to 137 pounds.

Racing from Canada to Tijuana and nearly every point in between, Exterminator won half of his 100 starts and earned $251,596, with eighty-four finishes on the board. Although the chestnut was capable of winning in sprints, it was over a distance of ground that Exterminator excelled. The gelding won eleven of twenty-two races at distances of one and a half to two and a quarter miles, setting two American distance records.

In one of his most dazzling performances, the 1922 Brooklyn Handicap, Old Bones battled head and head through the stretch with Grey Lag, the 1921 Belmont Stakes winner who was renowned for his ability to carry weight to victory. Carrying 135 pounds to Grey Lag's 126, Exterminator handed his younger rival the only loss of his season.

Race statistics alone, however, cannot depict the tenacious horse that was Exterminator, nor the emotion the public felt for him. Old Bones' courageous heart and iron body made him a legend. Perhaps his blood was not the bluest, nor his beginnings the most illustrious, but Exterminator was the epitome of the noble steed called the Thoroughbred, the exquisite blend of speed and stamina, the essence of class. The grand gelding was retired in 1924 and provided a pony companion named Peanuts.

On Sept. 26, 1945, the thirty-year-old relic of the Turf died in his stall. *The Thoroughbred Record* captured the day best: "A heart attack suffered by Exterminator...put the final footnote to the career of a horse that stirred more genuine affection in the hearts of men than any other Thoroughbred the American Turf has ever known." Exterminator was elected to the Racing Hall of Fame in 1957. — *J. W.*

MCGEE (GB), b, 1900	White Knight, 1895	Sir Hugo, 1889	Wisdom / Manoeuvre
		Whitelock, 1881	Wenlock / White Heather
	Remorse, 1876	Hermit, 1864	Newminster / Seclusion
		Vex, 1865	Vedette / Flying Duchess
EXTERMINATOR, chestnut gelding, 1915			
FAIR EMPRESS, blk, 1899	Jim Gore, 1884	Hindoo, 1878	Virgil / Florence
		Katie, 1872	Phaeton / Mare by War Dance
	Merrythought, 1893	Pirate of Penzance, 1882	Prince Charlie / Plunder
		Raybelle, 1889	Rayon d'Or / Blue Grass Belle

RACE and (STAKES) RECORD

YEAR	AGE	STS	1ST	2ND	3RD	EARNED
1917	at 2	4	2	0	0	$1,350
1918	at 3	15	7(6)	4(4)	3(3)	$36,147
1919	at 4	21	9(7)	6(5)	3(3)	$26,152
1920	at 5	17	10(10)	3(3)	2(2)	$52,905
1921	at 6	16	8(7)	2(2)	5(5)	$56,077
1922	at 7	17	10(10)	1(1)	1(1)	$70,575
1923	at 8	3	1(1)	1(1)	1(1)	$4,250
1924	at 9	7	3	0	2(2)	$4,140
Lifetime		100	50(41)	17(16)	17(17)	$251,596

Sysonby

THE NAME OF SYSONBY may be unfamiliar today to many who only recently have become involved with racing. In truth, those who have followed the Turf for several decades also might be excused for having only vague recognition of the name.

There was a time, however, when the name Sysonby comfortably made the list of top horses seen by an earlier generation of 20th Century horsemen. Later, the name was affixed to a distinguished race whose runnings included the 1948 Sysonby Mile won by Citation — three days before he won the Jockey Club Gold Cup at double the distance. In

1955, the Sysonby Stakes, at a mile and an eighth, was the vehicle by which Belmont Park hoped to entice Nashua and Swaps to another meeting some three weeks after their historic match race in Chicago. Lengthened from a mile and with an enhanced purse of $100,000, the Sysonby snagged match race winner Nashua, but he was upended by the older High Gun and Jet Action.

From 1947, the Sysonby's list of winners also included Armed, Tom Fool, Capot, and Cohoes, but pride of place among autumn weight-for-age races fell upon the Woodward, and the name Sysonby was dropped from the ranks of New York Racing Association stakes after 1958.

Such a fate was sadly consistent with the history of the horse himself, for Sysonby's arc across the sky of glory was brief, and a spiteful disease spelled an early death. Sysonby was sired by the 1885 Epsom Derby winner Melton and was out of the English mare Optime, daughter of Orme and granddaughter of the great, unbeaten Ormonde. The mating was arranged by Marcus Daly, whose good fortune at the Anaconda Copper mines had financed such niceties as the Bitter Root Stud in Montana and Apperfield Stud in England.

Optime was quartered at the English farm when Daly died, and the stock was brought to New York for auction. Wall Street wizard James R. Keene purchased Optime for $6,600, sent her to his Castleton Stud in Kentucky, and was thus the breeder of record of her 1902 foal. The Melton colt was named Sysonby (SY-sun-bee) for a hunting lodge which Keene's son, Foxhall, leased in the sporting English town of Melton Mowbray.

As a yearling observed in the Castleton paddocks, Sysonby reportedly would have merited the dismal description of small and unattractive, but slow. After Keene's trainer, James G. Rowe Sr., had been exposed to some early trials by the colt, however, he was so impressed that he resorted to trickery to make sure he kept Sysonby in his division of the Keene stable. When the time was at hand to send some of the Castleton two-year-olds to England, Sysonby was scheduled for the voyage, but Rowe wrapped the horse in blanket and bandages and convinced Keene that the colt was too ill to make the trip.

Thus retained for Rowe's further exploitation, Sysonby won his first start at two by ten lengths and got better from there. That season, he won a total of five of six races, including the Brighton Junior Stakes, Flash Stakes, Saratoga Special, and Junior Champion. Competing record keepers of the day tended to disagree over the results of these races, but the questions were hardly material: Did Sysonby win by ten lengths, or only six?

In the Futurity, Sysonby was third behind another star in the making, the filly Artful. Rowe later wrung from the colt's groom the confession that he had drugged Sysonby, which accounted for the impressive roll of bills the lad was seen brandishing.

At three, Sysonby won all nine of his races, including the opening feature at the grand Belmont Park, when he dead-heated with the older Race King in the Metropolitan Handicap. Sysonby also won the Tidal and Lawrence Realization, and was said to have overcome a seventy-five yard disadvantage in a ragged start to snatch the $50,000 Great Republic Stakes. He had a career mark of fourteen wins in fifteen races, and earnings of $184,438. At four, Sysonby was stricken by an outbreak of bloody sores. He was diagnosed as suffering from a liver disease and blood affliction called variola, and his condition proved fatal. His skeleton was later exhumed for display at New York's Museum of Natural History. — *E. L. B.*

Pedigree: SYSONBY, bay colt, 1902

MELTON, b, 1882	Master Kildare, 1875	Lord Ronald, 1867	Stockwell / Edith
		Silk, 1869	Plum Pudding / Judy Go
	Violet Melrose, 1875	Scottish Chief, 1861	Lord of the Isles / Miss Ann
		Violet, 1864	Thormanby / Woodbine
Optime, b, 1896	Orme, 1889	Ormonde, 1883	Bend Or / Lily Agnes
		Angelica, 1879	Galopin / St. Angela
	Daughter of, 1882	Speculum, 1865	Vedette / Doralice
		Nydia, 1875	Orest / Adelaide

RACE and (STAKES) RECORD

YEAR	AGE	STS	1ST	2ND	3RD	EARNED
1904	at 2	6	5(4)	0	1(1)	$40,058
1905	at 3	9	9(9)	0	0	$144,380
Lifetime		15	14(13)	0	1(1)	$184,438

Sunday Silence

HE WAS WORKING-CLASS ALL THE WAY, a hero for the common man. Once a horse that nobody wanted, he became one that few could beat. It was all there, the complete package, buried deep within his obsidian exterior. Sunday Silence had the guts, the fight, the drive. It took the skill of a master to expose it, but Charlie Whittingham found every last ounce of talent inside Sunday Silence's gleaming frame. What resulted was pure magic.

The year was 1989. As winter gave way to spring, and the classics loomed large on the horizon, the eyes of the nation centered on a fiery colt from the East, the next superhorse they called him. He was Easy Goer. Hardly a glance was being given to an eager son of

Halo, developing smoothly out West under Whittingham's Hall of Fame touch. But it was no wonder. Sunday Silence, after all, was the one you couldn't even give away.

Owner Arthur Hancock III had tried to sell his Kentucky-bred at auction — not once, but twice. There just weren't any takers. His pedigree wasn't stellar. Neither were his looks. But Whittingham sensed something special, and he bought in, along with Dr. Ernest Gaillard. From there, the fairy tale took wing.

While Easy Goer was running rampant from Florida to New York, defeating his competition with ease and with monotonous regularity, Sunday Silence was busy staking his own claim in California. A runaway jaunt in the Santa Anita Derby that April signaled that Easy Goer at least would have something to tangle with throughout the Triple Crown.

And so the stage was set. The clash was imminent, and it had the makings of a timeless saga. It was East versus West. Blue blood against blue collar. Easy Goer and Sunday Silence, head to head, in the grandest arena of them all — the 115th Kentucky Derby.

It was a piercing late afternoon when they finally squared off, the temperature hovering just above freezing. Though the conditions suggested otherwise, the 1989 Derby forever marked a beginning. The race was all but accorded to Easy Goer by most people, but Sunday Silence shocked his chestnut opponent that day. He relished the Churchill Downs mud, zigzagging to the wire for a clear two and a half-length victory. Easy Goer finished second. A rivalry had begun and would become one of the greatest match-ups the game has ever seen.

SUNDAY SILENCE, dark bay or brown colt, March 25, 1986

- **HALO, dkb/br, 1969**
  - Hail to Reason, 1958
    - Turn-to, 1951 — Royal Charger / Source Sucree
    - Nothirdchance, 1948 — Blue Swords / Galla Colors
  - Cosmah, 1953
    - Cosmic Bomb, 1944 — Pharamond II / Banish Fear
    - Almahmoud, 1947 — Mahmoud / Arbitrator
- **WISHING WELL, b, 1975**
  - Understanding, 1963
    - Promised Land, 1954 — Palestinian / Mahmoudess
    - Pretty Ways, 1953 — Stymie / Pretty Jo
  - Mountain Flower, 1964
    - Montparnasse II, 1956 — Gulf Stream / Mignon
    - Edelweiss, 1959 — Hillary / Dowager

The Preakness Stakes, quite simply, was one for the ages. Sunday Silence and Easy Goer engaged at the top of Pimlico's stretch, battling to the finish as one. They were inseparable, unwavering; neither was backing down. Sunday Silence prevailed by a head. The sport was now at the threshold of a Triple Crown. The Belmont Stakes, however, painted a much different picture. This time, it was all Easy Goer. There was no sweep in the cards for the Derby-Preakness winner. Back on his home turf, Easy Goer won by eight.

They would not meet again until late fall. With a Super Derby title added to his credentials, Sunday Silence stepped up for a rematch with Easy Goer in the Breeders' Cup Classic at Gulfstream Park. Together again, in their final bout, Sunday Silence left his rival behind on the far turn, then had enough to hold off Easy Goer's menacing late rush. At the end of ten furlongs, it came down to a neck. Now there were no doubts. Sunday Silence was the best three-year-old in the land. He was also best of all, honored as the 1989 Horse of the Year.

His career, however, was cut short by injury after just two starts at four. With victories in seven major stakes, spread from coast to coast, Sunday Silence walked away with earnings of nearly $5-million, third at the time only to Alysheba and John Henry. The horse that Whittingham once said couldn't stand getting beat had never finished worse than second.

Shortly after his retirement, Sunday Silence left for Japan, where he began his stud career. By 1995, Sunday Silence had become Japan's leading sire. A year later, he was inducted into the Racing Hall of Fame, modest bloodlines, awkward build, and all. But what Sunday Silence possessed was golden. A black beast with dazzling style and an iron will. It made him a champion. — C. H.

RACE and (STAKES) RECORD

YEAR	AGE	STS	1ST	2ND	3RD	EARNED
1988	at 2	3	1	2	0	$21,700
1989	at 3	9	7(6)	2(2)	0	$4,578,454
1990	at 4	2	1(1)	1(1)	0	$368,400
Lifetime		14	9(7)	5(3)	0	$4,968,554

Skip Away

SKIP AWAY'S REPUTATION AS AN IRON HORSE wasn't acquired simply by his steel-gray coat. The sturdy "Skippy," as he was called by Carolyn and Sonny Hine, his owner and trainer, respectively, was among the last horses from his crop still competing — and winning — at the highest levels when he retired in 1998.

In all, Skip Away won eighteen of thirty-eight starts and finished in the money a remarkable thirty-four times. He ranked second on the all-time leading money earner's list, behind Cigar, with a bankroll of $9,616,360. His consistency and durability earned him

and his connections a total of five Eclipse Awards.

Skip Away was foaled in Florida at Hilmer Schmidt's Indian Hill Farm. He is the first and only stakes winner bred by Massachusetts resident Anna Marie Barnhart, who inherited Ingot Way (by Diplomat Way), the dam of Skip Away, after her husband's death in 1984. Indian Hill then consigned the colt to a two-year-olds in training sale in Ocala, Florida. The Hines originally paid $30,000 for the son of Skip Trial, but a bone chip was found in his knee and the breeder agreed to accept $22,500 — the $7,500 representing the cost of surgery the colt never underwent.

Skip Away was stakes-placed even before he won a race. He finished second in the Gilded Time Stakes at Monmouth in July of his two-year-old year, then won his first race, an eight-furlong maiden event, the next month. Second-place finishes in the Cowdin and Remsen Stakes ended his first year at the track.

A commanding performance in the 1996 Toyota Blue Grass Stakes seemed to bode well for Skip Away's chances in the Kentucky Derby. But the colt apparently loathed the Churchill Downs surface — a dislike he would display again in the final race of his career — and he finished a dismal twelfth of nineteen. However, Skip Away's three-year-old cam-

SKIP TRIAL, b, 1982

Bailjumper, 1974
- Damascus, 1964 — Sword Dancer / Kerala
- Court Circuit, 1964 — Royal Vale / Cycle

Looks Promising, 1968
- Promised Land, 1954 — Palestinian / Mahmoudess
- Fluoresee, 1958 — Double Jay / Snow Flame

SKIP AWAY, gray or roan colt, April 4, 1993

INGOT WAY, gr, 1981

Diplomat Way, 1964
- Nashua, 1952 — Nasrullah / Segula
- Jandy, 1949 — Princequillo / Centenary

Ingot, 1971
- Iron Ruler, 1965 — Never Bend / Obedient
- Glorious Night, 1961 — Dark Star / Queen Fleet

paign rebounded, and he finished second in the Preakness and Belmont Stakes. One of Skip Away's biggest wins at three came at the expense of Cigar in the 1996 Jockey Club Gold Cup. Preakness Stakes winner Louis Quatorze took the lead early, with Skip Away following. Cigar, whose wins mainly came from off the pace, was about five lengths back in third. Both Skip Away and Cigar accelerated entering the stretch, but the younger runner outlasted his more seasoned rival to win by a head. That performance helped cement Skip Away's first Eclipse Award, for three-year-old male.

In 1997, the colt lost his first four starts. His one and a quarter-length loss to Formal Gold in the Donn Handicap had a particular sting to it, since it took place at his winter home, Gulfstream Park. Skip Away then beat that rival in the Massachusetts Handicap.

In his last two big races of the year, the Jockey Club Gold Cup and the Breeders' Cup Classic, Skip Away ran virtually unchallenged and won by daylight in both. At year's end, he had added nearly $4.1 million to his coffers, but he had won only four of his eleven starts and finished behind Formal Gold four times. Eclipse Award voters were not convinced. Skip Away earned the older horse title, and Carolyn Hine was named outstanding owner, but the Horse of the Year title went to the undefeated two-year-old Favorite Trick.

Personality was never lacking in the Skip Away camp and that came through loud and clear in 1998 when the big gray amassed seven wins in nine starts, including five grade I victories. His trainer, quick to bemoan imperfect race conditions or the lack of top-notch horses coming to face his big gray, never failed to give due credit to his horse. "He was a very generous horse," said Hine. "He always gave."

Skip Away competed at fourteen different tracks and withstood forty-two straight months of training and typically at least one race every eight weeks. Although the Hines hoped to surpass Cigar's earnings record with a victory in the 1998 Breeders' Cup Classic, Skip Away ran sixth on the Churchill Downs oval. Soon after the horse entered stud at Hopewell Farm near Lexington, Kentucky, Skip Away won the elusive Horse of the Year title as well as champion older horse honors. — *K. J. I.*

RACE and (STAKES) RECORD

YEAR	AGE	STS	1ST	2ND	3RD	EARNED
1995	at 2	6	1	3(3)	1(1)	$88,080
1996	at 3	12	6(5)	2(2)	2(2)	$2,699,280
1997	at 4	11	4(4)	5(5)	2(2)	$4,089,000
1998	at 5	9	7(7)	0	1(1)	$2,740,000
Lifetime		**38**	**18(16)**	**10(10)**	**6(6)**	**$9,616,360**

Assault

IN 1946, WHEN THE COUNTRY was recovering from a war and an epidemic hostility, Assault supplied the raw material for hope. Awkward and deformed, he had a most unlikely provenance, yet the little chestnut colt known as the "clubfooted comet" swept the Triple Crown and in doing so assumed a popular place in the public awareness.

Assault was bred, born, and raised in Texas, on the vast expanse once called the "Wild Horse Desert" but later famous as the King Ranch. As a weanling he stepped on a surveyor's spike, which ran through the frog of the right foot and out the hoof wall. The injury

left the foot deformed and the horse crippled. Even years later, Assault walked with a conspicuous limp. And he would sometimes stumble, even fall, when going to the racetrack. But once there, he ran with surprising grace and efficiency and, most of all, courage. Perhaps that was the source of his charisma. Overcoming his misfortune to become the seventh Triple Crown winner, he also became for many an embodiment of that same courageous spirit on which Americans had relied during the war.

Assault's injury was so severe that he was nearly destroyed. But the little colt was tough. And his pedigree insisted he be given a chance. He was a son of Bold Venture, who had won the 1936 Kentucky Derby. When Bold Venture's first two crops had failed to impress, his popularity sank in Kentucky. Robert Kleberg Jr., the president and manager of the family-owned King Ranch, then purchased the stallion for $40,000 and in 1941 brought him to Texas. Assault's dam was Igual, an unraced daughter of Hall of Famer Equipoise.

Assault was trained by Max Hirsch, himself a Texan, who at the age of ten hopped a train transporting a group of horses from the Morris Ranch in Fredericksburg to Baltimore. On his first day in Maryland, Hirsch became an exercise rider, years later a jockey, and in 1902 a trainer. In 1936, when Kleberg leaped into racing, he chose Hirsch as trainer for King Ranch.

Assault's deformed foot was so thin and brittle that he had to wear a special shoe that bent around the front of the hoof. But he trained well enough and he made his first start, on June 4, 1945 at Belmont Park, finishing twelfth. A month later he won for the first time, then captured the Flash Stakes at odds of 71-1. In his debut at three, Assault won the Experimental Free Handicap No. 1, then, eleven days later, the Wood Memorial. But after he ran fourth in the Derby Trial Stakes, he was given only a small chance in the Kentucky Derby.

Derby Trial winner Spy Song set the pace, with Knockdown and Assault stalking. At the top of the long Churchill Downs stretch, jockey Warren Mehrtens encouraged Assault with his whip, and they popped through an opening along the rail. At the wire, they had eight lengths on Spy Song, equaling the widest winning margin in Derby history. The next day, in the Washington *Post*, Walter Haight wrote: "Assault is the name, but he looked like Murder, Inc." Assault won the Preakness by a neck over fast-closing Lord Boswell. But the Belmont was probably his greatest moment. Out of the gate, he nearly fell and trailed by eight lengths as he entered the second turn. Assault brushed with Hampden, the early leader, as he swung to the outside, then drew off to win by three lengths. Mehrtens worried there might be a claim of foul. But there was no disputing Assault's dominance.

With Eddie Arcaro as his new rider, Assault went on to defeat Stymie in the Pimlico Special and to win the Westchester Handicap. With record earnings of $424,195, Assault was named Horse of the Year for 1946. Assault began 1947 with five consecutive victories, but injuries soon compromised him. "He never should have run" in the famous match race with Armed, according to Arcaro. Armed won by eight lengths, and Assault was never the same. But Arcaro always maintained that next to Citation, Assault was the best horse he ever rode.

After forty-two races, eighteen victories, and $675,470 in earnings, Assault retired to King Ranch, where in 1971 he died. — G. W.

RACE and (STAKES) RECORD

YEAR	AGE	STS	1ST	2ND	3RD	EARNED
1945	at 2	9	2(1)	2	1(1)	$17,250
1946	at 3	15	8(8)	2(2)	3(3)	$424,195
1947	at 4	7	5(5)	1	1(1)	$181,925
1948	at 5	2	1	0	0	$3,250
1949	at 6	6	1(1)	1	1(1)	$45,900
1950	at 7	3	1	0	1	$2,950
Lifetime		42	18(15)	6(2)	7(6)	$675,470

Easy Goer

FEW MODERN-DAY HORSES have stirred the dreams and expectations that were embodied in the powerful chestnut frame of Easy Goer. The regally bred scion of a racing dynasty met those expectations in authoring an unforgettable racing career, but his legacy ended all too soon.

Easy Goer died at the age of eight after having sired just 136 foals in four years. The son of Alydar just didn't have enough time to prove his worth, but Easy Goer hasn't been

forgotten. He is mentioned in the same breath with some of the greatest horses of all time, and whenever Triple Crown rivalries are discussed, the year 1989 comes to mind.

Owned and bred by Ogden Phipps and trained by Claude R. (Shug) McGaughey III, Easy Goer entered his three-year-old season wearing the crown as champion juvenile male of 1988. Foaled at the Hancock family's Claiborne Farm near Paris, Kentucky, where he later reported for stud duty, Easy Goer earned an Eclipse Award on the strength of four victories in six starts. He lost his career debut by a nose, and in his final start of the year, fell one and a half lengths shy of Is It True in a muddy Breeders' Cup Juvenile at Churchill Downs.

If the pride of New York was a good-looker at two, he struck an even more attractive picture at three. He looked the part and, in an early season tour de force, proved it on the racetrack. Easy Goer rattled off three almost-effortless wins, in the Swale Stakes at Gulfstream Park and the Gotham and Wood Memorial Stakes at Aqueduct in preparation for the Kentucky Derby.

With Pat Day in the saddle, Easy Goer was odds-on to win the Derby, but encountered a competitor that would set the table for one of the greatest rivalries in racing history. A colt from California named Sunday Silence got the best of Easy Goer that cold afternoon at Churchill Downs, and not for the last time.

The margin of victory in the Derby was two and a half lengths, but in the Preakness Stakes two weeks later, it was down to a nose after the duo battled stride for stride down the Pimlico stretch. Sunday Silence was two-thirds of the way home to a Triple Crown, but the pair was headed back to Belmont, where Easy Goer was almost perfect. "I guess I'm going to start hearing a lot of Affirmed-Alydar talk," McGaughey said in reference to the two horses that waged the Triple Crown battle of 1978. "In the Belmont, you've got a horse that's going to try to win the Triple Crown, and a horse that's going to try to stop him."

Hard as he tried, Easy Goer's father fell a head short of spoiling Affirmed's three-bagger. But that wasn't to be the case eleven years later.

The public, in anticipation of a sweep, made Sunday Silence the odds-on choice in the Belmont, with Easy Goer a close second. In the end, those numbers wouldn't compute. On the far turn of the sweeping Belmont track, Sunday Silence made his bid for the lead, but Easy Goer, with his long, powerful strides, assumed command near the top of the stretch. Easy Goer's lead expanded with ease in the final eighth of a mile to eight lengths at the wire, and his final time of 2:26 for one and a half miles — the fastest since Secretariat set the standard in the 1973 Belmont — left onlookers wondering if Easy Goer wasn't the better of the two. It's a debate that lingers to this day.

They would meet again in the Breeders' Cup Classic later that year, and in another thriller, Sunday Silence exacted his revenge by a neck. The 1989 Classic was the culmination of a superb end-of-the-decade run by Phipps, who also owned champion filly Personal Ensign, and McGaughey, who trained her. Only a year before, the filly had won the Breeders' Cup Distaff to conclude a perfect career.

By the numbers, Easy Goer wasn't perfect — he ended his racing career with fourteen victories in twenty starts, and never was worse than third — but in the eyes of his many fans, he was simply the best. For them, he was a champion long after his two-year-old season had ended. — T. L.

RACE and (STAKES) RECORD

YEAR	AGE	STS	1ST	2ND	3RD	EARNED
1988	at 2	6	4(2)	2(1)	0	$697,500
1989	at 3	11	8(8)	3(3)	0	$3,837,150
1990	at 4	3	2(2)	0	1(1)	$339,120
Lifetime		**20**	**14(12)**	**5(4)**	**1(1)**	**$4,873,770**

Pedigree of EASY GOER, chestnut colt, March 21, 1986

ALYDAR, ch, 1975
- Raise a Native, 1961
  - Native Dancer, 1950 — Polynesian / Geisha
  - Raise You, 1946 — Case Ace / Lady Glory
- Sweet Tooth, 1965
  - On-and-On, 1956 — Nasrullah / Two Lea
  - Plum Cake, 1958 — Ponder / Real Delight

RELAXING, b, 1976
- Buckpasser, 1963
  - Tom Fool, 1949 — Menow / Gaga
  - Busanda, 1947 — War Admiral / Businesslike
- Marking Time, 1963
  - To Market, 1948 — Market Wise / Pretty Does
  - Allemande, 1955 — Counterpoint / Big Hurry

Ruffian

HUMAN NATURE FORCES US TO REMEMBER the tragedy of Ruffian: The gallant, almost-black filly champion facing the Kentucky Derby-winning colt Foolish Pleasure in a match race that ended in death. That same nature allows us to get past the grieving and reflect on the accomplishments of one of the truly great Thoroughbreds of this century. Ruffian was perfect at two and her record was nearly so at three. In fact, in her entire career of eleven starts, the only time she lost a race was when she lost her life.

At two in 1974, Ruffian raced five times, winning every outing. She was a demon on the track in the mornings for trainer Frank Whiteley, and in the afternoons she was devastating from start to finish. After breaking her maiden — one of only two non-stakes starts in her career except for the fatal match race — she took the five and a half-furlong Fashion Stakes in 1:03, equaling Belmont's track record. In succession she then won the Astoria, Sorority, and Spinaway. In the last-named, she blew away to a thirteen-length victory, but in the process suffered a hairline fracture of her right hind ankle. She was considered a shoe-in for juvenile filly honors, and a strong contender for the Horse of the Year title (which went to Forego).

Owner Stuart S. Janney and his wife had no plans on racing their filly in the Kentucky Derby, holding to the school of thought that the one and a quarter-mile distance was too much, too soon for any three-year-old. However, they acknowledged that she would face the colts before the end of the year if all went well.

All went well.

After winning an allowance and the Comely Stakes in April, Ruffian's rudder was pointed toward the New York Filly Triple Crown: the Acorn, Mother Goose, and Coaching Club

American Oaks. Ruffian was not in competition with the other horses on the track during the series, for none could compete with her. In fact, Ruffian's time of 2:27⅗ in the CCA Oaks was two-fifths of a second faster than Avatar's winning Belmont Stakes time two weeks earlier while that colt was in a furious stretch battle with Foolish Pleasure. She did not come close to Secretariat's Belmont Stakes, track, and American record, but she did run her final quarter in time two-fifths of a second faster than Secretariat ran his.

REVIEWER, b, 1966	Bold Ruler, 1954	Nasrullah, 1940	Nearco / Mumtaz Begum
		Miss Disco, 1944	**Discovery** / Outdone
	Broadway, 1959	Hasty Road, 1951	Roman / Traffic Court
		Flitabout, 1945	Challedon / Bird Flower
SHENANIGANS, gr, 1963	Native Dancer, 1950	Polynesian, 1942	Unbreakable / Black Polly
		Geisha, 1943	**Discovery** / Miyako
	Bold Irish, 1948	Fighting Fox, 1935	Sir Gallahad III / Marguerite
		Erin, 1927	Transmute / Rosie O'Grady

RUFFIAN, dark bay or brown filly, April 17, 1972

At that point the match race was set. On July 6, 1975, the best filly in the country went out to meet the Kentucky Derby winner in a one and a quarter-mile match race that was nationally televised from Belmont Park, and stocked with $350,000 in purse money.

Ruffian was outbroken slightly by Foolish Pleasure, who was on the outside, but within a few strides she held a narrow lead. After a quarter-mile in a blazing :22⅕, they were nearly stride for stride. Ruffian appeared to be the aggressor in several bumping incidents early on, and she was beginning to edge away. Then, both jockeys heard a sickening crack. Foolish Pleasure swept by, and Ruffian went careening toward the outside rail. When she finally was stopped by Jacinto Vasquez, the truth was seen. Her right front ankle was gashed open and both proximal sesamoid bones were smashed.

What followed was a fight for her life. The decision was made for surgery at Dr. William O. Reed's nearby hospital. Anesthesia was touch and go because of the filly's stressed condition. It took an hour to get her stabilized before surgery could be performed, and another hour to perform the surgery and apply a cast and a special shoe. Then all there was left to do was wait for her to recover, and hope.

Ruffian lay quietly on the floor of the recovery stall for more than an hour, then began to struggle. As she became more violent, she began tossing her attendants around "like toys." First, the special shoe was torn loose; then the cast went flying. She was sedated, but the medication was fighting upstream against shock, stress, and a warrior's nature.

Janney gave the word. "Don't let her suffer any more." Ruffian was buried in the Belmont infield.

At three she received the title of champion filly of her age. She was inducted into the Racing Hall of Fame the following year. — K. H.

RACE and (STAKES) RECORD

YEAR	AGE	STS	1ST	2ND	3RD	EARNED
1974	at 2	5	5(4)	0	0	$134,073
1975	at 3	6	5(4)	0	0	$179,355
Lifetime		**11**	**10(8)**	**0**	**0**	**$313,428**

Gallant Man

POOR GALLANT MAN. Here is one of the most versatile horses of the 20th Century and what is he most often remembered for? The Kentucky Derby he didn't win.

It is a remarkable story, the way owner Ralph Lowe dreamed his jockey stood up early in the 1957 Derby only to see Bill Shoemaker go out and do just that. But there was a lot more to Gallant Man's career than that ignominious nose loss to Iron Liege.

The English-bred colt, named for a horse in a Don Ameche movie, was only a tad taller than 15 hands and battled bad feet and ankles his entire career. Yet he more than held his own in what is generally considered one of the best foal crops in history, one also including Round Table and Bold Ruler, both eventual Horses of the Year.

In that quirky Derby, for example, Gallant Man beat third-place Round Table by two and three-quarter lengths, while Bold Ruler finished fourth, still another three lengths back. After skipping the Preakness Stakes, trainer John Nerud sent Gallant Man out to annihilate the field assembled for the Belmont Stakes, winning the classic by eight lengths over Inside Tract and another four over Bold Ruler. His time for the mile and a half was 2:26⅗ — a track and an American record that held until Secretariat's 1973 Belmont.

Gallant Man's three-year-old season also included a track record-tying victory at six furlongs at Tropical Park and a victory over the two miles of the Jockey Club Gold Cup. He also won the '57 Travers and defeated five-year-old Dedicate in the Nassau County Handicap in track-record time. For the season, Gallant Man had eight wins from fourteen starts and four seconds, with earnings of $298,280.

Unfortunately, one of those defeats came in the season-ending showdown among Gallant

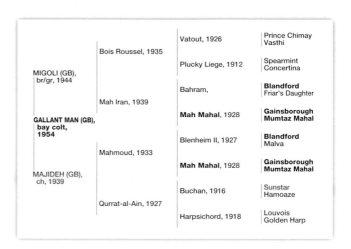

					Prince Chimay
			Vatout, 1926		Vasthi
	Bois Roussel, 1935				
			Plucky Liege, 1912		Spearmint
MIGOLI (GB),					Concertina
br/gr, 1944					
			Bahram,		**Blandford**
	Mah Iran, 1939				Friar's Daughter
			Mah Mahal, 1928		**Gainsborough**
GALLANT MAN (GB),					**Mumtaz Mahal**
bay colt,					
1954			Blenheim II, 1927		**Blandford**
	Mahmoud, 1933				Malva
			Mah Mahal, 1928		**Gainsborough**
MAJIDEH (GB),					**Mumtaz Mahal**
ch, 1939					
			Buchan, 1916		Sunstar
	Qurrat-al-Ain, 1927				Hamoaze
			Harpsichord, 1918		Louvois
					Golden Harp

Man, Round Table, and Bold Ruler in the Trenton Handicap at Garden State Park. Ralph Lowe was obsessed with beating Round Table, owned by rival oilman Travis Kerr. Shoemaker did as told, but when he was finished putting away Round Table he had nothing left for Bold Ruler, who had stolen away for a two and a quarter-length victory.

When the ballots for the year-end awards were counted, Gallant Man was left out in the cold. Nonetheless, Lowe should have realized he was lucky to have Gallant Man at all. If he had listened to his veterinarian instead of bloodstock agent Humphrey Finney, he would have never bought the colt.

Gallant Man was part of a group of horses (Nerud said ten; printed reports said nine) that Finney arranged to buy in 1955 from the Aga Khan. The price was $250,000 for the lot of them, or $25,000 per horse. The little brown colt was regally bred, sired by Prix de l'Arc de Triomphe winner Migoli out of Majideh, winner of both the Irish Oaks and Irish One Thousand Guineas. But the vet turned him down because of his size and his bad feet and ankles. "Ralph said, 'Well, hell, Finney, what do you think?'" Nerud remembered. "Finney said, 'Well, he's all right, I think. He's a good bred colt.' And so Ralph said, 'Ah, take him anyway.'" The vet was right as far as he went. But, Nerud remembered, "He had a wonderful stride."

Gallant Man ran just five times at age four. He opened the season with a third-place finish to Bold Ruler in the Carter Handicap, then beat his old nemesis in the Metropolitan Mile under 130 pounds. He then won the Hollywood Gold Cup under 130 and the Sunset under 132. In September 1958, Lowe sold a three-quarter interest in the colt to Spendthrift Farm for $1 million. Two days later, Gallant Man finished fifth in the Sysonby Handicap at Belmont Park and shortly after that developed a splint problem in his left foreleg.

Gallant Man was retired to a stud career every bit as good as his days racing. Among his progeny were fifty-one stakes winners, including Hall of Famer Gallant Bloom. His daughters produced eighty-eight stakes winners, among them four champions, including Genuine Risk. Gallant Man was pensioned before the start of the 1981 season and lived seven more years. — *P. S.*

RACE and (STAKES) RECORD

YEAR	AGE	STS	1ST	2ND	3RD	EARNED
1956	at 2	7	3	0	0	$7,075
1957	at 3	14	8(6)	4(4)	0	$298,280
1958	at 4	5	3(3)	0	1(1)	$205,000
Lifetime		**26**	**14(9)**	**4(4)**	**1(1)**	**$510,355**

Discovery

WHEN TALKING ABOUT THE GREAT WEIGHT CARRIERS of the 20th Century, no discussion is complete without mentioning Discovery. When discussing the great sire-line influences of the 20th Century, any lively banter that fails to include Discovery also isn't complete.

While Alfred Gwynne Vanderbilt's chestnut was a notch below the flashy Cavalcade at three in 1934, it was at four and five that the son of Display—Ariadne, by Light Brigade, made his indelible mark on the Turf. During the two-year run, Discovery made thirty-three

starts, running under an average of 131 pounds, and he won seventeen times. After a slow start in 1935, Discovery rattled off eight straight, with the pinnacle being a win under a back-breaking 139 pounds in the Merchants' and Citizens' Handicap. In all, he won nearly half of his starts, twenty-seven wins from sixty-three starts, and earned $195,287, a considerable figure for a Great Depression-era runner.

Bred by Walter J. Salmon Sr., raced at two for the Adolphe Pons stable, and trained by John R. Pryce, Discovery won but two of thirteen starts before being sold to a then twenty-one-year-old Vanderbilt for $25,000. In his first start for Vanderbilt and trainer J. H. (Bud) Stotler, and his last race at two, Discovery ran second to Chicstraw in the Walden Handicap at Pimlico.

In the spring and summer of his three-year-old year in 1934, Discovery faced Cavalcade on six occasions, and fell victim to the Brookmeade Stable runner each time. In the Kentucky Derby, Discovery held a two-length advantage after a mile and did his best to fight him off in early stretch, but Cavalcade prevailed by two and a half, handily. In the Preakness, Discovery was in tight quarters early and missed Cavalcade by a length. Calvacade, in turn, fell victim to his stablemate, High Quest, by a nose. Neither Discovery nor Cavalcade ran in the Belmont.

Discovery lost twice more to Cavalcade in the Midwest — in the American Derby and Detroit Derby — so it was time for a change of plan.

DISPLAY, b, 1923	Fair Play, 1905	Hastings, 1893	Spendthrift / Cinderella
		Fairy Gold, 1896	Bend Or / Dame Masham
	Cicuta, 1919	Nassovian, 1913	William the Third / Veneration II
DISCOVERY, chestnut colt, 1931		Hemlock, 1913	Spearmint / Keystone II
	Light Brigade, 1910	Picton, 1903	Orvieto / Hecuba
ARIADNE, br, 1926		Bridge of Sighs, 1905	Isinglass / Santa Brigida
	Adrienne, 1919	His Majesty, 1910	Ogden / Her Majesty
		Adriana, 1905	Hamburg / Kildeer

Stotler entered him against older horses in the Brooklyn Handicap. Discovery was to own the Brooklyn for three consecutive years, winning under successively heavier imposts.

He was beaten again by Cavalcade in the Arlington Classic, but won a pair of stakes at Saratoga, including the Whitney, which was another race he would win three times. After a win in the Rhode Island Handicap under 119 pounds, in which he set a world record of 1:55 for a mile and three-sixteenths, racing secretaries started to pack weight on. Discovery was assigned 128 for the Potomac Handicap and he won by four.

At four, Discovery started nineteen times and carried an average of 130 pounds, and after losing his first five starts, he finished the year with eleven victories. In a six-week period from late June to early August, the iron horse was unstoppable, winning eight consecutive races, including the Brooklyn Handicap, Detroit Challenge Cup, Butler Handicap, and the Arlington Handicap. The streak culminated with the Merchants' and Citizens' Handicap under 139, which was followed by a loss in the Narragansett Special, also under 139.

Discovery was the leading handicapper the next year as well, winning the San Carlos Handicap at Santa Anita, but he was unable to win a roughly run Santa Anita Handicap. After a rest, he came back to win the Brooklyn again, this time under 136, and he also accounted for the Saratoga Handicap under 132. Then the weight, and perhaps the age, began to catch up to him. Discovery was retired to Vanderbilt's Sagamore Farm, where he remained for the rest of his twenty-one-year stallion career.

Discovery sired just twenty-five stakes winners. Through his daughters the great weight carrier forever left his stamp. He was the sire of the dams of thirty-nine stakes winners, including Horses of the Year Bold Ruler and Native Dancer and champions Bed o' Roses, Intentionally, and Hasty Road. Native Dancer sired Raise a Native, a strong influence in the 1970s, who, in turn, sired the remarkable Mr. Prospector. — *E. H.*

RACE and (STAKES) RECORD

YEAR	AGE	STS	1ST	2ND	3RD	EARNED
1933	at 2	14	2	3(2)	5(3)	$8,397
1934	at 3	16	8(6)	3(3)	3(3)	$49,555
1935	at 4	19	11(11)	2(2)	2(2)	$102,545
1936	at 5	14	6(5)	2(2)	0	$34,790
Lifetime		63	27(22)	10(9)	10(8)	$195,287

Challedon

"MOST MEMORABLE OF ALL PREAKNESSES," wrote Humphrey S. Finney in a 1968 issue of *The Blood-Horse*, "was that of 1939, known to all loyal Marylanders as 'Challedon's Year.' " The first Maryland-bred to capture the Preakness Stakes in fifty years and the first two-time Horse of the Year since voting for the honor began, Challedon was something of a hero in his native Maryland.

The bay colt tallied some of his biggest scores in Maryland, but he parlayed his popularity in that state to success from coast to coast.

Foaled in April of 1936 at W. L. Brann and Robert S. Castle's Branncastle Farm, Challedon was the product of a mating between the partners' imported stallion Challenger II and Brann's undistinguished broodmare, Laura Gal, whom he had purchased for $2,050. By the time Challedon raced as a two-year-old, Castle's health caused him to drop out of the partnership. Brann then changed the name of the Maryland property to Glade Valley Farm, and Challedon was campaigned in his name alone.

As a two-year-old, Challedon captured four of his six starts, including a notable triple: the Maryland Futurity, New England Futurity, and Pimlico Futurity, in a span of less than a month. After the New England, it was reported Challedon came out of the race with badly bucked shins. If true, his Pimlico victory only fourteen days later became all the more impressive.

The first two starts of Challedon's three-year-old season resulted in losses. The Maryland-bred was third in the Chesapeake Stakes at Havre de Grace in late April to rivals Gilded Knight and Impound, then a well-beaten second in the Kentucky Derby, eight lengths behind Johnstown.

		John o' Gaunt, 1901	Isinglass / La Fleche
	Swynford, 1907	Canterbury Pilgrim, 1893	Tristan / Pilgrimage
CHALLENGER II (GB), b, 1927	Sword Play, 1921	Great Sport, 1910	Gallinule / Gondolette
		Flash of Steel, 1913	Royal Realm / Flaming Vixen
CHALLEDON, bay colt, 1936	Sir Gallahad III, 1920	Teddy, 1913	Ajax / Rondeau
		Plucky Liege, 1912	Spearmint / Concertina
LAURA GAL, b, 1929	Laura Dianti, 1923	Wrack, 1909	Robert le Diable / Samphire
		Lady Errant, 1911	Knight Errant / Outcome

Preakness day dawned gray and wet, and a muddy track faced the contenders. Challedon, Johnstown, and Gilded Knight battled through the final turn and the stretch head and head, but it was Challedon who pulled away by one and a quarter lengths to be the pride of Maryland that day. Trainer Schaefer had won the Preakness as a jockey in 1929, aboard Dr. Freeland, and confessed after Challedon's edition of the race that he felt he had ridden Challedon harder than he did his mount of ten years prior.

The bay colt did not contest the Belmont Stakes, as he had been removed from eligibility for the contest as a weanling. Nevertheless, other moments of elation awaited supporters of the horse, such as the setting of a new world record at Keeneland when he covered the one and three-sixteenths miles of the Tranter Purse in 1:54⅗.

Challedon traversed the country, traveling to Boston, Chicago, New York, and Los Angeles, among other places. He captured the Pimlico Special in 1939 and 1940, and the Hollywood Gold Cup in 1940, setting a new track record under 133 pounds. He was named Horse of the Year and champion three-year-old of 1939 and Horse of the Year and champion older horse at four.

Brann turned down a $350,000 offer for Challedon in the waning days of 1940, declining to sell his star for any price. As a five-year-old, Challedon ran into tendon trouble and quarter cracks. He only made three starts that year, failing to place and not earning a penny.

At six, Challedon won only two of his thirteen starts and toward the end of the year refused to extend himself in competition. In late 1942, Brann announced the once gallant horse's retirement and opted to stand Challedon at Ira Drymon's Gallaher Farm for a fee of $500. Challedon went to the breeding shed with earnings of $334,685 and a record of twenty wins from forty-four starts. His extra two years in training netted his connections less than $12,000 and dimmed his reputation considerably.

Syndicated in 1949, Challedon ultimately sired 282 foals, thirteen of which went on to be stakes winners. At age twenty-two, he broke a leg in a paddock accident and died. In 1977, Challedon was elected to the Racing Hall of Fame. — J. W.

RACE and (STAKES) RECORD

YEAR	AGE	STS	1ST	2ND	3RD	EARNED
1938	at 2	6	4(3)	0	1	$67,700
1939	at 3	15	9(9)	2(2)	3(3)	$184,535
1940	at 4	7	5(4)	1(1)	1(1)	$70,625
1941	at 5	3	0	0	0	$0
1942	at 6	13	2(1)	4(2)	1	$11,825
Lifetime		44	20(17)	7(5)	6(4)	$334,685

Armed

ARMED WAS BOTH A HORSE OF THE YEAR and a work horse during the glory days of Warren Wright's Calumet Farm in the 1940s. He won forty-one of eighty-one races during seven years of racing, captured ten or more races three consecutive years, and was Horse of the Year in 1947 and twice champion handicap male. He also reigned as the sport's leading money-earner, but only for two weeks in the fall of 1947.

Armed was foaled on May 1, 1941, at Calumet Farm near Lexington, Kentucky, and was a member of the first crop of foals sired by farm stallion Bull Lea. He was sent to Florida in mid-November of the following year to be prepared for his two-year-old season. Exhibiting a bit of studdishness while in Florida, Armed was gelded soon after arriving back at Calumet in March of 1943 and turned into a stable pony.

Around Thanksgiving, Armed again was on his way to Florida, and this time the lessons imparted by Calumet trainer Ben A. Jones seemed to stick. Armed won his first start by eight lengths at Hialeah in February of 1944 under Eddie Arcaro, then scored there again by three lengths, after which jockey Conn McCreary said to Jones, "Let's go with this one in the Derby, Ben; he'll win it."

Jones and McCreary instead won the 1944 Derby with Calumet homebred Pensive. Armed ended the year with only three wins from seven starts, and was placed in the hands of Jones' son, Horace A. (Jimmy) Jones. The younger Jones had returned to racing after spending time in the Coast Guard during World War II.

Armed won ten of fifteen races while racing from June to October his four-year-old season in 1945. After losing at Jamaica in his first start following a questionable ride, Armed won six consecutive races before finishing in the runner-up spot in four stakes. After that, he won the Washington Handicap at Laurel with top weight, followed by two overnight

				Teddy, 1913	Ajax Rondeau
		Bull Dog, 1927			
	BULL LEA, br, 1935			Plucky Liege, 1912	Spearmint Concertina
				Ballot, 1904	Voter Cerito
		Rose Leaves, 1916			
ARMED, brown gelding, May 1, 1941				Colonial, 1897	Trenton Thankful Blossom
				Fair Play, 1905	Hastings Fairy Gold
		Chance Shot, 1924			
	ARMFUL, blk, 1933			Quelle Chance, 1917	Ethelbert Qu'Elle est Belle II
				Luke McLuke, 1911	Ultimus Midge
		Negrina, 1921			
				Black Brocade, 1912	Neil Gow Black Velvet

races in preparation for the Pimlico Special. In the latter, he defeated Polynesian and Stymie.

Sent back to Florida, Armed won the 1946 Widener Handicap at Hialeah, emulating Bull Lea, who had won the 1939 running. Armed carried 128 pounds in the Widener, and in one ten-race stretch later that year he never carried less than 130 pounds, winning five of them. His big win came under 130 pounds in the Suburban Handicap at Belmont Park in May. Armed that year won his first championship.

Armed's six-year-old season in 1947 was more of the same. He won the Widener Handicap under 129 pounds, setting a track mark of 2:01⅗ for one and a quarter miles, and carried 130 pounds or more ten times. In one of the most anticipated races that year, Armed faced Assault in a match race in September and won by eight lengths. Although it was rewarding to the tune of $100,000 for the Calumet camp, the result meant next to nothing, since Assault's chances were compromised by a splint problem.

The following month, Armed won the Sysonby Mile, and boosted his earnings to a world-record $761,500. The record lasted sixteen days before Stymie passed him. Armed next finished third in the Pimlico Special and ended the year with eleven wins from eighteen starts. He was voted 1947 Horse of the Year and champion handicap male.

Armed raced three more seasons, but failed to win another stakes. He left racing the same way he came in — with a victory in Florida during the first part of the year. The win came at Gulfstream in March of 1950 and Armed's retirement was announced in June. At the time, he was the world's leading money-earning gelding, with $817,475. He had set or equaled nine track records.

Armed was elected to the Racing Hall of Fame in 1963 and died at Calumet on May 5, 1964. Years later, Jimmy Jones recalled, "Down the backstretch, going one and a quarter miles, he'd be in a horizontal position, but around the three and a half-furlong pole, it seemed to me, he'd drop down two inches and get digging," the Hall of Fame trainer said. "You couldn't help but admire that." — D. S.

RACE and (STAKES) RECORD

YEAR	AGE	STS	1ST	2ND	3RD	EARNED
1944	at 3	7	3	1	0	$4,850
1945	at 4	15	10(2)	4(4)	0	$91,600
1946	at 5	18	11(9)	4(4)	2(2)	$288,725
1947	at 6	17	11(8)	4(3)	1(1)	$376,325
1948	at 7	6	1	1(1)	2(2)	$12,200
1949	at 8	12	3	3(3)	5(2)	$36,250
1950	at 9	6	2	3(1)	0	$7,525
Lifetime		**81**	**41(19)**	**20(16)**	**10(7)**	**$817,475**

Busher

IT'S A SPECIAL KIND OF THREE-YEAR-OLD FILLY that can lay claim to Horse of the Year honors, and in the war-shortened racing year of 1945 Busher did exactly that. How good was she at three? Not only good enough to win ten of thirteen starts and beat older fillies and mares, but good enough to beat three-year-old colts and older males. She was good enough to finish her career with $334,035 in earnings — the most of any female up to that time.

During the World War II years, while America's best men were fighting overseas, it seemed the males were missing from racing as well. The year before Busher's tremendous campaign, Calumet Farm's Twilight Tear was voted Horse of the Year. Busher had the lineage to be a star. Bred by Col. E. R. Bradley, Busher was by 1937 Triple Crown winner War Admiral (by Man

o' War), out of Baby League, by 1926 Kentucky Derby winner Bubbling Over. Baby League, a half-sister to Bimelech, was a daughter of the great foundation mare, La Troienne.

Raced by Bradley's Idle Hour Stock Farm at two, Busher was a runner from the outset, winning three of her first four starts, including a two-length score in the Adirondack Stakes under Eddie Arcaro. Victories followed in the Matron Stakes and the Selima Stakes. Busher earned $60,300, tops in her division. She was voted champion two-year-old filly of 1944 and assigned 119 pounds on the Experimental Free Handicap.

Racing was put on hold from January to May of 1945 for the War effort, and Bradley sold many of his horses at this time. Movie mogul Louis B. Mayer purchased Busher for $50,000 in March of '45, a price, in retrospect, that turned out to be a bargain.

It didn't take Mayer long to get his investment back, as Busher made her three-year-old debut a winning one in an allowance race at Santa Anita on May 26. A week later, she dis-

		Fair Play, 1905	Hastings / Fairy Gold
	Man o' War, 1917		
WAR ADMIRAL, br, 1934		Mahubah, 1910	Rock Sand / Merry Token
		Sweep, 1907	Ben Brush / Pink Domino
	Brushup, 1929		
BUSHER, chestnut filly, 1942		Annette K., 1921	Harry of Hereford / Bathing Girl
		North Star III, 1914	Sunstar / Angelic
	Bubbling Over, 1923		
BABY LEAGUE, b, 1935		Beaming Beauty, 1917	**Sweep** / Bellisario
		Teddy, 1913	Ajax / Rondeau
	La Troienne, 1926		
		Helene de Troie, 1916	Helicon / Lady of Pedigree

mantled a field of fillies in the Santa Susana Stakes by seven. Trainer George Odom then set his sights on the boys in the one-mile San Vicente Handicap, and Busher came through with a length tally while carrying top-weight (by scale) of 121. She was then odds-on in the Santa Anita Derby under Johnny Longden and took the lead on the turn but fell short a half-length to Bymeabond.

Pitted against older fillies and mares for the first time, Busher won the Santa Margarita Handicap by one and a half lengths while carrying equal topweight. Then it was time to take her show on the road. After winning the Cleopatra Handicap in Chicago, she was assigned 113 pounds to take on older horses in the one and a quarter-mile Arlington Handicap. Going uncharacteristically for the lead under Longden, Busher led throughout, winning by nearly five lengths. Just when things couldn't be going any better for Busher, she promptly lost. Under 128 pounds, she was beaten by the four-year-old Durazna, the champion two-year-old filly of 1943, who carried 116.

Busher exacted revenge, beating Durazna in a match race by three-quarters of a length. Then, in her finest performance, Busher won the one and a quarter-mile Washington Park Handicap over top handicapper Armed in a track record 2:01⅖ while conceding four pounds. Busher also won the Hollywood Derby over colts, passing the $300,000 mark in earnings to become the first female to do so. After a victory in the Vanity Handicap, she developed swelling in a leg after a workout in mid-October of 1945 and raced no more that year. The year-end honors rolled in: best three-year-old filly, best three-year-old of either sex, best filly or mare in the handicap division, and Horse of the Year. She did not race in 1946, and, after finishing unplaced in her only start of 1947, the mighty Busher was retired.

On Feb. 27, 1947, Busher was sold as part of a dispersal for $135,000 to Neil S. McCarthy. Later that year, McCarthy sold Busher to Elizabeth Graham's Maine Chance Farm for a reported $150,000. As a broodmare, Busher produced five foals, including stakes winner Jet Action, by Jet Pilot. She died on March 22, 1955, from complications after giving birth to a Jet Pilot filly. — *E. H.*

RACE and (STAKES) RECORD

YEAR	AGE	STS	1ST	2ND	3RD	EARNED
1944	at 2	7	5(3)	1	0	$60,300
1945	at 3	13	10(9)	2(2)	1(1)	$273,735
1946	at 4	0	0	0	0	—
1947	at 5	1	0	0	0	$0
Lifetime		**21**	**15(12)**	**3(2)**	**1(1)**	**$334,035**

Stymie

STYMIE'S STORY REMAINS ONE OF THE MOST DEMOCRATIC and inspiring in horse racing. He was like the cinematic hero Rocky in that his career followed from humility to glory. Stymie began as a cheap claimer, laboring inconspicuously in the sort of races used to fill out a forgettable program. He ended his career as the richest racehorse in America, commanding attention and respect wherever he appeared.

Stymie was bred officially by the Hall of Fame trainer Max Hirsch, but that was only because of a delay in transferring ownership of the horse's dam, Stop Watch, to King

Ranch, the famous family-owned Texas ranch managed by Robert Kleberg Jr. Stymie was foaled there on April 4, 1941.

His appearance was unprepossessing, even ordinary. The chestnut ran with his head high, and he ran, at least to begin with, slowly. He made his debut May 7, 1943, at the old Jamaica racetrack in New York, for a claiming price of $2,500, and he finished seventh. Three weeks later, he was eleventh in a maiden race at Belmont Park.

Hirsch then dropped Stymie to $1,500, a price irresistible to trainer Hirsch Jacobs. In terms of victories, Jacobs had been one of the country's leading trainers for years, and generally his stable consisted of modest claimers. Maybe in Stymie he saw some potential — if so, it was well hidden and not about to emerge for several races. Or maybe Stymie's pedigree appealed to Jacobs. A son Equestrian, Stymie was a grandson of Equipoise, and he was inbred to the great Man o' War.

Claimed for $1,500, Stymie became one of the greatest bargains in racing history. Years later, visitors to King Ranch would be warned not to bring up the subject of Stymie.

With Jacobs as his trainer, Stymie made gradual improvement. He needed eleven more races before discovering the winner's circle, and then it was while racing for a $3,300 claiming price. In October, in his twenty-second start as a two-year-old, Stymie improved while stretching out to a mile. And in his twenty-eighth and final outing of the season, he won a mile and a sixteenth overnight handicap at Jamaica by five lengths.

As a three-year-old, Stymie competed, although with only moderate success, against many of the best horses of his generation. After two years of racing without respite, Stymie had made fifty-seven starts and had only seven victories, none of them stakes. Still, he already had proven to be an exceptional claim, for he had earned $52,260. But that was just the beginning. Stymie obviously had uncommon stamina, and in his best performances, when unhurried, he could muster a powerful charge. Returning rested when a wartime ban was lifted, Stymie won the Grey Lag Handicap in his third start as a four-year-old. It was the first of his twenty-five stakes victories.

Stymie became the champion of his division in 1945. From 1945 through 1947, he raced against the best horses of the time, some of the best of all-time — Armed, Assault, Gallorette, Devil Diver, Pavot, and Polynesian. He raced against them with courage and, in the end, distinction. During that three-year period, Stymie won twenty-four races and finished in the top three in fifty of his fifty-eight starts, earning $763,800.

In 1946, Stymie equaled Jamaica's record of 1:49⅗ for a mile and an eighth while again winning the Grey Lag Handicap. He defeated Polynesian and Trymenow in the Whitney and won the Saratoga Cup in a walkover. In the Gallant Fox, Stymie set a Jamaica record of 2:42⅘ for a mile and five-eighths while defeating King Ranch's Assault. Under jockey Conn McCreary, Stymie won the 1947 Gold Cup at Belmont.

In 1948, Stymie suffered a cracked sesamoid, but he returned briefly to race the next year. He retired with earnings of $918,485, which would remain a record until the sport saw its first millionaire: Citation. — G. W.

		Pennant, 1911	Peter Pan / Royal Rose
	Equipoise, 1928		
EQUESTRIAN, ch, 1936		Swinging, 1922	**Broomstick** / Balancoire II
		Man o' War, 1917	**Fair Play / Mahubah**
	Frilette, 1924		
STYMIE, chestnut colt, April 14, 1941		Frillery, 1913	**Broomstick** / Petticoat
		Colin, 1905	Commando / Pastorella
	On Watch, 1917		
STOP WATCH, blk, 1933		Rubia Granda, 1906	Greenan / The Great Ruby
		Man o' War, 1917	**Fair Play / Mahubah**
	Sunset Gun, 1927		
		Eventide, 1921	Uncle / Noontide

RACE and (STAKES) RECORD

YEAR	AGE	STS	1ST	2ND	3RD	EARNED
1943	at 2	28	4	8(1)	4(1)	$15,935
1944	at 3	29	3	5(1)	10(6)	$36,325
1945	at 4	19	9(8)	4(3)	4(4)	$225,375
1946	at 5	20	8(7)	7(5)	4(4)	$238,650
1947	at 6	19	7(7)	5(5)	2(2)	$299,775
1948	at 7	11	4(3)	3(3)	2(2)	$95,275
1949	at 8	5	0	1(1)	2	$7,150
Lifetime		131	35(25)	33(19)	28(19)	$918,485

Alysheba

CHRIS MCCARRON COULD FEEL THE SURGE OF POWER beneath him as he dashed by horses in the 1987 Kentucky Derby. Turning for home, all that stood between him and victory were the reddish orange silks of Robert Levy's Bet Twice. Beyond that, all McCarron could see were the Twin Spires beckoning in the distance.

As he prepared for the final surge that would propel him past Bet Twice, the scene suddenly changed. Bet Twice was now directly in his path. Then, in a heartbeat, the thousand pounds of horseflesh gave way under him. The mane of Alysheba no longer was blowing in his face. The Twin Spires in the corner of his eye were gone. All he could see was the ground rising up to meet him. All he could feel was the strain in his outstretched arms, as he fought to stay aboard.

Alysheba was fighting as well, using all his athletic ability to pick himself virtually off the ground. Then, just as quickly, everything was as it was before. Although Bet Twice drifted out in front of him on two more occasions, horse and rider this time were prepared, altering course both times. McCarron went to his left-hand whip and Alysheba kept coming. Both had survived one of the scariest moments in racing history and there would be no denying them.

Alysheba not only had won the 113th Kentucky Derby, he had gained the admiration of racing fans all over the country. The incident was enough to secure Alysheba's name in the annals of the sport. But it was only the beginning. His career would continue to skyrocket, culminating with an unforgettable performance in the following year's Breeders' Cup Classic, in which he was proclaimed "America's Horse."

Following the Derby, Alysheba, trained by Jack Van Berg and owned by Dorothy Scharbauer and her daughter Pam, defeated Bet Twice again in the Preakness, but could do no better than a well-beaten fourth in the Belmont Stakes. He lost a hard-fought battle with Bet Twice in a memorable running of the Haskell Invitational at Monmouth, then, after a dismal effort in the Travers over a sloppy track, he captured the Super Derby at Louisiana Downs.

ALYSHEBA, bay colt, March 3, 1984

ALYDAR, ch, 1975
- Raise a Native, 1961
  - Native Dancer, 1950 — Polynesian / Geisha
  - Raise You, 1946 — Case Ace / Lady Glory
- Sweet Tooth, 1965
  - On-and-On, 1956 — **Nasrullah** / Two Lea
  - Plum Cake, 1958 — Ponder / Real Delight

BEL SHEBA, b, 1970
- Lt. Stevens, 1961
  - Nantallah, 1953 — **Nasrullah** / Shimmer
  - Rough Shod II, 1944 — Gold Bridge / Dalmary
- Belthazar, 1960
  - War Admiral, 1934 — Man o' War / Brushup
  - Blinking Owl, 1938 — Pharamond II / Baba Kenny

Alysheba then fell a nose short of catching the previous year's Kentucky Derby winner, Ferdinand, in the Breeders' Cup Classic. The son of Alydar was voted champion three-year-old; the following year he matured into one of the great horses of his era.

First, Van Berg made an equipment change. Racing without blinkers, Alysheba won six grade I stakes; gained his revenge on Ferdinand; shattered the one and a quarter-mile track record at Meadowlands, running the fastest ten furlongs ever in the Northeast; and set a track record for one and a quarter miles at Belmont. He then defeated one of the strongest fields ever assembled in the Breeders' Cup Classic to clinch Horse of the Year honors.

By winning Belmont's Woodward Stakes over Forty Niner in a track-record 1:59⅖, then coming back and capturing the Meadowlands Cup in a record 1:58⅘, Alysheba became only the second horse to break 2:00 for one and a quarter miles on dirt at least three times — the other time being his 1:59⅖ Santa Anita Handicap — and the only horse of the modern era to break back-to-back track records at that distance.

Although his records and individual performances were enough to get him elected to the Racing Hall of Fame in 1993, what really flattered the colt was the company he kept. His heart-throbbing victories over Ferdinand in the Santa Anita Handicap and San Bernardino Handicap were memorable enough, but his intense, eight-race rivalry with Bet Twice (Alysheba finished first four times, and Bet Twice three times) really caught the nation's attention. The two had become so familiar with each other, Van Berg and Bet Twice's trainer Jimmy Croll insisted they would "nicker" and "holler" at each other whenever they crossed paths at the barn.

After his retirement in 1988, Alysheba was sent to Lane's End Farm in Versailles, Kentucky. He had sired fifteen stakes winners by June of 1999, but nothing even remotely close to himself.

— *S. H.*

RACE and (STAKES) RECORD

YEAR	AGE	STS	1ST	2ND	3RD	EARNED
1986	at 2	7	1	4(3)	1(1)	$359,486
1987	at 3	10	3(3)	3(3)	1(1)	$2,511,156
1988	at 4	9	7(7)	1(1)	0	$3,808,600
Lifetime		26	11(10)	8(7)	2(2)	$6,679,242

Northern Dancer

WINNING THE KENTUCKY DERBY and Preakness Stakes made Northern Dancer a hero in his native Canada. Becoming the stallion that he did made him a legend the world over.

Northern Dancer will always be remembered foremost for his extraordinary career as a sire and sire of sires. But his accomplishments on the racetrack hardly required apology. Indeed, sage observers will say that his racing class, combined with impeccable bloodlines, presaged Northern Dancer's later success.

Northern Dancer got a late start in life by Thoroughbred standards, entering the world on May 27, 1961. His dam Natalma, a stakes-placed Native Dancer mare, had been preparing for the Kentucky Oaks when a knee problem necessitated surgery. She then was bred late in the season to Canadian Horse of the Year Nearctic in his first year at stud.

Canadian industrialist E. P. Taylor owned Natalma, and Nearctic had raced in his colors. The founder of Woodbine Racecourse, Taylor had international aspirations for Canadian racing and breeding. His own breeding program derived from careful selection of European bloodstock, with horses such as Nearctic being an end result. Taylor wanted to promote his program and annually conducted pre-priced yearling sales at his farm in Oshawa, Ontario. Accordingly, he entered his Nearctic—Natalma yearling and set the reserve at $25,000. But the diminutive colt could find no buyers and Taylor kept him. Named Northern Dancer, he eventually joined the Windfields Farm stable under trainer Horatio Luro.

Northern Dancer vindicated his owner's faith with brilliant victories at two that included the Summer Stakes and Coronation Futurity in Canada and the Remsen Stakes in New York. His record of seven victories from nine starts led to Canadian juvenile honors.

		Pharos, 1920	Phalaris / Scapa Flow
NEARCTIC, br, 1954	Nearco, 1935	Nogara, 1928	Havresac II / Catnip
	Lady Angela, 1944	Hyperion, 1930	Gainsborough / Selene
		Sister Sarah, 1930	Abbots Trace / Sarita
NORTHERN DANCER, bay colt, May 27, 1961	Native Dancer, 1950	Polynesian, 1942	Unbreakable / Black Polly
		Geisha, 1943	Discovery / Miyako
NATALMA, b, 1957	Almahmoud, 1947	Mahmoud, 1933	Blenheim II / Mah Mahal
		Arbitrator, 1937	Peace Chance / Mother Goose

As a three-year-old, Northern Dancer swept the Triple Crown prep races with victories in the Flamingo Stakes, Florida Derby, and Blue Grass Stakes. Despite his record, Northern Dancer was sent off the second choice behind Hill Rise in the 1964 Kentucky Derby. Under a strong hold by rider Bill Hartack, the Canadian colt moved up steadily to gain the lead by the quarter pole. He prevailed by a neck over Hill Rise in then-record time of 2:00, a mark lowered only by Secretariat. Two weeks later, Northern Dancer confirmed his class with an emphatic victory in the Preakness Stakes. Trainer Luro worried about the colt's ability to get the one and a half miles of the Belmont Stakes, and Northern Dancer indeed came up short, finishing third behind Quadrangle and Roman Brother.

Northern Dancer returned to Canada to a hero's welcome, then sailed through the Queen's Plate to win by seven and a half lengths. Tenderness in a left front tendon discovered soon after ended his racing career. He retired with fourteen wins in eighteen starts and earnings of $580,647. He was named North America's champion three-year-old and Canadian Horse of the Year.

Northern Dancer initially stood at Taylor's Oshawa farm. His first crop yielded Canadian Horse of the Year Viceregal; the second crop, Nijinsky II, who for owner Charles Engelhard became the first horse in thirty-five years to win the English Triple Crown.

By then, Northern Dancer was standing at Taylor's Windfields Farm in Chesapeake City, Maryland, an outpost which would become a mecca for the world's top broodmares. Northern Dancer's success helped propel the stunning rise in yearling auction prices during the late 1970s and early '80s, and his offspring became the focus of legendary bidding battles between English horseman Robert Sangster and the Maktoums of Dubai.

At one point, Northern Dancer's stud fee soared to $1 million, and when the stallion was twenty, a European syndicate unsuccessfully offered $40-million to buy him. Northern Dancer's fertility waned in later years, and he was euthanized on Nov. 16, 1990, after a severe attack of colic. His final tally as a sire: 146 stakes winners. He also was the sire of the dams of 214 stakes winners. His legacy continues through the accomplishments of his descendants, both on the track and in the stud. — J. D.

RACE and (STAKES) RECORD						
YEAR	AGE	STS	1ST	2ND	3RD	EARNED
1963	at 2	9	7(6)	2(2)	0	$90,635
1964	at 3	9	7(6)	0	2(1)	$490,012
Lifetime		**18**	**14(12)**	**2(2)**	**2(1)**	**$580,647**

Ack Ack

FEW HORSES HAVE THE VERSATILITY to set sprint records and also win at classic distances under staggering imposts. Ack Ack did those things and more in a four-season career of remarkable range. For his five-year-old exploits, Ack Ack earned a rare triple to become Horse of the Year as well as champion sprinter and handicap male.

Named for the antiaircraft guns of World War II, Ack Ack was by the stallion Battle Joined out of the Turn-to mare Fast Turn. He was one of the last horses bred by Capt. Harry F. Guggenheim, the financier-philanthropist-publisher whose grandfather had amassed a

fortune in the mining business. Guggenheim owned 1953 Kentucky Derby winner Dark Star and bred a total of forty stakes winners in the United States, including Bald Eagle, Never Bend, and Crafty Admiral. None became a Horse of the Year, and Ack Ack would achieve that distinction only after Guggenheim's death.

Conditioned by Frank Bonsal, Ack Ack won one of three starts as a juvenile in the colors of Cain Hoy Stable and finished second in the other two. At three Ack Ack set a track record of 1:34⅖ in the mile Derby Trial Stakes but skipped the Kentucky Derby itself in pursuit of shorter distances. His other victories at three included a division of the Bahamas Stakes, the Arlington Classic, and Withers Stakes. He completed the year with seven wins and three seconds from eleven starts.

Guggenheim, in failing health, dispersed his Thoroughbred holdings in 1969, but retained several stallions as well as Ack Ack, on whom he reportedly had set a $1-million reserve. Ack Ack later that year went West to trainer Charlie Whittingham.

As a four-year-old, Ack Ack won the Los Angeles and Autumn Days Handicaps, and set a track record of 1:02⅕ for five and a half furlongs at Del Mar. In all, he won four of

		Alsab, 1939	Good Goods Winds Chant
	Armageddon, 1949		
		Fighting Lady, 1943	Sir Gallahad III Lady Nicotine
BATTLE JOINED, b, 1959			
		Revoked, 1943	Blue Larkspur Gala Belle
	Ethel Walker, 1953		
ACK ACK, **bay colt,** **February 24, 1966**		Ethel Terry, 1947	Reaping Reward Mary Terry
		Royal Charger, 1942	Nearco Sun Princess
	Turn-to, 1951		
		Source Sucree, 1940	Admiral Drake Lavendula
FAST TURN, b, 1959			
		Princequillo, 1940	Prince Rose Cosquilla
	Cherokee Rose, 1951		
		The Squaw II, 1939	Sickle Minnewaska

five starts. Although Ack Ack specialized in shorter distances, Whittingham saw the potential for longer efforts because of the colt's pedigree, which had the stayer Princequillo three generations back. Accordingly, the trainer set his sights on some of the rich handicap races of the following season. In Ack Ack, Whittingham molded the prototype of the West Coast handicap star.

Ack Ack began his five-year-old campaign by winning the San Carlos Handicap and running second in the Palos Verdes Handicap for Guggenheim. But Guggenheim did not live to see the full flowering of the best stakes winner he ever bred. He died in January of 1971. Whittingham persuaded E. E. (Buddy) Fogelson and his wife, the actress Greer Garson, to buy a majority interest in Ack Ack with the trainer retaining one-third. Thereafter, Ack Ack wore a patina of glamour bestowed by his Hollywood connections.

Ack Ack was undefeated for his new owners, winning six consecutive stakes in the colors of their Forked Lightning Ranch. In his first test beyond eight furlongs, Ack Ack won the San Pasqual Handicap at one and a sixteenth miles after stumbling at the start. Next came the San Antonio Stakes at a mile and an eighth. In the Santa Anita Handicap, Ack Ack, while carrying a hefty 130 pounds, defeated his talented stablemate Cougar II. Toting 130 pounds once again, Ack Ack won the five and a half furlong Hollywood Express Handicap, then set a course record of 1:47⅕ in the mile and an eighth American Handicap at Hollywood Park. In what was to be his final race, Ack Ack stretched his speed to win the mile and a quarter Hollywood Gold Cup under 134 pounds, the heaviest weight ever carried to victory in that event. He was retired later in 1971 after a life-threatening bout of colic.

Although he was done at mid-season and raced that year only in California, Ack Ack nevertheless was Horse of the Year and top sprinter and handicap male. Ack Ack entered stud at Claiborne Farm in 1972, where he sired a total of fifty-five stakes winners, including the French and North American champion Youth and multiple grade I winner Broad Brush. Daughters sired by Ack Ack have produced eighty-eight stakes winners, including champions North Sider and Benny the Dip. He died on Dec. 28, 1990. — J. D.

RACE and (STAKES) RECORD

YEAR	AGE	STS	1ST	2ND	3RD	EARNED
1968	at 2	3	1	2	0	$6,075
1969	at 3	11	7(4)	3(1)	0	$177,491
1970	at 4	5	4(2)	0	0	$59,775
1971	at 5	8	7(7)	1(1)	0	$393,300
Lifetime		27	19(13)	6(2)	0	$636,641

137

Gallorette

FILLIES DO BEAT THE COLTS EVERY NOW AND THEN, but perhaps the Kentucky Derby is proof of how difficult it can be. In 125 editions of the Derby, only three fillies — Regret (1915), Genuine Risk (1980), and Winning Colors (1988) — have won. The filly Gallorette was a three-year-old in 1945, but she didn't compete in the Kentucky Derby. In retrospect, she probably cut the boys a break.

On May 22 of that year, Gallorette, owned by William Leavitt Brann, won a $4,000 allowance test for three-year-olds at Jamaica. Fourth in that event was heavily favored Hoop, Jr., who the following month went on to win the Kentucky Derby.

A fluke? Not quite. In five years of racing, Gallorette won twenty-one of seventy-two starts, many of them against the boys. She padded her record with twenty seconds and thirteen thirds, and ended up with $445,535 in the bank — a good piece of change for the mid- to late-1940s and an earnings record for distaffers.

She was a filly, but she was made of iron. As a two-year-old, Gallorette was about 16.1 hands, and her sturdy frame would carry her to greatness. As written in *The Great Ones*: "She was a big mare; as big as most of the colts she raced against, tougher than some of them, faster than almost all of them."

Gallorette was bred by Preston M. Burch, who owned her dam, Gallette. Brann, one of Burch's friends, was a co-owner of the stallion Challenger II, sire of Preakness Stakes winner Challedon. Burch and Brann agreed to mate Gallette to Challenger II, and they struck a deal whereby Burch would own a foal, and Brann the next, for as long as Gallette produced.

Brann ended up with the first, and by far the best, one. Maryland-bred Gallorette finished third in her debut Sept. 14, 1944, at Laurel. She won her next two starts, then finished second to Petee Dee in the Maryland Futurity at Laurel. Gallorette then faced fillies in the Selima Stakes at Laurel, and finished third behind the victorious Busher.

	Swynford, 1907	John o' Gaunt, 1901	Isinglass / La Fleche
CHALLENGER II (GB), b, 1927		Canterbury Pilgrim, 1893	Tristan / Pilgrimage
	Sword Play, 1921	Great Sport, 1910	Gallinule / Gondolette
GALLORETTE, chestnut filly, 1942		Flash of Steel, 1913	Royal Realm / Flaming Vixen
	Sir Gallahad III, 1920	Teddy, 1913	Ajax / Rondeau
GALLETTE, b, 1929		Plucky Liege, 1912	Spearmint / Concertina
	Flambette, 1918	Durbar II, 1911	Rabelais / Armenia
		La Flambee, 1912	Ajax / Medeah

Horse of the Year Busher would hold the all-time earnings mark by a filly ($334,035) by the end of 1945. Gallorette later would smash that record by more than $100,000.

At three, Gallorette started thirteen times and won five races, including the Acorn Stakes, the Pimlico Oaks, and the Delaware Oaks against fillies. In July of that year, she defeated open company in the Empire City Stakes, a race that would set the tone for her career.

At four, Gallorette defeated males in the Metropolitan Handicap, the Brooklyn Handicap, and the Bay Shore Handicap. In the Brooklyn, she got the measure of the great Stymie, but in the Edgemere Handicap later in 1946, she finished second to him. Gallorette's final stakes victory of 1946 came in a division of the Beldame Handicap for fillies and mares. She was named champion handicap mare of that year.

In 1947, Gallorette defeated males twice in stakes company: in the Queens County Handicap and the Wilson Stakes. She also renewed her rivalry with Stymie. Gallorette handed him a loss in the Queens County, but Stymie turned the tables on subsequent occasions that year. In 1948, her final year of racing, Gallorette won four of fifteen starts, including the Carter Handicap, the Wilson Stakes, and the Whitney Stakes.

Gallorette was sold for $125,000 to Marie A. Moore of Virginia. She produced seven foals, two of them stakes winners, before she died at age seventeen at Moore's farm.

Eddie (Cocky) Simms, who broke Gallorette and worked with her during her career for trainer Ed Christmas, once told *The Blood-Horse*: "She's not only the greatest mare, but the greatest Maryland-bred of any sex…She had a long, tough career as a race mare, and if the jocks would have ridden her as instructed, she would have won a million instead of almost a half-million."

To believe Gallorette could have been any better than she was is quite a testament. — *T. L.*

RACE and (STAKES) RECORD

YEAR	AGE	STS	1ST	2ND	3RD	EARNED
1944	at 2	8	3	3(1)	2(1)	$7,950
1945	at 3	13	5(4)	2(2)	1	$94,300
1946	at 4	18	6(4)	5(4)	2(1)	$159,160
1947	at 5	18	3(2)	6(6)	5(5)	$90,275
1948	at 6	15	4(3)	4(3)	3(3)	$93,850
Lifetime		72	21(13)	20(16)	13(10)	$445,535

Majestic Prince

THE REGALLY NAMED MAJESTIC PRINCE holds the distinction of being the first horse to win the Kentucky Derby and Preakness Stakes while unbeaten. He also achieved fame as a record-priced auction yearling, selling for $250,000 to Canadian oilman Frank McMahon at the 1967 Keeneland July yearling sale. Central Kentucky horseman Leslie Combs II, who consigned Majestic Prince in the name of his Spendthrift Farm, was listed as the colt's official breeder. Unbeknownst to many, however, was the fact that McMahon owned Majestic Prince's dam, Gay Hostess, in partnership with Combs, making him the co-breeder.

The 1969 Derby field was one of the strongest ever, and Majestic Prince was the main attraction. Majestic Prince, whose big win had come in the one and an eighth-mile Santa Anita Derby five weeks before the Churchill classic, represented the West. Top Knight, Arts and Letters, and Dike were the big guns from the East. Veteran horsemen compared it to the 1957 Kentucky Derby, in which future Hall of Famers Bold Ruler, Gallant Man, and Round Table were bested by Iron Liege.

Top Knight, the previous year's champion two-year-old, was the big horse in Florida over the winter, winning the Flamingo Stakes and Florida Derby. Arts and Letters had run second in both those races, and came into Louisville with a fifteen-length win in the Blue Grass Stakes at Keeneland. Dike had won the Wood Memorial Stakes at Aqueduct.

That year's Run for the Roses attracted only eight contestants, the fewest since the Calumet powerhouse of Citation and Coaltown took on four rivals in the 1948 running. The 1969 Derby retained its elite status through the rest of the century. Since then, there hasn't been a Kentucky Derby with less than eight starters.

Trained by Johnny Longden, Majestic Prince tuned up for the one and a quarter-mile

		Polynesian, 1942	Unbreakable / Black Polly
	Native Dancer, 1950		
		Geisha, 1943	Discovery / Miyako
RAISE A NATIVE, ch, 1961			
		Case Ace, 1934	Teddy / Sweetheart
	Raise You, 1946		
		Lady Glory, 1934	American Flag / Beloved
MAJESTIC PRINCE, chestnut colt, March 19, 1966			
		Nearco, 1935	Pharos / Nogara
	Royal Charger, 1942		
		Sun Princess, 1937	Solario / Mumtaz Begum
GAY HOSTESS, ch, 1957			
		Alibhai, 1938	Hyperion / Teresina
	Your Hostess, 1949		
		Boudoir II, 1938	Mahmoud / Kampala

classic with a six-length triumph in the Stepping Stone allowance purse on opening day at the Churchill meeting. Majestic Prince went into the Derby with seven consecutive wins, and was sent away as the 7-5 favorite under rider Bill Hartack. Third down the backstretch, Majestic Prince rallied around the second turn and held off the closing charge of Arts and Letters to win by a neck. Dike finished third, with Top Knight ending up fifth. It was the fifth Derby triumph for Hartack, tying him with Eddie Arcaro.

All but Dike from the Fearsome Foursome were back for the Preakness, and five others joined in the fray. Majestic Prince, the 3-5 favorite, outlasted Arts and Letters to win by a head, with Top Knight running fourth.

Around this time it became public that McMahon had bred Majestic Prince with Combs. McMahon, who bid against Mrs. Bert Martin for Majestic Prince at the Keeneland sale, told *Sports Illustrated* that "I had a choice when Mrs. Martin went to $240,000: I could drop out and collect my $120,000 from the sale to Mrs. Martin or I could raise the bid to $250,000 and only be out $125,000. I wanted the colt so badly that's what I did."

Longden thought Majestic Prince should skip the Belmont Stakes. The hard-fought victories in the Derby and Preakness had taken a toll. But McMahon figured that he might never again have a chance to win the Triple Crown, and ordered Longden to get the colt ready for the one and a half-mile race. Never far back, but never really in the race, Majestic Prince finished five and a half lengths in second behind Arts and Letters.

Majestic Prince was returned to California and was fired for osselets. A knot appeared behind his left knee during the winter, and he was retired from racing. He had won nine of ten races and earned $414,200, but had failed to earn a championship. He was syndicated for $60,000 per share and entered stud at Spendthrift near Lexington, Kentucky that year.

Majestic Prince sired thirty-three stakes winners, including 1979 Belmont Stakes winner Coastal and major sire Majestic Light. He sired the dams of seventy-seven stakes winners, including three champions. Majestic Prince died on April 22, 1981, and was elected to the Racing Hall of Fame in 1988. Real Quiet, the 1998 Kentucky Derby and Preakness winner, traces in female family to Gay Hostess. — *D. S.*

RACE and (STAKES) RECORD

YEAR	AGE	STS	1ST	2ND	3RD	EARNED
1968	at 2	2	2	0	0	$5,500
1969	at 3	8	7(6)	1(1)	0	$408,700
Lifetime		10	9(6)	1(1)	0	$414,200

Coaltown

WHEN CALUMET FARM'S CITATION wore down stablemate Coaltown for a three and a half-length triumph in the 1948 Kentucky Derby, it typified the three-year-old campaigns of the two sons of Bull Lea.

After sustaining his first defeat in the Derby in what was his fifth start, Coaltown went on to post a respectable record of eight wins and five placings in thirteen trips to the post that year. But his accomplishments were overshadowed by Citation's great season in which he won nineteen of twenty starts and captured the coveted Triple Crown.

Unraced as a two-year-old due to respiratory and ankle problems, Coaltown broke his maiden in his first start before equaling Hialeah's six-furlong track record of 1:09⅗ with a twelve-length romp in allowance company. Sent to Keeneland, the colt defeated older stakes veterans sprinting in the Phoenix Handicap before setting a one and an eighth-mile track record of 1:49⅕ in the Blue Grass Stakes.

In the Derby, Coaltown held a six-length advantage after a half-mile in :46⅗ before Citation disposed of the pacesetter and won in a hand ride.

Following Coaltown's brief venture into classic company, the father-son training team of Ben and Jimmy Jones pointed the colt toward shorter races to take advantage of his brilliant speed. Coaltown responded favorably, winning the Jerome Handicap, Drexel Handicap, and Swift Stakes, and champion sprinter honors.

With Citation sidelined at four, Coaltown assumed the leadership role among Calumet's older horses in 1949, when he finished first or second in all fifteen starts while using his speed over longer distances. The colt won his first four starts, all at Hialeah in February. In his fifth outing of the year, Coaltown equaled the world record for one and a quarter miles when he carried 128 pounds to a seven-length win in the Gulfstream Park Handicap.

Although he could not be credited with records, Coaltown's first half-mile in :45 was two-fifths of a second faster than the then-existing world record and his mile time of 1:34⅕ bettered Equipoise's world standard by one-fifth of a second. That impressive

performance was not lost on the competition and in his next start, the Edward Burke Handicap, Coaltown won the Havre de Grace race in a walkover.

As Coaltown's reputation continued to build, so did the weight he was asked to carry. Jones held Coaltown out of the Dixie Handicap, for which he was assigned 136 pounds, and the Toboggan Handicap, where he would have had to tote 140 pounds. The trainer announced that 130, Coaltown's weight assignment in his walkover, would be the maximum under which he would race. Nevertheless, Coaltown shouldered 132 in the Equipoise Mile at Arlington Park, finishing second. He went on to post six more stakes wins under 130 pounds. Included in those victories was Washington Park's Whirlaway Stakes in which he set a world record of 1:34 for one mile. In post-season balloting, Coaltown shared Horse of the Year honors with Capot and was champion handicap horse.

Coaltown never regained his top form, however, winning one of four starts at age five and two of seven at six before being retired. He won twenty-three of thirty-nine starts, with six seconds, and three third-place finishes, while earning $415,675.

Although it was spelled differently when submitted to The Jockey Club, Coaltown was named by Calumet master Warren Wright for the Coletown area of Central Kentucky where his friend, Spendthrift Farm founder Leslie Combs II, was born. A slight horse at 16 hands and weighing just a little over 1,000 pounds, Coaltown was held in high esteem by his Hall of Fame trainers. "He's the fastest horse I've ever handled," said Ben Jones.

Jimmy Jones, who actually carried out the Calumet training with his father in a management role, said, "He had class right from the start."

Coaltown began his stud career at Calumet, where he averaged just eight foals a crop during four seasons. Sold to stand in France in 1955, Coaltown sired seventy foals prior to his death in 1965. He was inducted into the Racing Hall of Fame in 1983. — R. M.

RACE and (STAKES) RECORD						
YEAR	AGE	STS	1ST	2ND	3RD	EARNED
1948	at 3	13	8(5)	3(3)	2(2)	$104,650
1949	at 4	15	12(9)	3(3)	0	$276,125
1950	at 5	4	1	0	1(1)	$5,250
1951	at 6	7	2(2)	0	0	$29,650
Lifetime		39	23(16)	6(6)	3(3)	$415,675

Personal Ensign

FOUR LENGTHS WERE ALL THAT SEPARATED Personal Ensign from a perfect career. With an eighth of a mile to go in the 1988 Breeders' Cup Distaff, it seemed an impossible amount of ground for the bay filly to close on the leader, Winning Colors. It took about fourteen seconds for that final eighth to be run, but it seemed like an eternity.

Personal Ensign closed the gap relentlessly, inching slowly toward Winning Colors, and at the wire, she thrust a desperate nose in front of her younger rival.

The 1988 Distaff since has been hailed as one of the most exciting and gripping races of the 1980s, and perhaps of the century. But that race also marked the close of a remarkable career. Personal Ensign had become the first horse in the modern era to retire with a perfect record since the great Colin beat monstrous odds in the early 1900s to remain undefeated in fifteen starts. Personal Ensign faced monstrous odds during her career as well.

As a two-year-old in 1986, the upstart filly won her debut late that September at Belmont Park, and followed with a victory in the grade I Frizette Stakes a little more than two weeks later. But her path to greatness would take an unexpected turn that merely made it all the more impressive.

Personal Ensign figured to be one of the top picks in the 1986 Breeders' Cup Juvenile Fillies. But during a workout at Belmont only two days before she was to be shipped to Santa Anita Park, Personal Ensign fractured her left rear pastern. "We never thought she'd race again," trainer Claude R. (Shug) McGaughey III said later.

But this daughter of Private Account out of Grecian Banner was a special filly. The injury eventually healed, though five screws were inserted into Personal Ensign's leg. All eyes were on the bay filly when she made her return almost a year after her career debut. The date was Sept. 6, 1987, and she was back at Belmont, entered in a $31,000 allowance race. Personal Ensign didn't disappoint, winning by three and three-quarters lengths. The filly then took another allowance race, followed by the Rare Perfume and Beldame Stakes, all at Belmont.

The Beldame proved the biggest challenge to date for the filly owned and bred by Ogden Phipps. The Beldame was contested only eight days after the Rare Perfume and McGaughey admitted he didn't know what to expect. But Personal Ensign's smooth, two and a quarter-length tally must have come as no surprise to Randy Romero, the only jockey ever to ride her. "If she gets in trouble," Romero told *The Blood-Horse* after the Beldame, "she's so fast, she can get out of it."

The 1987 Breeders' Cup fell late in November, so Phipps and McGaughey passed on the grade I Distaff despite Personal Ensign's four-for-four season. In 1988, the filly won six consecutive races — five of them grade I events — with tallies in the Shuvee, Hempstead, Molly Pitcher, and Whitney Handicaps, and the Maskette and Beldame Stakes. In the Whitney at Saratoga, she took on males and defeated Gulch, who would go on to win the Breeders' Cup Sprint that year and be named champion sprinter.

Personal Ensign won those six races by an average of almost three lengths. The winning had come easy, but one more race remained: the Breeders' Cup Distaff at Churchill Downs in the thirteenth start of a thus far unblemished career. Phipps already had decided the Distaff would be the final race of the filly's career, and Personal Ensign saved the best for last, winning the race at the wire.

Personal Ensign finally took home a championship, as top older mare of 1988. She retired with thirteen wins in thirteen starts and earnings of $1,679,880. Later, she would be named Broodmare of the Year for 1996 as the dam of multiple graded stakes winners My Flag and Miner's Mark, and graded stakes-placed Our Emblem. She also achieved something no other prominent American Thoroughbred had in the previous eighty years: perfection. — *T. L.*

		Sword Dancer, 1956	Sunglow / Highland Fling
	Damascus, 1964		
		Kerala, 1958	My Babu / Blade of Time
PRIVATE ACCOUNT, b, 1976			
		Buckpasser, 1963	Tom Fool / Busanda
	Numbered Account, 1969		
		Intriguing, 1964	Swaps / Glamour
PERSONAL ENSIGN, bay filly, April 27, 1984			
		Tom Rolfe, 1962	Ribot / Pocahontas
	Hoist the Flag, 1968		
		Wavy Navy, 1954	War Admiral / Triomphe
GRECIAN BANNER, dkb/br, 1974			
		Aristophanes, 1948	Hyperion / Commotion
	Dorine, 1958		
		Doria, 1949	Advocate / Donatila

RACE and (STAKES) RECORD

YEAR	AGE	STS	1ST	2ND	3RD	EARNED
1986	at 2	2	2(1)	0	0	$174,600
1987	at 3	4	4(2)	0	0	$302,640
1988	at 4	7	7(7)	0	0	$1,202,640
Lifetime		**13**	**13(10)**	**0**	**0**	**$1,679,880**

Sir Barton

IT IS AN EXCLUSIVE FRATERNITY. Membership is limited and the initiation is taxing. There are only three stages to the ritual, but each is difficult in its own right. When taken as a whole, the degree of difficulty compounds. There are only eleven names inscribed on the membership roll of the Triple Crown.

Sir Barton was the first. His accomplishment came before there was an inclusive name to call the Kentucky Derby, the Preakness Stakes, and the Belmont Stakes. Perhaps what makes his feat even more amazing is that he entered the Kentucky Derby as a maiden.

Sir Barton's story combines some of the great names in the history of Thoroughbred racing during the early part of this century. Sir Barton was foaled at John Madden's

Hamburg Place near Lexington, Kentucky, in 1916. The chestnut colt was the son of leading sire Star Shoot and the Hanover mare Lady Sterling.

Madden trained and raced Sir Barton through the first four starts of the colt's two-year-old season. Although the youngster was highly regarded because of his breeding, Sir Barton did little to live up to his billing. For Madden he finished poorly in the Tremont, Flash, United States Hotel, and Sanford Memorial Stakes.

Madden sold his charge to J. K. L. Ross, a transplanted Canadian and one of the top owners of his day. Ross' stable was certainly not a one-horse operation; there were plenty of good horses in the barn and one of those was the Kentucky Derby contender Billy Kelly. Shipped to Kentucky along with his more famous stablemate, Sir Barton prepared for the race by working the full route of a mile and a quarter.

In the Kentucky Derby, Sir Barton had his white streaked nose in front the entire trip.

Shipped to Baltimore by train, Sir Barton was challenged by Eternal in the Preakness. Again he led all the way, this time carrying 126 pounds, and outfinished Eternal by four lengths. He won the Belmont Stakes by five lengths and set a new American record for the eleven-furlong distance. Thus, he was the first to be victorious in the triad of races which would become known as the Triple Crown.

SIR BARTON, chestnut colt, 1916	STAR SHOOT (GB), ch, 1898	Isinglass, 1890	Isonomy, 1875 — **Sterling** / Isola Bella
			Dead Lock, 1878 — Wenlock / Malpractice
		Astrology, 1887	Hermit, 1864 — Newminster / Seclusion
			Stella, 1879 — Brother to Strafford / Mare by Toxophilite
	LADY STERLING, ch, 1899	Hanover, 1884	Hindoo, 1886 — Virgil / Florence
			Bourbon Belle, 1869 — Bonnie Scotland / Ella D.
		Aquila, 1891	**Sterling**, 1868 — Oxford / Whisper
			Eagle, 1882 — Phoenix / Au Revoir

A loss in the Dwyer Stakes marred Sir Barton's three-year-old spring campaign. Afterward, he was given time off and didn't resume racing until the fall. His first start after this hiatus came in the Potomac Handicap. He lost to older horses in the Havre de Grace Handicap and won against his own age group in the Maryland Handicap. He finished the year with wins in the Pimlico Fall Serial Weight-for-Age races.

During the first half of Sir Barton's four-year-old year, he resumed his previous year's form. Following three unsuccessful efforts from four starts, Sir Barton reeled off four straight stakes victories, setting new track records in two handicaps and carrying top weight in each.

Rarely does the racing community experience the opportunity for the type of race that pits one outstanding animal against another: a match race. That was the case in 1920. There was a big red three-year-old who had established a reputation. What could be better than a showdown between the erstwhile three-year-old champion Man o' War and the champion older horse Sir Barton? The race took place Oct. 12 at Kenilworth Park in Windsor, Ontario, Canada. The value was $80,000, $75,000 in purse money and a gold cup; the distance was ten furlongs. The two combatants carried scale weight.

Perhaps like most things in life, the anticipation was greater than the event. Man o' War led throughout and was never really pressed. "Big Red" won by seven lengths and set a new track record for the mile and a quarter in 2:03, shaving over six seconds off the previous record. Sir Barton was retired to stud at the end of his four-year-old campaign.

Ross sold the colt, and Sir Barton stood first in Virginia and then in Kentucky without much success. In 1933 the first winner of the Triple Crown was sent to the U.S. Army Remount. He was transported to Wyoming where he died of colic in 1937.

— *T. H.*

RACE and (STAKES) RECORD

YEAR	AGE	STS	1ST	2ND	3RD	EARNED
1918	at 2	6	0	1(1)	0	$4,113
1919	at 3	13	8(8)	3(1)	2(2)	$88,249
1920	at 4	12	5(5)	2(2)	3(3)	$24,495
Lifetime		31	13(13)	6(4)	5(5)	$116,857

Dahlia

DON'T LET HER ELEGANCE, pretty looks, and gentle disposition fool you. Dahlia, the charming temptress who graced racetracks all over Europe and America in the early to mid-1970s, was a fierce warrior who lured many an unsuspecting colt to his demise.

When her racing career concluded in the fall of 1976, Dahlia had left a legacy that has continued to grow over the years. International competition is pretty much taken for granted these days. But it wasn't always that way. The only opportunity Americans once had of seeing top-class international stars came in the Washington, D.C., International each year.

In 1974, Dahlia, having already conquered Europe, was sent to America for a fall campaign, which consisted of the Man o' War Stakes at Belmont Park, the Canadian International Championship at Woodbine, and the Washington, D.C., International at Laurel. Never before had a European champion, at the height of his or her success, come to America to compete in a series of fall races. The daughter of Vaguely Noble captured the first two before finishing a fast-closing third at Laurel.

This was not the first time American racing fans were treated to the brilliance of Dahlia. The year before, with the legendary Secretariat about to depart for stud duty at Claiborne Farm, Dahlia came to Laurel and annihilated a top international field with one of the most awesome bursts of speed ever seen in this country. But beating colts was already old hat to the three-year-old filly.

Earlier in the year, in the King George VI and Queen Elizabeth Stakes, she had stunned English racing fans with an explosion of speed and power not seen in Europe since the days of Sea-Bird and Ribot. Not only did her electrifying rush from last to first carry her to a six-length victory, but in her wake were the winners of the English, French, and Irish

Derbys and the subsequent winner of the Prix de l'Arc de Triomphe.

When she arrived at Laurel, there was concern in the Dahlia camp. The filly had wrenched a leg muscle in the Prix Vermeille and that accounted for her poor effort two weeks later in the Arc. Although trainer Maurice Zilber still was confident of victory at Laurel despite acknowledging that Dahlia was not back to her summer form, the filly's jockey, Bill Pyers, pleaded with him not to run her. But run she did, and when it was over, Dahlia's legend had spread across the Atlantic.

The following year, she defeated colts in three more group I stakes, including another decisive victory in the King George. Following her fall campaign in America that year, she returned to Europe once again, and in 1975, captured a second Benson and Hedges Gold Cup, defeating English Derby winner Grundy and Arc de Triomphe winner Star Appeal.

By the time she was sent to America in October of 1975 to close out her career, she was already past her prime and feeling the effects of four years of travel and an amazing total of thirty-one group or grade I stakes. Although a shell of her former self, she still managed to win the Hollywood Invitational Handicap in May of 1976 at the age of six.

When she retired, she had logged almost 30,000 miles of traveling, defeated no less than nine classic-winning colts, and was the only horse ever to win group or grade I stakes in five different countries. She captured seven championships, including two Horse of the Year titles in England.

She was retired to owner Nelson Bunker Hunt's Bluegrass Farm outside Lexington, Kentucky, and became one of the most successful broodmares of her time, producing six graded stakes winners, including an amazing four grade I winners: Dahar, Rivlia, Delegant, and Dahlia's Dreamer, and one grade I-placed horse. In all, her progeny won or placed in eighteen grade or group I stakes in five different countries. At twenty-nine, she was living out her remaining days at Allen Paulson's Brookside Farm near Versailles, Kentucky. Paulson bought her for $1,100,000 at Hunt's massive 1988 dispersal. — S. H.

	Vienna, 1957	Aureole, 1950	**Hyperion** Angelola
VAGUELY NOBLE (GB), b, 1965		Turkish Blood, 1944	Turkhan Rusk
	Noble Lassie, 1956	Nearco, 1935	Pharos Nogara
DAHLIA, chestnut filly, March 25, 1970		Belle Sauvage, 1949	Big Game Tropical Sun
	Honeys Alibi, 1952	Alibhai, 1938	**Hyperion** Teresina
CHARMING ALIBI, ch, 1963		Honeymoon, 1943	Beau Pere Panoramic
	Adorada II, 1947	Hierocles, 1939	Abjer Loïka
		Gilded Wave, 1938	Gallant Fox Ondulation

RACE and (STAKES) RECORD

YEAR	AGE	STS	1ST	2ND	3RD	EARNED
1972	at 2 in Fr	4	1(1)	1(1)	0	$17,144
1973	at 3 in Fr, Eng,Ire,NA	10	6(6)	1(1)	1(1)	$446,779
1974	at 4 in Fr, Eng, NA	10	5(5)	0	3(3)	$631,991
1975	at 5 in Fr, Eng, It, NA	11	1(1)	1(1)	2(2)	$152,690
1976	at 6 in NA	13	2(1)	0	1(1)	$178,750
Lifetime		48	15(14)	3(3)	7(7)	$1,427,354

Susan's Girl

THERE WAS SOMETHING BRAND NEW in North American racing in 1973 — the grading of stakes races. The system was borrowed from Europe to assess the quality of races, and thus, the quality of the horses who run in them.

The quality of Susan's Girl needed no ranking, though. She won nine stakes in 1972 and was named champion three-year-old filly. But in the first year of graded stakes, she confirmed her class in accordance with the new system, winning six graded races in all, four being the most elite run — grade I.

Raced by Fred Hooper and bred in Florida by his son, Fred Hooper Jr., Susan's Girl was by Quadrangle out of Quaze, by Quibu. Fred Hooper had bought her second dam, Heavenly Sun, as a yearling in 1953 for $10,500. Susan's Girl just happened to debut in the summer of 1971, when a filly named Numbered Account was in complete control of the division. The eventual champion defeated Susan's Girl in the Frizette and Gardenia Stakes.

The next year, with Numbered Account hampered by a splint condition, Susan's Girl took charge, winning nine of thirteen starts and never finishing worse than third. She won early in the year, taking three straight stakes at Santa Anita (Pasadena, Santa Ynez, and Santa Susana), and late in the season, winning two in a row at Belmont (Gazelle and Beldame). She also won in between, capturing the La Troienne Stakes at Churchill Downs a mere seven days before winning the Kentucky Oaks, a race her dam, Quaze, had finished second in twelve years earlier.

Returning in 1973 at four, with a championship and more than $500,000 in earnings, Susan's Girl twice finished fifth in open company to begin the year. Returned to races against her own sex, she resumed her spot at the top of her division, winning the Santa Maria, Santa Margarita, and Santa Barbara Handicaps.

Pedigree of SUSAN'S GIRL, bay filly, March 23, 1969:

- QUADRANGLE, b, 1961
  - Cohoes, 1954
    - Mahmoud, 1933 — Blenheim II / Mah Mahal
    - Belle of Troy, 1947 — Blue Larkspur / La Troienne
  - Tap Day, 1947
    - Bull Lea, 1935 — Bull Dog / Rose Leaves
    - Scurry, 1937 — Diavolo / Slapdash
- QUAZE, ch, 1957
  - Quibu, 1942
    - Meadow, 1936 — Fairway / Silver Mist
    - Querendona, 1934 — Diadochos / Querella
  - Heavenly Sun, 1952
    - Olympia, 1946 — Heliopolis / Miss Dolphin
    - Daffy, 1932 — The Porter / Lady Pike

After losses in three stakes at Hollywood Park, Susan's Girl was given a brief rest, then shipped East, where she won the Susquehanna Handicap at Liberty Bell, and the Delaware Handicap at Delaware Park. Trying to win the Beldame for the second straight year, she finished second to Desert Vixen, then ran third in the Matchmaker before winning Keeneland's Spinster Stakes and her second consecutive championship.

Now champion older filly or mare, Susan's Girl had earnings of $843,658, second only to Shuvee's $890,455. Hooper had one thing in mind — seeing Susan's Girl become the first distaffer to win a million dollars. In February of 1974, however, she chipped a bone in her left foreleg. Many would have given up the plan; not Hooper. After noted equine surgeon Dr. Robert Copelan removed three chips, Susan's Girl was sent to Hooper's farm near Ocala, Florida. Every day for two months, she was vanned to nearby Lake Weir to swim for ten minutes. Nine months later, she was ready to return to the races.

By then, however, two distaffers racing in Europe had passed the $1-million mark: first Dahlia, then Allez France. Hooper still aspired to the North American record, however.

In one of racing's great comeback stories, Susan's Girl won the Falls City Handicap in November, then was as good as ever as a six-year-old. She got the $1 million in earnings, won six stakes, and placed in eight others. She won her second Delaware Handicap, second Beldame, and second Spinster. She had her leading money-winning season ($361,951) in 1975 to retire with twenty-nine wins (twenty-four of them stakes), fourteen seconds, and eleven thirds in sixty-three starts and earnings of $1,251,668. Susan's Girl won her second championship as older filly or mare. She is the only female of the 20th Century to win a three-year-old championship and two subsequent championships in the handicap division. She was trained at various times throughout her career by Leland R. Fenstermaker, T. W. Kelley, Chuck Parke, John Russell, and Robert Smith.

The first big winner of grade I races among females, Susan's Girl went on to produce a grade I winner: Copelan (named for Dr. Copelan), by stablemate Tri Jet. Susan's Girl died at Hooper Farm on Oct. 18, 1988. — D. L.

RACE and (STAKES) RECORD

YEAR	AGE	STS	1ST	2ND	3RD	EARNED
1971	at 2	13	5(2)	5(3)	0	$150,484
1972	at 3	13	9(9)	2(2)	2(2)	$352,678
1973	at 4	14	6(6)	2(2)	3(3)	$340,496
1974	at 5	6	2(1)	1(1)	2(1)	$46,059
1975	at 6	17	7(6)	4(4)	4(4)	$361,951
Lifetime		63	29(24)	14(12)	11(10)	$1,251,668

Twenty Grand

TWENTY GRAND WAS A LOT OF MONEY in 1928 — the year before the stock market crash and the beginning of the Great Depression. But the equine Twenty Grand, foaled in the spring of 1928, proved plenty good enough to do justice to his name, competing on equal terms with the likes of Equipoise.

The colt was a bit of an experiment. He was from his sire's second crop, and from the first crop of youngsters foaled and raised on his owner's farm. But when the sire is an English "Cup" horse purchased for $125,000, the owner-breeder is named Whitney, and the farm is Greentree, experiments tend to work out well.

Thus it was with Twenty Grand.

Payne Whitney selected and bought Twenty Grand's sire, St. Germans, for his wife. A mating to a mare named Bonus resulted in the colt who would set records and provide drama for years.

Twenty Grand ran for the first time at Jamaica racetrack in New York on April 30, 1930, winning by five lengths. In his next start, he bucked shins and trainer Tom Murphy put him away. The colt won his return race in September, then finished fourth in his first stakes try, the Babylon Handicap at Aqueduct. Few handicappers gave him a chance when he hooked Equipoise in his next start — the Junior Championship at Aqueduct — and when he won, beating Equipoise in deep stretch, he became a star. Twenty Grand again whipped Equipoise in a furious stretch duel in the Kentucky Jockey Club Stakes at Churchill Downs.

Equipoise turned the tables in the Pimlico Futurity. Although both Equipoise and Twenty Grand got off to slow starts in the race, Equipoise caught Mate, another prominent two-year-old, near the wire. Twenty Grand was second, beating Mate by a neck under the wire. Mate, who had defeated Equipoise in the Champagne, then took the measure of Twenty Grand in the Walden Handicap at Pimlico. That defeat left Twenty Grand with a juvenile record of four wins, two seconds, and a third from eight starts. Still, he earned $41,380 — more than twice his "name."

ST. GERMANS, b, 1921	Swynford, 1907	John o' Gaunt, 1901	Isinglass / La Fleche
		Canterbury Pilgrim, 1893	Tristan / Pilgrimage
	Hamoaze, 1911	Torpoint, 1900	Trenton / Doncaster Beauty
TWENTY GRAND, bay colt, 1928		Maid of the Mist, 1906	Cyllene / Sceptre
	All Gold, 1908	Persimmon, 1893	St. Simon / Perdita II
BONUS, b, 1919		Dame d'Or, 1899	Bend Or / Dame Masham
	Remembrance, 1913	Broomstick, 1901	Ben Brush / Elf
		Forget, 1893	Exile / Forever

At age three, Twenty Grand truly came into his own. The colt won his first start, the Wood Memorial, then finished second to Mate in the Preakness Stakes after being bumped, then blocked. He was the odds-on favorite in the Kentucky Derby, run after the Preakness at that time, and justified the support. After trailing early, he surged past his rivals at the top of the stretch and won by four lengths in a track record 2:01⅘. Twenty Grand faced only Jamestown and Sun Meadow in the Belmont Stakes, winning by ten lengths.

Twenty Grand suffered a minor injury to his back while winning the Dwyer, then finished third in his next start, the Classic at Arlington Park. He was given time to recover and came back to win the Travers, Saratoga Cup, Lawrence Realization, and the Jockey Club Gold Cup. He injured his left front pastern in the Gold Cup, but this time, he did not respond to treatment and was only a shadow of his former greatness in two starts at age four. In his final race that year, he pulled up lame after losing to Mad Frump.

Returned to Greentree for his second career, Twenty Grand for the first time failed to live up to his name. The horse proved sterile, and he was put back in training at age seven in 1935. The goal was the inaugural running of the Santa Anita Handicap and, again, he faced the likes of Mate and Equipoise. All had passed peak form but, still, Twenty Grand wasn't up to the challenge after his two-year layoff and finished a humiliating tenth. He then ran twice in England without success. Finally, the old warrior was returned to Greentree, where he died in 1948.

Twenty Grand made twenty-five starts, won fourteen, and was off the board only four times. His career earnings totaled $261,790. The gallant runner was inducted into the Racing Hall of Fame in 1957. — B. K.

RACE and (STAKES) RECORD

YEAR	AGE	STS	1ST	2ND	3RD	EARNED
1930	at 2	8	4(2)	2(1)	1(1)	$41,380
1931	at 3	10	8(8)	1(1)	1(1)	$218,545
1932	at 4	2	1	1	0	$915
1933	at 5	0	0	0	0	—
1934	at 6	0	0	0	0	—
1935	at 7 in NA, Eng	5	1	0	1	$950
Lifetime		**25**	**14(10)**	**4(2)**	**3(2)**	**$261,790**

Sword Dancer

IT'S DIFFICULT TO DISCERN which accomplishment garnered Sword Dancer greater admiration: his exploits during his own Hall of Fame racing career or his siring of an even more accomplished Hall of Fame son, Damascus. Sword Dancer's name can scarcely be mentioned without also breathing that of Damascus, yet his own career was meritorious enough to stand alone.

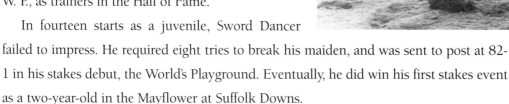

The chestnut Sword Dancer, small in stature but embellished with eye-catching chrome, was foaled in April of 1956 in Virginia. A son of Sunglow and the unraced mare Highland Fling, Sword Dancer would campaign as a homebred for his breeder, Isabel Dodge Sloane's Brookmeade Stable. His dam was sold for $2,000 at the Keeneland fall sale when Sword Dancer was a yearling and resold for $80,000 in 1959 at the height of the colt's prowess. Sword Dancer would be the first champion trained by Elliott Burch, who one day would join his father, Preston, and grandfather, W. P., as trainers in the Hall of Fame.

In fourteen starts as a juvenile, Sword Dancer failed to impress. He required eight tries to break his maiden, and was sent to post at 82-1 in his stakes debut, the World's Playground. Eventually, he did win his first stakes event as a two-year-old in the Mayflower at Suffolk Downs.

Sword Dancer would get a four-month respite prior to his sophomore season, partly due to a fever that encouraged Burch to take it easy with the colt. Burch and Sloane considered selling Sword Dancer, fielding offers as high as $175,000 when the colt captured an allowance event prior to his second-place finish in the Florida Derby. When no offers were received for the colt's asking price of $200,000, the team decided to take a gamble. Sword Dancer was no longer for sale.

In an overnight event a week before the Kentucky Derby at Churchill Downs, Sword Dancer won at the expense of the previously undefeated filly, Silver Spoon. In the Derby, Sword Dancer and Tomy Lee staged a furious stretch battle, with neither willing to relinquish the lead. The head bob did not fall in Sword Dancer's favor; the sophomore was also second in the Preakness.

SUNGLOW, ch, 1947	Sun Again, 1939	Sun Teddy, 1933	Teddy / Sunmelia
		Hug Again, 1931	Stimulus / Affection
	Rosern, 1927	Mad Hatter, 1916	Fair Play / Madcap
		Rosedrop, 1907	St. Frusquin / Rosaline
SWORD DANCER, chestnut colt, April 24, 1956			
HIGHLAND FLING, br, 1950	By Jimminy, 1941	Pharamond II, 1925	Phalaris / Selene
		Buginarug, 1934	Blue Larkspur / Breakfast Bell
	Swing Time, 1935	Royal Minstrel, 1925	Tetratema / Harpsichord
		Speed Boat, 1930	Man o' War / Friar's Carse

Before finally capturing a classic victory in the Belmont, Sword Dancer defeated older horses in the Metropolitan Handicap. He would defeat older rivals again in the Monmouth Handicap, finish second in the Brooklyn, and take the Travers before winning the Woodward, billed as the race of the year. In the Woodward, Sword Dancer stole through along the inner rail, and Eddie Arcaro piloted him to a dramatic head victory over Hillsdale.

Sword Dancer's Woodward also dethroned the reigning Horse of the Year, Round Table. Not long after, Sword Dancer added icing to the cake when he posted a seven-length triumph in the Jockey Club Gold Cup, then contested at two miles.

Honored as Horse of the Year in 1959, in addition to champion three-year-old colt and handicap male titles, Sword Dancer failed to run to the same form in 1960. He flashed moments of his past brilliance, setting a track record at Aqueduct in the Suburban and winning a second Woodward, reducing his own track record by two-fifths of a second.

In November, Sword Dancer wrenched an ankle. Already syndicated for stud duty at John W. Galbreath's Darby Dan Farm near Lexington, Kentucky, the decision was made to retire him. Sword Dancer retired with fifteen wins and eleven placings from thirty-nine starts. His career earnings were $829,610.

Sword Dancer was not as resounding of a success at stud as he had been on the racetrack. He sired a total of 282 foals, of which fifteen were stakes winners and two were champions: Lady Pitt and Damascus. The latter emulated his sire as Horse of the Year (1967), champion three-year-old colt, and champion handicap male. Damascus was elected to the Racing Hall of Fame in 1974, three years before Sword Dancer.

In 1970, Sword Dancer was leased by a group of French breeders and left the country. The champion died in France in 1984. — J. W.

RACE and (STAKES) RECORD

YEAR	AGE	STS	1ST	2ND	3RD	EARNED
1958	at 2	14	3(1)	2	3(1)	$60,531
1959	at 3	13	8(6)	4(4)	0	$537,004
1960	at 4	12	4(3)	1(1)	1(1)	$232,075
Lifetime		39	15(10)	7(5)	4(2)	$829,610

Grey Lag

WHEN JOHN E. MADDEN bought fifteen-year-old Star Shoot as a proven sire, he tripled the stallion's book of mares, breeding both his good and not-so-good mares to him. From one of the good mares, Lady Sterling, he got Sir Barton, first winner of the Triple Crown. From one of the mediocre mares, Miss Minnie, a non-winner who had only produced non-winners, he got Grey Lag. Madden, "The Wizard of the Turf" who bred 182 stakes winners during three decades at his

Hamburg Place near Lexington, Kentucky, later called Grey Lag the best horse he had ever bred.

Foaled in 1918, Grey Lag was not gray at all with the exception of an odd-shaped gray patch on his side that was hidden whenever he wore a saddlecloth. The colt was actually chestnut, with three white feet and a large blaze. His name was derived from the wild geese, called grey lags, of northern Europe.

Madden sold Grey Lag as a yearling to trainer Max Hirsch in a package deal with a filly for $10,000. Grey Lag didn't break his maiden until his fifth start as a two-year-old. After a third-place finish in the Futurity, trainer Sam Hildreth, buying racing stock for oilman Harry F. Sinclair, inspected Grey Lag at a quoted sale price of $40,000. When Hildreth, superstitious to the core, laid eyes on Grey Lag's unusual patch of gray, he refused the colt.

Shortly afterwards, Grey Lag romped home by six lengths in the Champagne Stakes, the first added-money victory of his career. On his way to the winner's circle, Hirsch was stopped by Sinclair, who asked the trainer to name a price on the Champagne winner. Hirsch, thinking quickly, added $20,000 for the colt's gray spot to his original price, and the deal was done. Sinclair purchased Grey Lag for $60,000. Grey Lag made six more starts as a juvenile under his new team, adding the Remsen Handicap and Autumn Day Stakes.

Grey Lag was prepared for the Kentucky Derby at Sinclair's Rancocas Farm in New Jersey. Shipped to Louisville, Grey Lag bruised a heel while galloping forty-eight hours before the race, and was withdrawn.

Grey Lag instead made his three-year-old debut at Belmont Park in the Freeport Handicap, victorious in spite of carrying twenty pounds more than his closest opponent. Two days later, he finished third in the Withers, then won eight consecutive races. Included in the streak were the Belmont Stakes, the Brooklyn Handicap, in which he faced older horses for the first time, including the iron gelding Exterminator, and the Dwyer Stakes. Perhaps the most impressive victory came in the Knickerbocker Handicap, in which Grey Lag carried 135 pounds to a near track-record victory.

At four, Grey Lag's lone loss came to old rival Exterminator, who defeated him by a head in the Brooklyn Handicap. At five, Grey Lag again suffered defeat only once. He closed out his racing career with victory in the Suburban under 135 pounds. Grey Lag retired to stud with the distinction of having won all the major Eastern handicaps. He also won championships at three, four, and five.

As a stallion, Grey Lag failed miserably, siring only nineteen foals before becoming sterile. At age nine, Grey Lag was returned by Hildreth to the track. He won both his starts that year, but only one start the following season. Retired again, Grey Lag was given to a veterinarian as a riding horse. Shortly after, the new owner died and Grey Lag was sold through his estate. Put back in training as a thirteen-year-old, Grey Lag ran in cheap claiming races in Canada. Public outcry for the elderly champion's loss of dignity was harsh, and an embarrassed Sinclair sent a representative to Canada to repurchase Grey Lag. Grey Lag had twenty-five wins from forty-seven starts, fifteen placings, and earnings of $136,375. —J. W.

		Isonomy, 1875	Sterling / Isola Bella
STAR SHOOT (GB), ch, 1898	Isinglass, 1890	Dead Lock, 1878	Wenlock / Malpractice
	Astrology, 1887	Hermit, 1864	Newminster / Seclusion
GREY LAG, chestnut colt, 1918		Stella, 1879	Brother to Stafford / Mare by Toxophilite
	Meddler, 1890	St. Gatien, 1881	The Rover / Saint Editha
MISS MINNIE, ch, 1908		Busybody, 1881	Petrarch / Spinaway
	Spectrum, 1896	Orvieto, 1888	Bend Or / Napoli
		False Sight, 1891	Melton / Mirage

RACE and (STAKES) RECORD

YEAR	AGE	STS	1ST	2ND	3RD	EARNED
1920	at 2	13	4(4)	5(3)	2(2)	$17,202
1921	at 3	13	9(8)	2(2)	1(1)	$62,346
1922	at 4	6	5(5)	1(1)	0	$26,937
1923	at 5	5	4(4)	1(1)	0	$26,900
1924	at 6	0	0	0	0	—
1925	at 7	0	0	0	0	—
1926	at 8	0	0	0	0	—
1927	at 9	2	2	0	0	$1,400
1928	at 10	4	1(1)	0	2(1)	$1,550
1929	at 11	0	0	0	0	—
1930	at 12	0	0	0	0	—
1931	at 13	4	0	0	1	$40
Lifetime		47	25(22)	9(7)	6(4)	$136,375

157

Devil Diver

DEVIL DIVER HOLDS TWO RECORDS that might never be broken. During the 1940s, he won three consecutive runnings of the historic Metropolitan Handicap for Greentree Stable, and one of those triumphs came under a still-standing record of 134 pounds.

The Metropolitan win under 134 pounds came in 1944 and was one of seven stakes victories that year for Devil Diver. A five-year-old that season, Devil Diver carried 130 pounds or more in the first four of those triumphs.

Under Ted Atkinson, Devil Diver won the six-furlong Paumonok Handicap under 130 pounds at Jamaica in April. A month later, he took another six-furlong feature, the Toboggan Handicap at Belmont Park, while toting 134 pounds, including Eddie Arcaro. It was Devil Diver's second consecutive Toboggan win. Five days after the Toboggan, Devil Diver came through with his historic Metropolitan Handicap victory under Atkinson. Sent off as the 1-2 favorite while coupled

with stablemate Four Freedoms, Devil Diver got up to win by one and a half lengths over Alquest, who was in receipt of twenty-five pounds.

Devil Diver next carried 136 pounds to victory in the American Legion Handicap at seven furlongs at Belmont Park. After that, his next two stakes wins — the Whitney and the Wilson — were achieved under feathery weights of 117 pounds in August.

Devil Diver's last stakes win of 1944 came in the Manhattan Handicap under 125 pounds at Belmont Park in September. The day after the Manhattan, it was announced that Greentree owner Mrs. Payne Whitney had died, and the stable passed into the hands of Mrs. Whitney's son, John Hay (Jock) Whitney, and her daughter, Joan Shipman Payson. At the time of his mother's death, Jock Whitney was with the Allied Army in Europe, having recently escaped from a German prison train.

A week after the Manhattan, Devil Diver ran third in the two-mile Jockey Club Gold Cup at Belmont. A month later, he finished second behind subsequent Horse of the Year Twilight Tear in the Pimlico Special. Devil Diver was named champion handicap male for 1944.

DEVIL DIVER, bay colt, 1939	ST. GERMANS (GB), b, 1921	Swynford, 1907	John o' Gaunt, 1901 — Isinglass / La Fleche
			Canterbury Pilgrim, 1893 — Tristan / Pilgrimage
		Hamoaze, 1911	Torpoint, 1900 — Trenton / Doncaster Beauty
			Maid of the Mist, 1906 — Cyllene / Sceptre
	DABCHICK, dk b, 1931	Royal Minstrel, 1925	Tetratema, 1917 — The Tetrarch / Scotch Gift
			Harpsichord, 1918 — Louvois / Golden Harp
		Ruddy Duck, 1925	Touch Me Not, 1918 — Celt / Dainty Dame
			Briony, 1921 — Dominant / Cardamine

Devil Diver was a member of the same Greentree foal crop as Shut Out. As a two-year-old, Devil Diver beat Shut Out in the 1941 Hopeful Stakes, and also won the Breeders' Futurity and Sanford Stakes that year. Devil Diver opened his three-year-old season by winning the six-furlong Phoenix Handicap at Keeneland over the previous year's Triple Crown winner Whirlaway as a prep for the Kentucky Derby. Both Shut Out and Devil Diver were pointed toward the 1942 Derby, and Greentree trainer John Gaver gave Arcaro his choice of mounts. Arcaro chose Devil Diver, and finished sixth behind winner Shut Out.

The Phoenix was Devil Diver's sole stakes win as a three-year-old, but he won four stakes as a four-year-old in 1943. In addition to the Metropolitan and Toboggan, he captured the Brooklyn and Carter Handicaps and shared champion handicap male honors with Market Wise. At the end of his five-year-old season, Devil Diver was supposed to enter stud at Greentree near Lexington, but stayed in training after it was determined that he was the outfit's only championship prospect. Devil Diver didn't disappoint, either. He raced five times in 1945, winning his third Metropolitan, his second Paumonok, and his first Suburban Handicap. The Suburban was special altogether. Ridden by Arcaro and carrying 132 pounds, Devil Diver beat Stymie while giving him thirteen pounds.

Devil Diver was retired after reinjuring his right front foot during a workout at Belmont Park in August of 1945. He had won twenty-two of forty-seven starts and earned $261,064.

Devil Diver sired eighteen stakes winners, including the filly Anchors Aweigh. Devil Diver was euthanized at The Stallion Station near Lexington, Kentucky, on Nov. 16, 1961, after breaking his left hind leg. He was elected to the Racing Hall of Fame in 1980. — *D. S.*

RACE and (STAKES) RECORD

YEAR	AGE	STS	1ST	2ND	3RD	EARNED
1941	at 2	12	4(3)	7(3)	1(1)	$65,359
1942	at 3	9	4(1)	1(1)	1(1)	$10,535
1943	at 4	9	4(4)	1	0	$48,900
1944	at 5	12	7(7)	1(1)	1(1)	$64,265
1945	at 6	5	3(3)	2(2)	0	$72,005
Lifetime		47	22(18)	12(7)	3(3)	$261,064

Zev

ZEV WAS JUST THE SECOND HORSE TO WIN the Kentucky Derby and Belmont Stakes, but even those two classic triumphs took a back seat to his victory in the international match race against Epsom Derby winner Papyrus in 1923. American horses for years had been sent to England to run in that country's top races (witness the example of Pierre Lorillard's Iroquois winning the 1881 Epsom Derby), but never before had an English horse bearing such high credentials risked life and limb to make the trip to the United States.

Zev, who raced for Harry F. Sinclair's Rancocas Stable, and Papyrus were matched at one and a half miles at Belmont Park that October. Papyrus' expenses were paid in full, and the winner would get $80,000 of the $100,000 purse. Zev had contracted a skin disease, and it was feared that he might not be able to run. My Own, owned by Adm. Cary Grayson, was to substitute, but Zev's trainer, Sam Hildreth, assured officers of The Jockey Club that the Sinclair colt would be ready to race.

The track came up heavy the day of the match and New York trainer Andrew Jackson Joyner suggested to Papyrus' trainer, Basil Jarvis, that mud caulks might help Papyrus negotiate the muddy going. Papyrus never had worn mud caulks, and Jarvis feared that the horse might cut himself. Zev was outfitted with them, and some felt that might have made all the difference.

Earl Sande was aboard 4-5 favorite Zev, and Steve Donoghue, who was on Papyrus in the Epsom Derby, rode that colt. Papyrus took an early lead, but Sande hustled Zev to the front before the first quarter mile. They stayed there until the end and won by five lengths.

Zev next won the Autumn Championship Stakes, but lost to three-year-old rival In Memoriam in the one and three-quarters-mile Latonia Championship. The loss provided the impetus for another match race, one that ended in controversy.

After the Latonia Championship, Zev took the Pimlico Serial Weight-for-Age Race No. 3. Sinclair and In Memoriam's owner, Carl Weidemann, then put up $10,000 each for the match, and the Kentucky Jockey Club, which had proposed the race, also put up $10,000.

Zev and In Memoriam met at a mile and a quarter at Churchill Downs. In Memoriam, under Mack Garner, led through the first six furlongs. Jockey Sande caught Garner napping and shot favored Zev into a two-length lead with a quarter-mile remaining. In Memoriam closed with a rush, but it appeared that Zev won by a nose. Three of the five judges gave the decision to Zev, but slow-motion films showed In Memoriam apparently winning (although the angle of filming was questionable). The judges' decision, however, was final.

Zev ended the year with a dozen wins from fourteen starts and record earnings for a single season, $276,408. His lone off the board effort came in the Preakness Stakes, which was contested before the Kentucky Derby. Zev was 1923 Horse of the Year, but shared champion three-year-old male honors with In Memoriam.

Sinclair had bought Zev as a yearling from the colt's breeder, John Madden, and named him for his counsel, Colonel Zeverley. Zev started out as a two-year-old with five consecutive wins, including the Albany Handicap and Grand Union Hotel Stakes at Saratoga. He later ran third in the Hopeful Stakes, and second in the Futurity Stakes. He passed out after the Futurity, and was put away for the remainder of the year after suffering an injury training for the Pimlico Futurity. He was named champion two-year-old male.

Zev's victory in the Kentucky Derby came as a complete surprise to Sinclair and Hildreth, who did not attend. Zev's poor performance in the Preakness had cautioned the two men not to expect too much from the colt at Churchill Downs. Sent away the fifteenth choice in the Derby field of twenty-one, Zev led throughout. Zev was retired at four with twenty-three wins from forty-three starts. His world-record earnings mark of $318,048 lasted until Gallant Fox surpassed it in 1930. Zev stood at Rancocas Stud and sired only two stakes winners. He died in Virginia in 1943 and was inducted into the Racing Hall of Fame in 1983. — *D. S.*

THE FINN, blk, 1912	Ogden, 1894	Kilwarlin, 1884	Arbitrator / Hasty Girl
		Oriole, 1887	Bend Or / Fenella
	Livonia, 1907	Star Shoot, 1898	Isinglass / Astrology
		Woodray, 1897	Rayon d'Or / Wood-nymph
MISS KEARNEY, b, 1906	Planudes, 1897	St. Simon, 1881	Galopin / St. Angela
		Lonely, 1882	Hermit / Anonyma
	Courtplaster, 1902	Sandringham, 1896	St. Simon / Perdita II
		Set Fast, 1894	Masetto / Bandala

ZEV, brown colt, 1920

RACE and (STAKES) RECORD

YEAR	AGE	STS	1ST	2ND	3RD	EARNED
1922	at 2	12	5(2)	4(1)	2(1)	$24,674
1923	at 3	14	12(11)	1(1)	0	$276,408
1924	at 4	17	6(3)	3(3)	3(3)	$16,966
Lifetime		43	23(16)	8(5)	5(4)	$318,048

Riva Ridge

RIVA RIDGE IN THE EYES OF MANY should have been the ninth Triple Crown winner. A homebred for Virginia breeder-owner Christopher T. Chenery, Riva Ridge started off by winning the 1972 Kentucky Derby as the 3-2 favorite, then couldn't handle a sloppy track in the Preakness Stakes as the 3-10 favorite and finished fourth. He redeemed himself with a seven-length victory in the Belmont Stakes as the 8-5 favorite, and the question of "If it only had been dry for the Preakness?" soon popped up.

Riva Ridge, who was foaled at Arthur B. (Bull) Hancock Jr.'s Claiborne Farm near Paris, Kentucky, had been the previous year's champion two-year-old male. He first was placed

under the care of trainer Roger Laurin, then was transferred to Laurin's father, Lucien, after the son was offered the job of training for Ogden Phipps and members of his family in the spring of 1971.

Stabled in New York, Riva Ridge was ridden in his first four races by Chuck Baltazar before Ron Turcotte took over as the colt's regular rider. Turcotte had approached Lucien and suggested an arrangement whereby he would work the conditioner's horses in hopes of riding them later. Laurin agreed, and Turcotte first rode Riva Ridge in the Flash Stakes at Saratoga at the time Baltazar was serving a suspension. Riva Ridge won the six-furlong stakes in 1:09⅖.

Riva Ridge dominated the division the rest of the year. That fall, he won the Futurity Stakes over favored Windjammer; took the Champagne Stakes by seven lengths; scored by eleven in the Pimlico-Laurel Futurity; and captured the Garden State Stakes over Ogden Phipps' filly Numbered Account. His victory in the Futurity Stakes had come over a sloppy track, but it later became obvious that he had trouble over wet tracks.

For the year, Riva Ridge won seven of his nine races and earned $503,263. Thirteen years earlier, his sire, First Landing, had been champion two-year-old male for Chenery.

In March of 1972, Laurin announced that Riva Ridge would run only three times prior to the Kentucky Derby. Disbelief set in among seasoned Turf writers and fellow trainers, who were used to seeing Derby hopefuls run several more times than that. Riva Ridge ended up winning the Hibiscus Stakes, then finished unplaced in the Everglades Stakes over a sloppy surface at Hialeah. Nine days before the Derby, he won the Blue Grass Stakes at Keeneland. The fact that Riva Ridge won the Derby off only three prep races is a testament to the colt's ability and Laurin's training acumen. Laurin tried it the following year with the Chenery family's Secretariat, and that colt won the Triple Crown.

Following the Triple Crown, Riva Ridge ran in the Hollywood Derby three weeks later. He eked out a neck win, but the effort took too much out of him, and he failed to win again in five starts that year. He not only failed to get the Horse of the Year title, but lost out on the three-year-old male championship to Key to the Mint.

Riva Ridge raced the following year and earned a championship as best older male. His major wins came in the Massachusetts and Brooklyn Handicaps in consecutive starts in the summer of 1973. In late summer, Riva Ridge finished second to stablemate Secretariat in the inaugural Marlboro Cup Invitational Handicap at Belmont Park. The race initially was scheduled to be a match race between those two, but was switched to an invitational event after both horses lost leading up to it.

Riva Ridge was retired that fall with seventeen wins from thirty starts and earnings of $1,111,497. He had been bred in the name of Meadow Stud, raced in the name of Meadow Stable, and was raised at The Meadow in Virginia. Riva Ridge entered stud in 1974 at the Hancock family's Claiborne Farm amidst concerns about his fertility. He went on to sire twenty-nine stakes winners, including Alada, the granddam of filly champion Saratoga Dew. Riva Ridge died of a heart attack on April 21, 1985. He was elected to the Racing Hall of Fame in 1998. — D. S.

RACE and (STAKES) RECORD

YEAR	AGE	STS	1ST	2ND	3RD	EARNED
1971	at 2	9	7(5)	0	0	$503,263
1972	at 3	12	5(5)	1(1)	1(1)	$395,632
1973	at 4	9	5(3)	2(1)	0	$212,602
Lifetime		30	17(13)	3(2)	1(1)	$1,111,497

Slew o' Gold

LIKE A FINE WINE, Slew o' Gold got better as he got older. Slew o' Gold was inducted into the Racing Hall of Fame in 1992, eight years after his final campaign. In 1984, he had been named champion older horse. He also had been so impressive at three that he was named champion colt even though he didn't win either of the two classics in which he raced.

Slew o' Gold, bred by Claiborne Farm, was a member of the first crop of foals sired by Triple Crown winner Seattle Slew. He was produced from a fine female family that traced back to Bourtai. That stakes-placed mare produced five stakes winners, including Delta

and Levee, both of whom were stakes winners and eventual Broodmares of the Year. Bourtai also produced champion Bayou, second dam of Slew o' Gold.

At two, Slew o' Gold was not remarkable. He broke his maiden in mid-October at Aqueduct, won an allowance race there, then finished sixth in the Remsen Stakes. At three, Slew o' Gold finished off the board twice, when he was fourth in Sunny's Halo's Kentucky Derby and sixth in the Haskell Invitational. He started the year with a third in a minor stakes at Tampa Bay Downs, then was second in the Budweiser Tampa Bay Derby. Shipped back to Aqueduct, Slew o' Gold won an allowance race by nearly eight lengths on April 13, and ten days later won the Wood Memorial.

After his Derby failure, Slew o' Gold skipped the Preakness and instead raced in the Peter Pan Stakes, which he won by twelve lengths. That performance convinced his group of owners (including primary partners Jim and Sally Hill and Mickey and Karen Taylor, who had raced Seattle Slew) and trainer Sid Watters to try the Belmont Stakes.

Slew o' Gold was sent away the favorite in the Belmont, but finished second to Caveat.

			Boldnesian, 1963	Bold Ruler
		Bold Reasoning, 1968		Alanesian
	SEATTLE SLEW,		Reason to Earn, 1963	Hail to Reason
	dkb/br, 1974			Sailing Home
			Poker, 1963	Round Table
		My Charmer, 1969		Glamour
SLEW o' GOLD,			Fair Charmer, 1959	Jet Action
bay colt,				Myrtle Charm
April 19, 1980			Tom Fool, 1949	Menow
		Buckpasser, 1963		Gaga
	ALLUVIAL,		Busanda, 1947	War Admiral
	ch, 1969			Businesslike
			Hill Prince, 1947	Princequillo
		Bayou, 1954		Hildene
			Bourtai, 1942	Stimulus
				Escutcheon

Slew o' Gold next finished sixth in the Haskell Invitational, followed by a runner-up effort in the Travers. He then took on older horses in the Woodward Stakes, beating the older Bates Motel by a nose. That put Slew o' Gold in line to win a $1-million bonus if he could capture the Fall Championship Series, consisting of the Woodward, Marlboro Cup Invitational, and Jockey Club Gold Cup. Slew o' Gold couldn't quite make the trio his in 1983, finishing second by a neck to Highland Blade in the Marlboro before winning the Gold Cup by three lengths in his final outing of the year.

There was a change in trainers in early 1984 for "disagreements over general policies." Eight horses belonging to the Taylors, Hills, and their partners were taken away from Watters and several, including Slew o' Gold, were given to John Hertler.

Slew o' Gold didn't start his four-year-old campaign until July, when he took an allowance race at Belmont by seven and a half lengths. Earlier in the year, he had been beset by problems, including hoof cracks and frog trouble that required bar shoes. But once he was back, he seemed to be his old self. Slew o' Gold's victory in the Whitney Stakes in his next outing marked trainer Hertler's first graded stakes score. The champion next swept the Fall Championship Series and took the $1-million bonus home. His earnings leap placed him second to John Henry on the all-time leading money earners' list.

In his racing finale, the inaugural Breeders' Cup Classic, Slew o' Gold was sent away the heavy favorite. However, an abscess had been discovered and drained just prior to the Breeders' Cup, and more patching was required on the injured foot. There was heat in the colt's ankle the morning of the race, but all felt he could run safely.

In the roughly run Classic, Wild Again crossed the wire a head in front of Gate Dancer, with Slew o' Gold a half-length back in third. However, Gate Dancer was disqualified for bumping Slew o' Gold and placed third. Second money was enough to give Slew o' Gold a single-season earnings record.

Slew o' Gold was retired to Robert N. Clay's Three Chimneys Farm in Kentucky. He has sired seven grade I/group I winners and three millionaires (Dramatic Gold, Gorgeous, and Thirty Six Red) from twenty-three stakes winners to date. — K. H.

RACE and (STAKES) RECORD

YEAR	AGE	STS	1ST	2ND	3RD	EARNED
1982	at 2	3	2	0	0	$22,200
1983	at 3	12	5(4)	4(4)	1(1)	$883,390
1984	at 4	6	5(4)	1(1)	0	$2,627,944
Lifetime		21	12(8)	5(5)	1(1)	$3,533,534

Twilight Tear

WHEN THE JUGGERNAUT that was the Calumet Farm stable began its Shermanesque march through the 1940s racing scene, among its vanguard was a bay filly with the euphonic name Twilight Tear. Foaled in 1941 from the first crop of Bull Lea, whose development as a leading sire helped Calumet dominate two decades of American racing, Twilight Tear was produced from the Blue Larkspur mare Lady Lark. Although she won only once, Lady Lark possessed enough credentials as a broodmare prospect that Calumet owner Warren Wright Sr. retained her for his growing broodmare band. Lady Lark's third dam, Mannie Himyar, was a sister to the legendary Domino as well as to the great race mare Correction.

Twilight Tear began her racing career under the tutelage of Ben A. Jones, winning a maiden race for two-year-old fillies in come from behind style. Eight days later Twilight Tear returned in the Arlington Lassie Stakes and raced to a two and half-length victory over her stablemate, Miss Keeneland. In winning, Twilight Tear became the first stakes winner for Bull Lea.

Rested until the fall, Twilight Tear traveled to Pimlico for the Selima Stakes. There she ran into a nemesis that plagued her throughout her career: a wet track. In a prep race on a sloppy track, she finished third. Four days later in another prep, she won on a fast track. In the Selima Stakes a week later, Miss Keeneland, with an eight-pound weight advantage, overtook Twilight Tear in the muddy stretch and posted a length victory.

Twilight Tear ran once more at two, beating Miss Keeneland at even weights, ironically on a sloppy track. Twilight Tear finished her two-year-old season with four victories, a second, and a third in six starts and earnings of $34,610. She shared year-end honors with Durazna, also a daughter of Bull Lea from a Blue Larkspur mare.

As good as Twilight Tear was at two, at three she was phenomenal. After finishing third to older horses in her first start, she reeled off eleven straight victories. Included in this skein was a win in the six-furlong Rennert Handicap at Pimlico, in which the filly defeated stablemate and future Horse of the Year Armed. This victory began a streak of four stakes wins in twenty-four days; she also won the Pimlico Oaks, Acorn Stakes, and Coaching Club American Oaks.

Jones shipped the filly back to Arlington where, after a month's rest, she defeated five three-year-old fillies in the Princess Doreen Stakes. Twilight Tear next took on and defeated the colts in the seven-furlong Skokie Handicap in track record time of 1:22⅗, then took the Arlington Classic Stakes. The next stop was venerable Saratoga for the Alabama Stakes, in which Twilight Tear fell victim to a brisk, pressured pace to finish second.

A long rest for the well-traveled, hard-raced filly ensued. She resumed her campaign at Belmont Park, winning at five and a half furlongs, then taking the Queen Isabella Handicap. In Laurel's Maryland Handicap she finished off the board for the only time in two years. Her 130-pound impost and a muddy track were to blame for her fourth-place finish. In her final start of the year, Twilight Tear defeated champion Devil Diver by six lengths.

The depth and scope of her fourteen victories in seventeen starts and earnings of $167,555 were impressive enough for her to be named champion three-year-old filly, champion handicap mare, and, in a rare honor for the distaff half (especially three-year olds), Horse of the Year. A bleeding problem hampered Twilight Tear's four-year old season, and she was retired with totals of twenty-four starts, eighteen wins, two seconds, two thirds, and earnings of $202,165.

Twilight Tear's success as a broodmare nearly equaled her success on the racetrack. She produced outstanding stakes winners in Bardstown, A Gleam, and Coiner.

Twilight Tear died in 1954. Although she never produced a champion, the championship blood of Twilight Tear did come full circle. Twilight Tear is the third dam of Calumet Farm's 1981 champion two-year-old filly Before Dawn.

— T. H.

Pedigree Chart

	Bull Dog, 1927	Teddy, 1913	Ajax / Rondeau
BULL LEA, br, 1935		Plucky Liege, 1912	Spearmint / Concertina
	Rose Leaves, 1916	Ballot, 1904	Voter / Cerito
TWILIGHT TEAR, bay filly, 1941		Colonial, 1897	Trenton / Thankful Blossom
	Blue Larkspur, 1926	Black Servant, 1918	Black Toney / Padula
LADY LARK, b, 1934		Blossom Time, 1920	North Star III / Vaila
	Ladana, 1928	Busher, 1916	Trap Rock / Lady Lane
		Adana, 1908	Adam / Mannie Himyar

RACE and (STAKES) RECORD

YEAR	AGE	STS	1ST	2ND	3RD	EARNED
1943	at 2	6	4(1)	1(1)	1	$34,610
1944	at 3	17	14(9)	1(1)	1	$167,555
1945	at 4	1	0	0	0	$0
Lifetime		24	18(10)	2(2)	2	$202,165

Native Diver

NATIVE DIVER WAS A STAR, plain and simple. Everyone knows stars are made in California, and Native Diver was California's equine version of a matinee idol. He was a fan favorite, claimed by the public as its own. The nearly black gelding exuded audacity and vitality and the intangible quality known as heart.

More brilliant horses have competed, but Native Diver had a charisma and scarcely harnessed energy that drew people to him. The perception that he only tolerated the bridle and merely indulged his rider added to his mystique. It was "The Diver" who had control. Rivals

found it impossible to catch the free-wheeling gelding when he was alone on the lead, but found it even more futile to attempt to run with him. His strategy was simple: run as fast as you can as far as you can. No one who saw The Diver run doubted he loved his profession. Native Diver so enjoyed running that he rarely felt his rider's whip.

Native Diver was a wild horse at heart, injuring his back in a spree of impetuous behavior as a yearling. As a result, he ran with his head held high to accommodate the injury. His fractiousness left his connections no choice but to geld him, but the operation did little to calm his spirit. Spectators always watched him with anticipation, waiting for their hero to display some of the tempestuousness for which he was known.

L. K. Shapiro and his wife bred the gelding, having claimed his dam, Fleet Diver, for $3,500 in January, 1954. Fleet Diver had another claim to fame other than foaling Native Diver; she was the horse on whom jockey Johnny Longden won his 4,000th race in May, 1952, at Hollywood Park. Native Diver's sire, Imbros, also found fame when he set a world record of 1:41 for one and a sixteenth miles in the Californian Stakes in 1954.

Shapiro owned Mar-Dor Company, one of the country's largest manufacturers of women's coats, and was co-founder and president of the Western Harness Racing Association. But it was Native Diver, born in 1959, who "has brought us all the greatest thrills anyone has ever had," said Shapiro.

Pedigree of NATIVE DIVER, brown colt, April 16, 1959

IMBROS, ch, 1950	Polynesian, 1942	Unbreakable, 1935	Sickle / Blue Glass
		Black Polly, 1936	Polymelian / Black Queen
	Fire Falls, 1942	Bull Dog, 1927	Teddy / Plucky Liege
		Stricken, 1932	Pennant / Moody Mary
FLEET DIVER, b 1950	Devil Diver, 1939	St. Germans, 1921	Swynford / Hamoaze
		Dabchick, 1931	Royal Minstrel / Ruddy Duck
	Our Fleet, 1946	Count Fleet, 1940	Reigh Count / Quickly
		Duchess Anita, 1940	Count Gallahad / French Duchess

Native Diver won his first three starts as a two-year-old for trainer M. E. (Buster) Millerick by a combined margin of twenty-three and three-quarters lengths, including his first career stakes event, the El Camino Handicap at Tanforan. As a sophomore, he set the first of six career track records, winning Bay Meadows' Hillsdale Handicap in 1:08⅖ for the six furlongs. Yet The Diver's potential had barely been tapped.

During his career, Native Diver won six times carrying 130 pounds or more, setting three track records toting that burden. The Diver also could sprint or carry his speed and set track records at distances from six to nine furlongs. Winning thirty-four stakes events over seven seasons of racing, The Diver made each performance an event. He won a stakes race at each of California's six major tracks, only the second horse to accomplish such a feat. Only once did he race outside of California, finishing sixth in the Washington Park Handicap in Chicago in 1965.

For three consecutive years, The Diver captured the Hollywood Gold Cup, running it faster each time. Native Diver gave no hint of slowing down, but Shapiro vowed to retire him the moment he showed he was losing a step. The opportunity never came. After equaling the track record for nine furlongs in the 1967 Del Mar Handicap, Native Diver became ill. Transported to the University of California at Davis, The Diver succumbed to enterio toxemia, or intestinal colic. He was buried at Hollywood Park near the grandstand.

Native Diver never won a championship, nor a race outside California. He lost more races than he won, winning thirty-seven of his eighty-one starts. Nevertheless, he captured the public's imagination, claimed the distinction of being the first California-bred to reach millionaire status, and was elected to the Racing Hall of Fame in 1978. — J. W.

RACE and (STAKES) RECORD

YEAR	AGE	STS	1ST	2ND	3RD	EARNED
1961	at 2	5	3(1)	0	1(1)	$17,400
1962	at 3	11	6(1)	0	1(1)	$68,225
1963	at 4	15	5(1)	3(1)	1(1)	$108,125
1964	at 5	15	6(1)	0	4(1)	$127,250
1965	at 6	10	7(7)	1(1)	1(1)	$241,650
1966	at 7	12	4(4)	1(1)	1(1)	$205,750
1967	at 8	13	6(6)	2(2)	3(3)	$258,100
Lifetime		81	37(21)	7(5)	12(9)	$1,026,500

Omaha

OMAHA — THE ONLY TRIPLE CROWN WINNER sired by a Triple Crown winner — was a late starter. The trait was as true of his career as it was of his normal running style. Omaha was a product of the first stud season by his sire, Gallant Fox. Like his sire, Omaha was bred and owned by William Woodward Sr. He was foaled at Claiborne Farm in Kentucky and sent to the Belair Stud in Maryland.

Trained by Jim Fitzsimmons, the chestnut colt ran for the first time on June 18, 1934,

at Aqueduct, finishing second with a late rush, running somewhat erratically. A mere five days later, he returned to post his only victory in nine starts as a juvenile, winning by a head while running five furlongs in :58⅗. At Saratoga, Omaha continued to show promise while closing well in the late stages of races — but without winning. He was fourth in the United States Hotel Stakes, fourth again in the Saratoga Special, and second in the Sanford.

After finishing fourth yet again in the Hopeful, Omaha ran an atypical race in the Champagne Stakes. Eschewing his usual slow start, the colt went right out after pace-setting Balladier and missed only by a nose while Balladier shaved four-fifths of a second off the Belmont Park record for six and a half furlongs.

It was back to his old tricks in the Futurity as Omaha reported home fourth. And, after finishing second in the Junior Champion Stakes in his final start of the year, Omaha was regarded as a prospect for the following year but, certainly not *the* prospect.

As a three-year-old, Omaha made good on the promise of his juvenile year and the genes of his sire. He got his second career win in his first start of the year. But put back into stakes company in the Wood Memorial, Omaha got off in eleventh position and, despite his usual good closing punch, finished third. For a change, Omaha's penchant for a slow start may have been a help in the Kentucky Derby. Facing seventeen rivals and starting from the num-

		Teddy, 1913	**Ajax**
			Rondeau
	Sir Gallahad III, 1920		
		Plucky Liege, 1912	Spearmint
GALLANT FOX,			Concertina
b, 1927		Celt, 1905	Commando
			Maid of Erin
	Marguerite, 1920		
OMAHA,		Fairy Ray, 1911	Radium
chestnut colt,			Seraph
1932			
		Robert le Diable, 1899	Ayrshire
			Rose Bay
	Wrack, 1909		
		Samphire, 1902	Isinglass
FLAMBINO,			Chelandry
b, 1924		Durbar II, 1911	Rabelais
			Armonia
	Flambette, 1918		
		La Flambee, 1912	**Ajax**
			Medeah

ber ten post, jockey Willie Saunders kept Omaha to the outside and out of trouble through the stretch for the first time, around the first turn, and onto the backstretch. He took the lead turning for home and won by one and a half lengths.

Again coming from off the pace, Omaha took the Preakness by storm, winning by six lengths and just missing the Pimlico track record. After finishing second to Rosemont in the Withers at one mile, Omaha came back to whip four challengers soundly in the Belmont, beating Firethorn by one and a half lengths with Rosemont a distant third.

Omaha's sweep of the Kentucky Derby, Preakness, and Belmont — repeating the feat of his sire — cemented the concept of a "Triple Crown" comprised of that trio of races for three-year-olds. Although Sir Barton had won all three races in 1919, the accomplishment was not acknowledged by name until the father-son duo of Gallant Fox and Omaha presented sportswriters an opportunity for a catchy — and type-saving — accolade. On two weeks' rest, Omaha was set out against the handicap division in the Brooklyn Handicap and quickly proved incapable of dealing with that class rise, finishing third.

Returning to his own age group, Omaha won the Dwyer Stakes only a week after the Brooklyn. He then shipped west to Chicago, where he faced two top fillies — Black Helen and Bloodroot — in the Arlington Classic. He responded with an impressive effort, starting slowly as usual but rolling home one and a half lengths in track-record time of 2:01⅖.

A long bout of unexplained physical problems prevented Omaha from running again as a three-year-old and, at age four, Woodward shipped the colt to England, hoping his late-running style and ability to get a distance of ground would prove effective in that country's premier races. He won a minor stakes at Kempton in his first try, then captured the Queen's Plate. In his ultimate test, the Ascot Gold Cup, Omaha battled gallantly but lost by a nose after two and a half miles to the filly Quashed. He finished second in his last race, the Princess of Wales's Stakes at Newmarket.

Omaha was not a successful sire for Claiborne and wound up his stallion career in Nebraska, standing for $25. Sire of only seven stakes winners, he died in Nebraska in 1959 and was buried near the entrance to Ak-Sar-Ben. — B. K.

RACE and (STAKES) RECORD

YEAR	AGE	STS	1ST	2ND	3RD	EARNED
1934	at 2 in NA	9	1	4(3)	0	$3,850
1935	at 3 in NA	9	6(5)	1(1)	2(2)	$142,255
1936	at 4 in Eng	4	2(1)	2(2)	0	$8,600
Lifetime		22	9(6)	7(6)	2(2)	$154,705

Cicada

VOTING FOR CHAMPIONSHIPS BEGAN IN 1936, and Cicada became the first female to be voted a champion at two, three, and four. She was a second-generation dividend for sportsman/industrialist Christopher T. Chenery from his purchase of Hildene for $700 from the E. F. Simms dispersal of 1939.

Hildene failed to win for Chenery, but produced his first champion, Hill Prince, and a later champion, First Landing, as well as additional stakes winners Mangohick, Prince Hill, and Third Brother. Cicada was foaled from one of Hildene's non-distinguished runners, the Bossuet filly Satsuma. Her sire was Bryan G., a high-class campaigner for Chenery, but without championship pretensions.

J. H. (Casey) Hayes served a long stint as trainer for Chenery's Meadow Stable horses, and he had under his shedrow both Sir Gaylord and Cicada as their two-year-old season of 1961 dawned. Both began early, in winter three-furlong dashes at Hialeah. Sir Gaylord quickly moved to the top of his division, but could not sustain his status. Cicada scrimmaged on more or less even terms with several other stakes-winning fillies early, then took firm control of her division at Saratoga and won her last six races in succession.

Cicada's first championship was clinched in that sequence, which included the Spinaway, Matron, Astarita, Frizette, and Gardenia. Only a few fillies could test her severely, one being Firm Policy, who got to within a head of her in the Astarita. Firm Policy would be around to test Cicada for two more years, occasionally beating the champion. Cicada concluded her campaign with a ten-length waltz in the Gardenia. She had won eleven of sixteen at two and earned $384,676, then a record for a two-year-old filly.

Hayes liked tough horses, and Cicada was as tough as he could have wished. In the winter of her three-year-old season, Cicada took on older fillies and mares in the Black Helen, then faced colts in the Florida Derby. She won neither, but her narrow loss to Ridan after a furious struggle in the latter added to, rather than detracted from, her status. In the spring, Cicada won the Kentucky Oaks, although it was assumed she might have been entered in the Kentucky Derby had Hayes and Chenery known a few hours earlier that their Derby favorite, the revitalized Sir Gaylord, would turn up lame. Cicada then won the Acorn and Mother Goose, but in the Coaching Club American Oaks, she was prevented by Bramalea from becoming the first winner of the New York Filly Triple Crown.

Through the rest of her three-year-old season, the stern trials were unrelenting. In addition to major races in her own division, Cicada faced older distaffers in the Delaware Handicap and colts in the Travers. She suffered five losses, but was admirable in most, especially the Delaware, in which she was beaten only a head by the older Seven Thirty, with Bramalea and Primonetta in their wake. Cicada rebounded to win the Beldame from a field of the year's best distaffers, including Primonetta, Firm Policy, Bramalea, and Seven Thirty. She won eight of seventeen races at three to earn her second year-end championship.

At four, Cicada expanded her venue to turf when she won the one and a sixteenth-mile Sheepshead Bay Handicap under 128 pounds. She also won the Columbiana, Distaff, and Vagrancy. In the Vagrancy, she carried 127 pounds and defeated old rival Bramalea.

Cicada was voted older distaff champion, for her third consecutive year as a titlelist. She was retired, but failed to get in foal and was returned to training. Cicada made but a brief comeback, then was retired again with the distafff earnings record of $783,674. She had won twenty-three of forty-two races. Cicada had been tested as thoroughly as virtually any modern filly or mare and had stood up to every challenge with speed, grit, and an unwavering fortitude.

RACE and (STAKES) RECORD

YEAR	AGE	STS	1ST	2ND	3RD	EARNED
1961	at 2	16	11(8)	2(2)	3(2)	$384,676
1962	at 3	17	8(6)	4(4)	2(2)	$298,167
1963	at 4	8	4(4)	2(2)	1(1)	$100,481
1964	at 5	1	0	0	0	$350
Lifetime		42	23(18)	8(8)	6(5)	$783,674

Cicada's first foal was by former stablemate Sir Gaylord. Named Cicada's Pride, the colt won the Juvenile Stakes at two, providing a positive beginning. Sadly, Cicada then suffered through years of reproductive problems, eventually having only six foals, none of the others distinguished as runners. Cicada died in 1981 at age twenty-two. — E. L. B.

Silver Charm

BUT FOR THREE-QUARTERS OF A LENGTH, Silver Charm would be sitting a lot higher on the list of the 20th Century's top 100 horses as the nation's twelfth Triple Crown champion. That's the meager distance by which Touch Gold beat the iron gray son of Silver Buck in the 1997 Belmont Stakes to deny him the third jewel of the crown. And, to this day, most of Silver Charm's fans believe he never would have allowed Touch Gold to pass if he'd seen him coming way out in the middle of the track. But Chris McCarron, with one of the savviest Triple Crown rides in history, blind-sided Silver Charm

and Gary Stevens as they concentrated on putting away familiar nemesis Free House, who was blocking the view.

More than 70,000 of New York's tough fans treated Silver Charm to a standing ovation anyway. They'd already fallen in love with the Kentucky Derby and Preakness Stakes winner with a penchant for gritty, tight finishes. As Silver Charm's career continued, so, too, did his narrow victories and losses, whether it was Free House or Swain, Wild Rush or Awesome Again. Silver Charm always seemed to enjoy the eyeball-to-eyeball competition as much as victory itself. And it seems for that reason, along with his beautiful color and what trainer Bob Baffert called his "ham sandwich price," Silver Charm became one of the most popular horses of the 1990s. Coming on the heels of Cigar, he gave racing a much-needed lift, attracting newspaper and television coverage as well as more fans.

Silver Charm wasn't so popular as a youngster. His Florida breeder, Mary Lou Wootton, let him slip away for $16,500 to pinhookers Randy Hartley and Dean De Renzo at the 1995 Ocala Breeders' Sales Co.'s August yearling sale. Canadian horseman C. J. Grey then purchased the gray privately for $30,000 early in the colt's two-year-old season and entered him in the OBS April two-year-olds-in-training sale. Silver Charm failed to bring the $100,000 reserve, though, so Grey bought him back.

By this time, however, pinhookers J. B. and Kevin McKathan, Florida talent scouts for Baffert, had sent the Southern California trainer a tape of Silver Charm's pre-sale work. Baffert liked what he saw and purchase of the colt was negotiated. Bob and Beverly Lewis ended up paying the $85,000 — a pittance compared to the $6.9 million he had won through June 1999.

It didn't take long for Silver Charm to build a small fan club in Southern California. After a second and a first in maiden special weights, Silver Charm won the first of his famous photo finishes, by a head over Gold Tribute, in the Del Mar Futurity. Then Baffert paid Silver Charm the ultimate compliment: He put him away to rest up and grow before the Triple Crown campaign the following season. Baffert did the same thing after the 1997 Belmont: He rested the colt until December, when the son of Silver Buck finished second by a half-length in the Malibu Stakes after a troubled trip. That left him with three wins and four seconds in seven starts for the year as well as the three-year-old championship.

Silver Charm's goal for 1998 was to knock off favored Skip Away for the handicap championship. He didn't quite pull it off as he won six of nine starts and finished second twice. But his fans had plenty of thrills along the way: an uncharacteristic four-length romp in the Strub, an incredible trip to race in and win the $4-million Dubai World Cup by a nose over Swain, a dead-heat victory with Wild Rush in the Kentucky Cup Classic, and then the $4-million Breeders' Cup Classic, in which he lost to Awesome Again by three-quarters of a length.

In 1999, Silver Charm managed just one victory, in the San Pasqual Handicap. He ran third to Puerto Madero in the Donn Handicap and third to old foe Free House in the Santa Anita Handicap. Then he headed to Dubai, where the second time was not the Charm. Instead, he bled and finished sixth, the worst showing of his career. In June, the Lewises and Baffert decided to retire Silver Charm after he finished fourth in the Stephen Foster Handicap at Churchill Downs.

— P. S.

Pedigree of SILVER CHARM, gray or roan colt, February 22, 1994

SILVER BUCK, gr, 1978	Buckpasser, 1963	Tom Fool, 1949 — Menow / Gaga
		Busanda, 1947 — War Admiral / Businesslike
	Silver True, 1964	Hail to Reason, 1958 — Turn-to / Nothirdchance
		Silver Fog, 1944 — Mahmoud / Equilette
BONNIE'S POKER, dkh/br, 1982	Poker, 1963	Round Table, 1954 — Princequillo / Knight's Daughter
		Glamour, 1953 — Nasrullah / Striking
	What a Surprise, 1968	West Margin, 1950 — Market Wise / One Ripple
		Militant Miss, 1951 — Faultless / Miss Militant

RACE and (STAKES) RECORD						
YEAR	AGE	STS	1ST	2ND	3RD	EARNED
1996	at 2 in NA	3	2(1)	1	0	$177,750
1997	at 3 in NA	7	3(3)	4(4)	0	$1,638,750
1998	at 4 in NA, UAE	9	6(6)	2(2)	0	$4,696,506
1999	at 5 in NA, UAE	5	1(1)	0	2(2)	$431,363
Lifetime		**24**	**12(11)**	**7(6)**	**2(2)**	**$6,944,369**

Holy Bull

ON THE SAME DAY THAT RACHEL CARPENTER, who operated under the name Pelican Stable, died at age 78 on Aug. 14, 1993, her homebred gray colt Holy Bull broke his maiden at Monmouth Park. Hall of Fame trainer Warren A. (Jimmy) Croll, who had known the late owner-breeder since 1957, found out several days after Holy Bull's initial victory that the colt was among six horses left to him in Carpenter's will.

Thus began the storybook rise to racing glory for the game horse and his adopted owner. When injury ended his career prematurely one and a half years later, Holy Bull retired to stud with a Horse of the Year title and thirteen victories in sixteen starts. He earned $2,481,760.

A Florida-bred son of Great Above, Holy Bull led at every call in winning all four juvenile starts in 1993. At three, the colt picked up where he had left off, posting an impressive win in the Hutcheson Stakes. Holy Bull sustained his first loss in the Fountain of Youth Stakes when he finished sixth, twenty-four and a quarter lengths behind winner Dehere, the previous year's champion two-year-old male. Despite the setback, the colt rebounded in the Florida Derby, setting quick fractions in a front-running five and three-quarters-length victory.

With "the Bull" starting to attract a fan base, Croll shipped the colt to Keeneland for the Blue Grass Stakes in his final Kentucky Derby prep. On the eve of the Blue Grass, Holy Bull worked three furlongs in a quick :34, the fastest time of the day among twenty-nine horses working that distance. The following day he led from start to finish to win the Blue Grass by three and a half lengths.

Since it had worked well in Lexington, on the day before the May 7 Derby Croll sent Holy Bull to the track for another "blow out," although the three-eighths of a mile in :36⅗ was

			Rough'n Tumble, 1948	Free For All Roused
		Minnesota Mac, 1964		
	GREAT ABOVE, dkb/br, 1972		Cow Girl II, 1949	Mustang Ate
			Intentionally, 1956	Intent My Recipe
		Ta Wee, 1966		
HOLY BULL, gray colt, January 24, 1991			Aspidistra, 1954	Better Self Tilly Rose
			The Axe II, 1958	Mahmoud Blackball
		Al Hattab, 1966		
	SHARON BROWN, gr, 1980		Abyssinia II, 1953	Abernant Serengeti
			Grey Dawn, 1962	Herbager Polamia
		Agathea's Dawn, 1970		
			Agathea, 1955	I Will Alxanth

slower than the trainer wanted. After a poor start in the Derby, Holy Bull raced in close quarters rounding the first turn before recovering. He went on to finish twelfth in the fourteen-horse field as the favorite.

The inexplicable performance left Croll puzzled. "I just can't explain that race," the trainer said. "If I had to do it all over again, I would not have run him. He looked fine physically and was eating normally. But on the track he did not have the pep and vigor he had shown before."

Rather than continue on the classic route, Croll decided to let his three-year-old test older horses in the Metropolitan Handicap, commonly known as the Met Mile. The Bull ran off with the race, stopping the timer in 1:33⅗, four-fifths of a second off Conquistador Cielo's stakes mark. Holy Bull continued to excel, winning the Dwyer Stakes, Haskell Invitational, and Travers, the last confirming the colt's ability to go one and a quarter miles. Prior to the Travers, Croll sold one-quarter interest in Holy Bull to John A. Bell III's Jonabell Farm to secure the colt as a future stallion.

With Holy Bull not nominated to the Breeders' Cup, the colt's final start of the season would be against older horses in the Woodward Stakes. The 9-10 favorite, Holy Bull had to rally from behind to pass Devil His Due for a five-length triumph. With eight wins from ten starts and seasonal earnings of $2,095,000, Holy Bull was voted Horse of the Year and champion three-year-old, despite not winning any leg of the Triple Crown and not running in the Breeders' Cup.

After winning the Olympic Handicap in his first outing at age four, Holy Bull was sent off the 3-10 choice in the Donn Handicap at Gulfstream Park. With the Bull stalking then-rising star Cigar early in the race, he apparently took a bad step and was pulled up. A post-race veterinary examination revealed a severe strain of the flexor tendon, but no broken bones, in his left front leg. Rather than wait for the injury to heal, the decision was made to retire the horse.

Holy Bull entered stud at Jonabell Farm near Lexington, Kentucky. From his initial two crops to race, Holy Bull has sired stakes winners Confessional, Holywood Picture, Holy Golightly, Crash Course, and Smokey Mirage. — R. M.

RACE and (STAKES) RECORD

YEAR	AGE	STS	1ST	2ND	3RD	EARNED
1993	at 2	4	4(2)	0	0	$335,760
1994	at 3	10	8(8)	0	0	$2,095,000
1995	at 4	2	1(1)	0	0	$51,000
Lifetime		16	13(11)	0	0	$2,481,760

177

Alsab

IF ALSAB HAD THE LOOK OF EAGLES as a young horse, hardly anybody noticed it. His sire and dam — Good Goods and Winds Chant — were modest stock. And when breeder Tom Piatt sold him as a yearling at Saratoga in 1940, Alsab brought only $700, well below the $1,369 average for Piatt's twenty-four-horse consignment.

The price proved to be one of racing's biggest bargains ever for trainer August (Sarge) Swenke and his client, Chicago attorney Albert Sabath, president of Hawthorne Racecourse. Carrying the colors of Mrs. Sabath, Alsab earned championships at two and three. So impressive were his efforts that some said he deserved to be named Horse of the Year in both seasons over Triple Crown winner Whirlaway, whom he beat twice in three meetings in 1942.

As a juvenile, Alsab captured fifteen of his twenty-two races. At first, he was dismissed as a "Midwest Flash" by Turf writers, but he stamped himself as a serious 1941 title contender with dominating victories over one of New York's best, Requested. The two first met in a match race, which was proposed by Belmont Park president Alfred G. Vanderbilt because neither runner was eligible for the prestigious Futurity. Requested set a fast pace in the six and a half-furlong test while jockey Bobby Vedder kept Alsab under a good hold until they reached the three-eighths pole. Vedder then went to his whip, Alsab roared up to challenge, then surged ahead to win by three and a half lengths. His time of 1:16 was more than a second faster than the Belmont record set by the four-year-old Audacious twenty-one years earlier.

Eleven days after the match win, Alsab showed the effort was no fluke when he returned to the starting gate for the Champagne Stakes. None of the first four finishers in the Futurity — Some Chance, Devil Diver, Caduceus, and Ramillies — showed up, but Requested, getting six pounds, was ready to try again. At the wire, Alsab was seven lengths

GOOD GOODS, b, 1931	Neddie, 1926	Colin, 1905	Commando **Pastorella**
		Black Flag, 1919	Light Brigade Misplay
	Brocatelle, 1915	Radium, 1903	Bend Or Taia
		Pietra, 1905	Pietermaritzburg Briar-root
ALSAB, bay colt, 1939			
WINDS CHANT, br, 1931	Wildair, 1917	Broomstick, 1901	Ben Brush Elf
		Verdure, 1910	Peter Pan **Pastorella**
	Eulogy, 1913	Fair Play, 1905	Hastings Fairy Gold
		St. Eudora, 1898	St. Simon Dorothea

in front of Requested, completing the mile in 1:35⅖, the fastest of the year and a world record for a two-year-old.

Alsab, who won twice more before the season ended, was given 130 pounds on the Experimental Free Handicap. Previously, only Bimelech, the undefeated champion two-year-old male of 1939, had received that much.

At three, Alsab got off to a slow start. Eight times he tried, and eight times he failed. But he was no disgrace, with his efforts including a runner-up finish to Shut Out in the Kentucky Derby. In the Preakness, Alsab finished a length in front of his old rival, Requested. After a romp in the Withers, Alsab was favored for the Belmont Stakes, but wound up two lengths behind Shut Out. Five days later, it was discovered that Alsab was suffering from a blind splint.

Two months off did not seem to diminish his competitive fire, and Albert Sabath soon decided that Alsab was strong enough to tackle the great Whirlaway. The Narragansett Special was chosen for the showdown, but at the last minute, Alsab was withdrawn. Narragansett Park management then proposed a match race for the following Saturday: one and three-sixteenths miles, $25,000, weight for age, with Whirlaway carrying 126 pounds and Alsab toting 119. Alsab defeated his determined older rival by a short nose.

Next, during an eleven-day period in New York, Alsab faced three stiff tests and handled them like a true professional. In the Lawrence Realization, he gave the top filly Vagrancy eleven pounds and triumphed by three and a half lengths. In the two-mile Jockey Club Gold Cup, he was second, beaten only three-quarters of a length, by Whirlaway. In the two and a quarter-mile New York Handicap, Alsab matched strides with Whirlaway in the final turn and through the upper stretch before putting him away, then survived a late rush by longshot Obash to win by a head.

After three more races, Alsab closed out his three-year-old campaign with nine victories in twenty-three races and earnings of $234,565. After frustrating seasons at four and five, he ended his career with earnings of $350,015. Alsab sired sixteen stakes winners, including Myrtle Charm, the champion juvenile filly of 1948. — D. B. B.

RACE and (STAKES) RECORD

YEAR	AGE	STS	1ST	2ND	3RD	EARNED
1941	at 2	22	15(12)	3(1)	1	$110,600
1942	at 3	23	9(9)	7(7)	3(3)	$234,565
1943	at 4	5	1	1(1)	1(1)	$4,650
1944	at 5	1	0	0	0	$200
Lifetime		51	25(21)	11(9)	5(4)	$350,015

Top Flight

GOOD RACEHORSES sometimes come from unexpected sources — unexceptional performers whose genetic potential lies waiting to erupt. C. V. Whitney's champion filly Top Flight is such an example.

International racing and breeding in the decades before and after World War I were the exclusive province of the very rich. Certainly, Harry Payne Whitney, the breeder of Top Flight, fit that category. Following the lead of his father, W. C. Whitney, the younger Whitney often sent runners abroad.

The pedigree of Top Flight reveals this global nature of racing. Her bloodline is filled with both American and European influences. Top Flight's sire, Dis Donc, did little on the racetrack to merit the best mares. What he did have was a European pedigree that would add stamina. Top Flight's dam, Flyatit, descended from one of the premier families in the American Stud Book, that of Maggie B.B. Flyatit's second dam was Matinee, a full sister to the outstanding runner and sire Whisk Broom II. A daughter of Peter Pan and the Prince Palatine mare Afternoon, Flyatit won five of her ten starts. Thus, both of Top Flight's parents were lackluster in performance but gleamed with genetic possibilities.

In 1929, Flyatit foaled a brown filly with a blazed face and less than perfect conformation. The filly would later demonstrate the superior genetic material she received from her parents. Unfortunately, H. P. Whitney would never see the foal, named Top Flight, race. When the elder Whitney died in 1930, his son Cornelius Vanderbilt Whitney inherited his legacy in racing, as well as the filly who possessed in her movement a touch of European grace with the essence of effortless American speed.

Top Flight began her racing career in the 1931 Clover Stakes at Aqueduct. She led the entire five furlongs and won by a length on the muddy track. Next, trainer Thomas J.

		Prestige, 1903	Le Pompon / Orgueilleuse
	Sardanapale, 1911		
DIS DONC, b, 1918		Gemma, 1903	Florizel II / Agnostic
		Hamburg, 1895	Hanover / Lady Reel
	Lady Hamburg II, 1908		
TOP FLIGHT, dark brown filly, 1929		Lady Frivoles, 1894	St. Simon / Gay Duchess
		Commando, 1898	Domino / Emma C.
	Peter Pan, 1904		
FLYATIT, b, 1922		Cinderella, 1888	Hermit / Mazurka
		Prince Palatine, 1908	Persimmon / Lady Lightfoot
	Afternoon, 1917		
		Matinee, 1908	Broomstick / Audience

Healey took the two-year-old filly to the Midwest, where she won the Lassie Stakes at Arlington Park.

Top Flight then was sent to try Saratoga. In the Saratoga Special, she challenged the colts and the result remained the same: she was first under the wire. A week later she easily beat fillies in the Spinaway Stakes, then extended her perfect record by winning the Matron Stakes at Belmont.

In her final two juvenile starts, Top Flight once again faced the colts. In the Futurity Stakes at Belmont, eleven colts lined up against her, but it proved to be no contest. In the beaten field languished Col. E. R. Bradley's Burgoo King, the future winner of the Kentucky Derby. She then won the Pimlico Futurity by a neck over Tick On and Burgoo King. Top Flight completed a perfect season and was named champion two-year-old filly.

Such talent brought comparisons to another Whitney filly from the past — Regret. Would Top Flight be the second filly and the second Whitney filly to win the Kentucky Derby? Her three-year-old campaign was mapped with that goal in mind. However, Top Flight failed to live up to her press. Healey chose the Wood Memorial at Jamaica for Top Flight's return, but she finished a well-beaten fourth and Derby plans were scrapped.

Instead, Top Flight contested the Acorn Stakes. She was never challenged, winning by six lengths. In the Coaching Club American Oaks, Top Flight defeated a top notch field by three-quarters of a length. She followed up with a victory in the Arlington Oaks. In the Arlington Classic, she again faced colts and turned in her worst performance, finishing fifth. This race began a series of seesaw races which Top Flight either won or finished off the board. At Saratoga she won the Alabama Stakes, then finished fourth in the Delaware Handicap, but rebounded to win the Ladies Handicap at Belmont. In the final start of her career, the Potomac Handicap for three-year-olds, she struggled home in fourth place. She retained her championship crown, being named champion three-year-old filly in 1932.

Retired to the Whitney broodmare band, Top Flight produced seven foals, one of which was a stakes winner. She also foaled three stakes-producing daughters, the best of which was the Mahmoud filly White Lady. Top Flight died in 1949 and was buried at the Whitney farm in Kentucky. — *T. H.*

RACE and (STAKES) RECORD

YEAR	AGE	STS	1ST	2ND	3RD	EARNED
1931	at 2	7	7(7)	0	0	$219,000
1932	at 3	9	5(5)	0	0	$56,900
Lifetime		**16**	**12(12)**	**0**	**0**	**$275,900**

Arts and Letters

VIRGINIA SPORTSMAN PAUL MELLON got plenty more than he bargained for when he purchased the Battlefield mare All Beautiful for $175,000 at the William du Pont Jr. dispersal at Timonium, Maryland, in February of 1966. Through trainer Elliott Burch, Mellon bought the mare with the intention of breeding her that season to European champion Sea-Bird. All Beautiful at that time was in foal to another European champion, undefeated Ribot, and she produced a colt on April 1 at Mellon's Rokeby Farms in Virginia. Under the name of Arts and Letters, the son of Ribot proved to be the best runner ever raced by Mellon in the United States.

Arts and Letters was a stamina-filled iron horse during his three-year-old season in 1969, which culminated in Horse of the Year honors. He raced from January to October, running first or second in thirteen of fourteen races and earning more money than any other horse that year. The highlight came in a six-race win streak, in which he won in succession the Metropolitan Handicap, Belmont Stakes, Jim Dandy Stakes, Travers Stakes, Woodward Stakes, and Jockey Club Gold Cup.

Lightly raced as a two-year-old, Arts and Letters raced in the shadow of Top Knight in Florida in the winter of 1969, then behind the shadow of Majestic Prince in May, before taking complete control. Arts and Letters won the Everglades Stakes at Hialeah, but ran second behind Top Knight in Florida's two big races for three-year-olds: the Flamingo Stakes and Florida Derby. From there, it was on to Keeneland, where he cruised home in the Blue Grass Stakes by fifteen lengths under Bill Shoemaker.

Shoemaker was scheduled to ride Arts and Letters in the Kentucky Derby, but he suffered an injury during Derby week and Burch secured the services of Braulio Baeza. Arts and Letters gave it his best shot in both the Derby and the Preakness, but his trademark

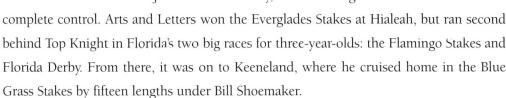

closing rush fell short of unbeaten Majestic Prince in both races.

Burch wanted to restore some confidence in Arts and Letters, and he ran him against older runners in the Metropolitan Handicap before the Belmont. In receipt of eighteen pounds from the older Nodouble, Arts and Letters won the mile race by two and a half lengths over that handicap star.

In the Belmont Stakes, Arts and Letters roared to a five and a half-length victory over Majestic Prince. Arts and Letters was rested until Saratoga and came back to win the Jim Dandy and Travers Stakes at that upstate New York track. His time of 2:01⅗ in the one and a quarter-mile Travers equaled the track record.

The Woodward Stakes and Jockey Club Gold Cup followed. Arts and Letters defeated Nodouble in both races, taking the Woodward by two lengths and the Jockey Club by fourteen lengths in his final two starts of the year. He earned $555,604 that year and was voted Horse of the Year and champion three-year-old colt.

Rested over the winter, Arts and Letters raced three times as a four-year-old in 1970, winning the Grey Lag Handicap in the second of those starts before suffering a career-ending injury in the Californian Stakes at Hollywood Park in May. His injury came within a week of the announcement that he was being pointed toward the Prix de Saint-Cloud in France in July. Arts and Letters was retired with a record of eleven wins from twenty-three starts and earnings of $632,404. He was syndicated for $100,000 per share and entered stud for a fee of $20,000 at Greentree Stud near Lexington, Kentucky, in 1971.

Arts and Letters was elected to the Racing Hall of Fame in 1994, joining Mellon, Burch, and Baeza in the Hall. He sired twenty-nine stakes winners, including 1980 Preakness Stakes winner Codex, whose son, Lost Code, has carried on the male line. Arts and Letters also is the broodmare sire of fifty-one stakes winners, including Breeders' Cup Classic winner Alphabet Soup.

Arts and Letters was placed under the management of Gainesway Farm later in his stallion career. He was pensioned in 1995 and died in the fall of 1998, several months before Mellon died on Feb. 1, 1999. — *D. S.*

RIBOT (GB), b, 1952	Tenerani, 1944	Bellini, 1937	Cavaliere d'Arpino / Bella Minna
		Tofanella, 1931	Apelle / Try Try Again
	Romanella, 1943	El Greco, 1934	Pharos / Gay Gamp
ARTS AND LETTERS, chestnut colt, April 1, 1966		Barbara Burrini, 1937	Papyrus / Bucolic
	Battlefield, 1948	War Relic, 1938	Man o' War / Friar's Carse
ALL BEAUTIFUL, ch, 1959		Dark Display, 1941	Display / Dark Loveliness
	Parlo, 1951	Heliopolis, 1936	Hyperion / Drift
		Fairy Palace, 1945	Pilate / Star Fairy

RACE and (STAKES) RECORD

YEAR	AGE	STS	1ST	2ND	3RD	EARNED
1968	at 2	6	2	1	0	$18,898
1969	at 3	14	8(8)	5(5)	1	$555,604
1970	at 4	3	1(1)	0	0	$57,902
Lifetime		23	11(9)	6(5)	1	$632,404

All Along

ALL ALONG WAS A RACING PIONEER in more ways than one. She was the first horse, male or female, to win the East's three major turf events in the fall in the same year. In the process, she became the first horse to earn a $1-million bonus. All Along also was the first horse to be named Horse of the Year off a campaign conducted exclusively on turf.

All Along dominated the East's three big turf races in 1983, taking the Rothmans International Stakes at Woodbine, the Turf Classic at Aqueduct, and the Washington, D.C., International at Laurel. All that came after the four-year-old filly had humbled males in

France's greatest race, the Prix de l'Arc de Triomphe at Longchamp, under Walter Swinburn. A homebred for Daniel Wildenstein of France, she was an easy choice for Horse of the Year and for champion grass mare. She also was a French champion that year.

All Along, who won those four races in the span of six weeks, arrived from France for the one and five-eighths-mile Rothmans International

five days before the race. Not unexpectedly, she was sent away the favorite, going off at 8-5 in the field of eleven. Ridden once again by Swinburn, All Along raced near the back for the first part before making her move around the far turn. She took over in the stretch and won by two lengths over longshot Thunder Puddles while completing the distance over a yielding course in the slow time of 2:45.

Wildenstein's son, Alex, represented his father at Woodbine and said his father was "overjoyed" with the victory. The younger Wildenstein had telephoned his father at Longchamp, where another Wildenstein homebred, Sagace, won the important Prix du Conseil de Paris earlier in the day. (Sagace won the Arc in 1984, then finished first again the following year, only to be disqualified to second.)

French trainer Patrick-Louis Biancone sent All Along to New York to prepare for the rich Turf Classic two weeks later. Ridden by Swinburn, All Along won by eight and three-quarters

		Princequillo, 1940	**Prince Rose** Cosquilla
	Round Table, 1954		
TARGOWICE, b, 1970		Knight's Daughter, 1941	Sir Cosmo Feola
		Bold Ruler, 1954	Nasrullah Miss Disco
	Matriarch, 1964		
ALL ALONG (Fr), **bay filly,** **April 17, 1979**		Lyceum, 1948	Bull Lea Colosseum
		Brantome, 1931	Blandford Vitamine
	Vieux Manoir, 1947		
AGUJITA (Fr), b, 1966		Vieille Maison, 1936	Finglas Vieille Canaille
		Coastal Traffic, 1941	Hyperion Rose of England
	Argosy, 1950		
		Prosodie, 1942	**Prince Rose** Protein

lengths as the odds-on favorite. Thunder Puddles again finished second, and he was followed by 3-1 second choice Erins Isle and eight others. The race was contested over a yielding course, which resulted in another slow time, 2:34, nearly nine seconds slower than the course record. The Turf Classic, with a gross value of $585,700, was the richest race ever run in New York, and it made All Along a millionaire.

The Nov. 12 Washington, D.C., International was next for the team of All Along and Swinburn, and a victory in the one and a half-mile event would be worth an extra $1 million because of the bonus. Thunder Puddles dropped out of the hunt, but Majesty's Prince returned, and six others gave chase. The 2-5 favorite, All Along led by six lengths in the stretch, and scored by three and a quarter lengths over a yielding course. The time, 2:35, was eleven and a half seconds slower than the course mark.

The winner's share of $150,000, coupled with the $1-million bonus, boosted her earnings to $2,441,955, which was the fourth-highest at the time. All Along became the first female to earn sole possession of Horse of the Year honors since Busher in 1945. (The filly Moccasin shared top honors in 1965.)

All Along raced in 1984, and managed to run second in the inaugural Breeders' Cup Turf, plus third in the Arc and fourth in the Turf Classic and Rothmans International in four starts. She was retired with nine wins from twenty-one races and earnings of $3,018,420 (this includes the $1-million bonus) from racing in Europe, North America, and Japan, where she had run second in the 1982 Japan Cup. The earnings were a record for a female.

Wildenstein boards All Along at Mr. and Mrs. Robert N. Clay's Three Chimneys Farm near Midway, Kentucky. All Along, who was elected to the Racing Hall of Fame in 1990, has produced eleven foals through 1999, including French stakes winner Along All. — D. S.

RACE and (STAKES) RECORD

YEAR	AGE	STS	1ST	2ND	3RD	EARNED
1981	at 2 in Fr	1	1	0	0	$2,895
1982	at 3 in Fr, Eng, Jpn	9	4(3)	2(2)	0	$301,802
1983	at 4 in Fr, NA	7	4(4)	1(1)	1(1)	*$2,137,258
1984	at 5 in Fr, NA	4	0	1(1)	1(1)	$576,465
Lifetime*		**21**	**9(7)**	**4(4)**	**2(2)**	**$3,018,420**
* includes $1-million bonus						

Noor

JUDGING FROM HIS RECORD during his formative years racing in England for the Aga Khan, Noor hardly seemed likely to end his career as one of the century's top racehorses. At two and three, the English-bred from the first crop of Nasrullah, out of the Bahram mare Queen of Baghdad, had won four of thirteen races and had placed third in the 1948 Epsom Derby and Eclipse Stakes — a nice record, but hardly one with the stamp of greatness. He was to make his indelible mark on the Turf in his magical, world-record breaking campaign of 1950, not only on the other side of the

Atlantic, but on the other side of the continent, in California, where he defeated the mighty Citation in four consecutive meetings.

Purchased by California horseman Charles S. Howard from the Aga Khan as the lesser part of a package that included Irish Derby winner Nathoo (also by Nasrullah), Noor was shipped to Northern California in the fall of 1948, but didn't start until late in 1949 for trainer Burley Parke. Howard's literal claim to fame in the Thoroughbred business was as the owner of Seabiscuit, whom he had claimed for $8,000 at Saratoga in 1936.

While racing under Howard's colors, Noor won but once in six starts in 1949, hardly the record of a champion, but in 1950, he earned championship honors as handicap male with a miraculous season.

In his first start, he finished second to Solidarity in the San Pasqual Handicap at Santa Anita, flashing signs of brilliance while defeating Citation's stablemate, Ponder, who finished third. Next came the San Antonio Handicap, which marked the return of the five-year-old Citation after his inactive four-year-old year. Under 130 pounds, Citation finished second to Ponder, with Noor third, a half-length back under 114.

The Big 'Cap — Santa Anita Handicap — was the race in which Noor made the big time, winning by one and a quarter lengths over Citation, with another Calumet star, Two

Lea, back in third. While there was quite a weight spread — Noor carried 110 to Citation's 132 — weights would narrow in matches to come. A week later in the San Juan Capistrano Handicap, the gap narrowed to thirteen pounds, Noor's 117 to Citation's 130, and the two fought neck and neck down the Santa Anita stretch. Noor again prevailed, this time by a nose, with the English-bred setting a new American record of 2:52⅕ for one and three-fourths miles. Noor became the first horse to do two things: win the Big 'Cap and the San Juan Capistrano in the same year, and beat Citation twice.

It was on to Northern California for their next two meetings, and Noor defeated the 1948 Triple Crown winner in both races: the Forty-Niners Handicap, with a five-pound pull in the weights at 128 to 123, and the Golden Gate Handicap, in which Noor was asked to spot Citation weight, 127 pounds to 126. Sent postward the favorite for the first time over the Calumet star, Noor proved his backers right in the Golden Gate to win by three lengths. The time of 1:58⅕ was a second world record in as many tries.

After a win in the American Handicap at Hollywood Park in July, Noor was shipped East, and next appeared in the Harmonicon Handicap at Belmont under highweight of 128 pounds, but was beaten by Greentree Stable's 107-pound toting One Hitter. Five days later, in the one and a half-mile Manhattan Handicap, Noor again fell short of One Hitter, who only picked up three pounds. A four-length loss to eventual Horse of the Year Hill Prince in the two-mile Jockey Club Gold Cup ended a rough East Coast excursion.

Noor redeemed himself, winning a prep for the one and a quarter-mile Hollywood Gold Cup on Dec. 9. Then under 130 pounds, same as Hill Prince, Noor won the Gold Cup by a length in 1:59⅘, establishing a new track record in what was his final race.

While Noor was among the first to show the power of Nasrullah as a sire, he was not a success himself. While standing at his owner's ranch at San Ysidro, California, then later at the Loma Rica Ranch near Grass Valley, California, Noor sired thirteen stakes winners. Suffering from heart problems and other infirmities, Noor was euthanized on Nov. 16, 1974, at the age of twenty-nine. — *E. H.*

RACE and (STAKES) RECORD						
YEAR	AGE	STS	1ST	2ND	3RD	EARNED
1947	at 2 in Eng	7	2(2)	1	1(1)	$6,629
1948	at 3 in Eng	6	2(2)	0	2(2)	$20,399
1949	at 4 in NA	6	1	1(1)	2(2)	$10,000
1950	at 5 in NA	12	7(6)	4(4)	1(1)	$346,940
Lifetime		**31**	**12(10)**	**6(5)**	**6(6)**	**$383,968**

 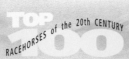

Shuvee

SHE LOOKED LIKE A STALLION, ate like a stallion, and trained like a stallion. Best of all, Shuvee could race like a stallion, too. Twice she beat the nation's top male handicappers in the Jockey Club Gold Cup in New York — something no other filly or mare has done even once in the eighty-year history of the race. And she did so in 1970 and 1971, when the distance was two miles. That, however, is only one of the reasons this daughter of Nashua—Levee, by Hill Prince, is remembered as one of the century's best horses.

She was, quite simply, one of the best and most durable mares in racing history. Between 1968 and 1971, she started in forty-four races and won sixteen of them — fifteen of them major stakes — at distances ranging from eight furlongs to two miles. When she retired to Whitney and Anne Stones' Morven Stud as a broodmare, her career earnings of $890,445 were an all-time record for a filly or mare.

Her career accomplishments also included an eight and a half-furlong track record at old Liberty Bell (1:43⅕) and what was just the second sweep in history of the series once known as the Filly Triple Crown. Together, the Acorn, Mother Goose, and Coaching Club American Oaks, all run in New York, now are known as the Filly Triple Tiara.

"Boy, she was tough," her trainer, W. C. "Mike" Freeman, remembered years after the end of her career. "You couldn't make her back off the feed tub or anything. She'd eat anything you put in front of her. And she needed more training than any filly I saw."

Her breeder-owners Whitney and Anne Stone, the former an engineer, had high hopes from the start for the golden chestnut because of her regal pedigree. Freeman, however, had his doubts. A combination of her big, masculine build — eventually she would stand

16.1 hands, weigh 1,100 pounds and have a girth of seventy-six inches — and her conformation did not auger a long, sound career. But his fears proved groundless. "She never took a bad step in her life and never had any physical problems at all through her

NASHUA, b, 1952			
	Nasrullah, 1940	Nearco, 1935	Pharos / Nogara
		Mumtaz Begum, 1932	Blenheim II / Mumtaz Mahal
	Segula, 1942	Johnstown, 1936	Jamestown / La France
		Sekhmet, 1929	Sardanapale / Prosopopee
SHUVEE, chestnut filly, January 22, 1966			
LEVEE, ch, 1953	Hill Prince, 1947	Princequillo, 1940	Prince Rose / Cosquilla
		Hildene, 1938	Bubbling Over / Fancy Racket
	Bourtai, 1942	Stimulus, 1922	Ultimus / Hurakan
		Escutcheon, 1927	Sir Gallahad III / Affection

racing career," he said. "Real extraordinary mare — for a big filly, particularly...Never bucked her shins. Just a real freak," he said.

The only problem Shuvee did have was learning what the game was about. The come-from-way-back runner needed seven starts to break her maiden. For her seventh start, Freeman stuffed Shuvee's ears with cotton to muffle the sounds of the other horses and the crowd. He never figured out if the cotton was the reason she finally won that day but used it the rest of her career.

Despite her slow start, Shuvee got into the hunt for the 1968 juvenile filly championship by charging from ninth to defeat top filly Gallant Bloom in the Frizette Stakes. She followed that with an upset of highly regarded Process Shot in the Selima Stakes at Laurel. The race was a betless exhibition. But Gallant Bloom avenged her loss to Shuvee in the Gardenia at Garden State Park and, with a more consistent record, was voted *Daily Racing Form*'s divisional champion. Thoroughbred Racing Associations voted for Process Shot.

Despite her sweep of the Triple Tiara, much the same thing happened to Shuvee at three. Process Shot tailed off at three, but Gallant Bloom won a showdown in the Delaware Oaks and then Shuvee went into a mild slump. She lost to Gallant Bloom in the Gazelle, then to older horses in the Beldame and Vosburgh. Gallant Bloom was again champion.

Little Gallant Bloom was not as durable as Shuvee, though, and was retired early at four. That left Shuvee to dominate the older mares — and score those Gold Cup upsets — during the second half of her career. She was voted champion handicap female in 1970 and 1971. Shuvee was inducted into the Racing Hall of Fame in 1975.

Though she was sent to the top sires of her era, Shuvee never reproduced herself. Out of eleven live foals, three were stakes winners: Tom Swift, Shukey, and Benefice. Shuvee died in 1986 of complications from foaling. — *P. S.*

RACE and (STAKES) RECORD						
YEAR	AGE	STS	1ST	2ND	3RD	EARNED
1968	at 2	13	3(2)	4(1)	3(1)	$209,396
1969	at 3	12	6(6)	2(2)	2(2)	$312,894
1970	at 4	10	4(4)	1(1)	0	$201,852
1971	at 5	9	3(3)	3(2)	1(1)	$166,303
Lifetime		44	16(15)	10(6)	6(4)	$890,445

Regret

WHEN HARRY PAYNE WHITNEY'S CHESTNUT FILLY with the bold white stripe stepped onto the Churchill Downs racing surface on that eighth day of May in 1915, she was poised to challenge the widely held belief that no filly could win the Kentucky Derby. Regret's winning performance that spring afternoon confirmed her place in the annals of racing lore, and for sixty-five years, she had no peer. In 1980, another filly who bore a striking resemblance to Regret added the name Genuine

Risk to the list of Derby winners. In the one hundred and twenty-five runnings of the Kentucky Derby, thirty-eight fillies have gone postward. Of those, only three have won: Regret, Genuine Risk, and Winning Colors (in 1988).

Regret's win should have surprised no one in the crowd of more than 49,000; she sported a flawless record. The New Jersey-bred filly had, in fact, made an auspicious beginning to her career by winning a stakes race and breaking her maiden all in her first start, when she easily won the Saratoga Special. Seven days later Regret returned in the Sanford Memorial Stakes, carrying 127 pounds and winning by one and a half lengths.

In the final start of her juvenile season, Regret moved from well back to win the appropriately named Hopeful Stakes at Saratoga under a 127-pound impost. In the span of fourteen days in August, Regret had won three stakes races and established herself as more than a hopeful for the following year's campaign.

Trainer James Rowe chose for Regret's three-year-old debut a little race in Kentucky that was growing in stature and popularity — the Kentucky Derby. Would a filly with no race since a six-furlong sprint the previous August be ready for the grueling stint of the mile and a quarter Derby? With other trainers, an unfit horse might be the case, but with Rowe,

		Bramble, 1875	Bonnie Scotland / Ivy Leaf
	Ben Brush, 1893		
BROOMSTICK, b, 1901		Roseville, 1888	Reform / Albia
	Elf, 1893	Galliard, 1880	Galopin / Mavis
REGRET, chestnut filly, 1912		Sylvabelle, 1887	Bend Or / Saint Editha
	Hamburg, 1895	Hanover, 1884	Hindoo / Bourbon Belle
JERSEY LIGHTNING, ch, 1905		Lady Reel, 1886	Fellowcraft / Mannie Gray
	Daisy F., 1895	Riley, 1887	Longfellow / Geneva
		Modesty, 1881	War Dance / Ballet

there was little doubt. A hard taskmaster, Rowe had the reputation that if any horse survived his training methods, it was indeed a racehorse. Breaking from the second post position, Regret under jockey Joe Notter returned to her old running style and led throughout the race. At the finish line she was two lengths ahead of Pebbles after covering the distance in 2:05⅖. She started once more at three. In the Saranac Handicap at Saratoga, she assumed the lead at the start and won easily, remaining undefeated. Although she had only run twice, she topped the championship polls at three.

In her four-year-old debut, Regret suffered her first defeat when she finished last in the Saratoga Handicap. In her only other start that season, Regret won an allowance race, the first time she had started in anything other than a stakes.

At five, Regret made four starts and won three. After taking an allowance race against fillies and mares at Belmont Park in late May, Regret resumed her campaign against the best of her generation in the Brooklyn Handicap. Included in the stellar field were Old Rosebud, Roamer, Omar Khayyam, Ormesdale, and Chiclet. As was her wont, Regret led throughout. In the final strides, she was caught by her entrymate Borrow, who was in receipt of five pounds, and defeated by a nose.

Returned to the distaff ranks, Regret next won the Gazelle Handicap at Aqueduct. On Sept. 25, 1917, the Whitney colorbearer faced the starter for the final time in what was little more than an exhibition race. Carrying 127 pounds, Regret had only one opponent, Ima Frank, who carried 109. Regret set a new track record of 1:24⅕ for the seven furlongs.

The daughter of Broomstick retired to stud with nine wins and a second in eleven starts. Unplaced only once, she earned $34,093. At stud, she helped perpetuate the myth that good race mares do not make good producers. She failed to replicate herself, producing only a minor stakes winner from eleven foals.

Regret died in 1934 and was buried at the Whitney farm, which by that time was in the care of C. V. Whitney, H. P. Whitney's son and heir, and the third generation of Whitneys to own a member of Regret's family. — *T. H.*

RACE and (STAKES) RECORD

YEAR	AGE	STS	1ST	2ND	3RD	EARNED
1914	at 2	3	3(3)	0	0	$16,390
1915	at 3	2	2(2)	0	0	$12,500
1916	at 4	2	1	0	0	$560
1917	at 5	4	3(1)	1(1)	0	$4,643
Lifetime		**11**	**9(6)**	**1(1)**	**0**	**$34,093**

Go for Wand

GO FOR WAND'S BRILLIANCE on the racetrack could not be denied. For two brief seasons, the bay filly dominated the distaff scene to win seven grade I events, ranging in distance from seven to ten furlongs. She battled older mares twice before the Breeders' Cup and easily won both times. Her accomplishments earned her two Eclipse Awards. Thus, it came as no surprise when a mere six years after her tragic death in the 1990 Breeders' Cup Distaff, Go for Wand was inducted into the Racing Hall of Fame in her first year of eligibility.

"She raced with such joy and abandon. That's what I want people to remember about

her," Jane du Pont Lunger told *The Blood-Horse* in 1996 before the Hall of Fame induction ceremony that August.

A daughter of Deputy Minister out of the Cyane mare Obeah, Go for Wand was bred and raced in the name of Christiana Stables, owned by Mrs. Lunger and her late husband, Harry, who died in 1976. The Lungers began their stable in 1937 and were repre-

sented by their first stakes winner in 1939 when Miss Ferdinand won the Matron Stakes. Christiana raced more than forty stakes winners, including Go for Wand's dam, Obeah. With a penchant for picking unusual names, Mrs. Lunger derived Go for Wand's name from the phrase "going for a wand to protect yourself from an obeah or 'voodoo' curse."

Throughout her career, Go for Wand was trained by William Badgett Jr. and ridden by Randy Romero. The Pennsylvania-bred filly made her debut on Sept. 14, 1989, at Belmont Park and won a six-furlong maiden race by four lengths. In her next start, she demolished an allowance field by eighteen and a quarter lengths going a mile in the slop at Belmont. After suffering her only loss of the season in the Frizette Stakes, Go for Wand rebounded to capture the Breeders' Cup Juvenile Fillies by two and three-quarters lengths at Gulfstream Park. She was named champion two-year-old filly.

Go for Wand began her three-year-old campaign in the Beaumont Stakes at Keeneland. Going seven furlongs, the bay filly rocketed to an eight and a half-length victory, then returned eleven days later to take the Ashland Stakes by five lengths over Charon. Go for Wand missed a beat with a second-place effort in Seaside Attraction's Kentucky Oaks, but the champion filly quickly got back on track with a victory in the Mother Goose Stakes at Belmont.

She next took on Saratoga. First came the seven-furlong Test Stakes which she aced by two lengths, then the ten-furlong Alabama Stakes. She won the Alabama by seven lengths, just nine days after the Test. Moving back to Belmont, Mrs. Lunger's filly captured the Maskette Stakes at a mile in her first test against older mares. The Maskette was renamed for Go for Wand two years after her death and was moved to Saratoga in 1994.

In her last start before the fateful Breeders' Cup, Go for Wand dismissed older rivals in the Oct. 7 Beldame Stakes, winning the nine-furlong contest by four and three-quarters lengths. The Breeders' Cup Distaff was run twenty days later. Go for Wand had a slight lead in the nine-furlong race over Bayakoa before they hooked up in a stretch duel. Tragedy struck at the sixteenth pole when Go for Wand, on the inside, went down suddenly. Bayakoa raced clear and went on to win. Go for Wand had suffered a compound injury in her right front ankle and had to be euthanized.

"There just is not anything you can do after this," trainer Badgett told *The Blood-Horse* the morning after the accident. "Anytime you lose a horse it takes away a little part of you, but to lose a horse like that..."

Two days after the Distaff, Go for Wand was buried in the infield at Saratoga, where earlier in the year she had so easily won the Test and Alabama. Go for Wand compiled a record of ten victories and two second-place finishes in thirteen starts and earned $1,373,338. She received an Eclipse Award posthumously as the champion three-year-old filly.

"I'm very grateful for having owned such a lovely filly," said Mrs. Lunger. — *J. L. M.*

RACE and (STAKES) RECORD

YEAR	AGE	STS	1ST	2ND	3RD	EARNED
1989	at 2	4	3(1)	1(1)	0	$548,390
1990	at 3	9	7(7)	1(1)	0	$824,948
Lifetime		13	10(8)	2(2)	0	**$1,373,338**

Johnstown

JOHNSTOWN'S PLACE IN RACING HISTORY was hard to define during his racing career, mainly because he was the "third man through the door," for both owner William Woodward and trainer James (Sunny Jim) Fitzsimmons. Johnstown, a foal of 1936 by Jamestown—La France, by Sir Gallahad III, was the third Kentucky Derby winner of the decade for Woodward's Belair Stud's champion-producing factory, following Triple Crown winners Gallant Fox in 1930 and Omaha in 1935.

Purchased from breeder A. B. Hancock Sr. as a yearling, Johnstown had a successful campaign at two, winning seven of twelve starts, including the Remsen Handicap and Breeders' Futurity, then became a star at three. A three-race winning streak carried Johnstown to Churchill Downs for the Kentucky Derby as the shortest-priced horse in thirty-four years. Impressive wins in the Paumonok Handicap and an eight-length win in the Wood Memorial made him 3-5 for the Derby. Those odds hadn't been matched since Agile won in 1905 at 1-3.

Only seven horses challenged, the fewest in twenty-one years, since Exterminator won in 1918. Known for his front-running ability, Johnstown, under the twenty-four-year-old Jimmy Stout, went right for the front and stayed there. William Ziegler Jr.'s El Chico, the leading two-year-old of 1938, tried to run with him early, but backed up after six furlongs. In control throughout, Johnstown won the Derby by eight lengths and in the third-fastest clocking, to that date, of 2:03⅖. The runner-up was Challedon.

Johnstown was unable to emulate his Belair Triple Crown-winning predecessors of the '30s due to a fifth-place performance in the Challedon-won Preakness, where a muddy track may have been his undoing. But he rebounded spectacularly to win the Withers, then the Belmont by five lengths. His time for the one and a half miles was 2:29⅗, one second off War Admiral's track record, but he did get the first mile in the same time as War Admiral (1:37⅕), and was not pressured the rest of the way.

Two weeks later, Johnstown was challenged early by Challedon in the Dwyer, but his rival was only able to

JAMESTOWN, b, 1928	St. James, 1921	Ambassador IV, 1911	Dark Ronald / Excellenza
		Bobolink II, 1913	Willonyx / Chelandry
	Mlle. Dazie, 1917	Fair Play, 1905	Hastings / Fairy Gold
		Toggery, 1909	Rock Sand / Tea's Over
LA FRANCE, b, 1928	Sir Gallahad III, 1920	Teddy, 1913	**Ajax** / Rondeau
		Plucky Liege, 1912	Spearmint / Concertina
	Flambette, 1918	Durbar II, 1911	Rabelais / Armenia
		La Flambee, 1912	**Ajax** / Medeah

JOHNSTOWN, bay colt, 1936

hang with him for the opening quarter mile. Turning for home, Johnstown had a four-length advantage and won by a length over the closing Sun Lover. The time, 1:48⅖ for the one and one-eighth miles, tied the stakes mark set the year before by The Chief.

The Dwyer would be the last victory for Johnstown, as he went down to defeat once again to Challedon in the Classic Stakes in Chicago. Fitzsimmons took the blame for the loss. "I let Johnstown work too fast and it took too much out of him when it came to the race. I made a mistake in letting him make such a fast move before he went to Chicago and again when he made another fast move just two days before the race."

Johnstown worked a mile in 1:35⅕ at Aqueduct before shipping to Chicago, besting the six-furlong, seven-furlong, and mile track records in the process. Before the Classic, he worked a half in a blistering :45⅕.

Johnstown was declared out of the Lawrence Realization, and an announcement of his retirement followed. Woodward even issued a statement, that in part said: "Johnstown has not been himself since the Dwyer. He was carefully prepared for the Travers and would have started had it been dry. He then had a short spell of coughing and on his return to Aqueduct, cast a front shoe which cut his hock. Returning to training, he responded well, when a slight quarter crack showed itself. This could be cared for on a dry track, but not a wet one such as there is today. We would run on the dry but feel it is unfair both to the horse and to the public to run under these handicaps."

Johnstown retired with a record of fourteen wins from twenty-one starts and earnings of $169,315. He returned to Hancock's Claiborne Farm near Paris, Kentucky, to serve stud duty, but Johnstown was not nearly as successful a sire as he was a racehorse. He sired 227 foals and just six stakes winners, but he did have the reputation of siring consistent runners. He died at Claiborne at the age of fourteen on May 14, 1950, after suffering a cerebral hemorrhage. He was buried in the Claiborne horse cemetery. — E. H.

RACE and (STAKES) RECORD

YEAR	AGE	STS	1ST	2ND	3RD	EARNED
1938	at 2	12	7(4)	0	2(2)	$31,420
1939	at 3	9	7(6)	0	1(1)	$137,895
Lifetime		**21**	**14(10)**	**0**	**3(3)**	**$169,315**

Bald Eagle

CAPT. HARRY F. GUGGENHEIM'S HOMEBRED BALD EAGLE twice won the Washington, D.C., International when the race was the most important turf event in North America, and he remains the sole two-time winner. A son of Nasrullah, Bald Eagle won that rich invitational grass race in 1959 and 1960, and also captured other important events such as the Widener, Metropolitan, Suburban, Gulfstream Park, Aqueduct, Saratoga, and Gallant Fox Handicaps those two years.

Before all that, however, Guggenheim had sent Kentucky-bred Bald Eagle to England in pursuit of one of his dreams. Guggenheim had won the 1953 Kentucky Derby with Dark Star, and the thought of winning the English Derby as well created quite an impression in his mind. Bald Eagle's considerable size, and a pedigree sprinkled with foreign ancestors, made the colt a reasonable candidate for the English race. Guggenheim sent Bald Eagle to English trainer Capt. Cecil Boyd-Rochfort to be prepared for the 1958 Epsom Derby.

Bald Eagle created a favorable impression as a two-year-old by winning the 1957 Duke of Edinburgh Stakes in his only racecourse appearance. He was favored in the Two Thousand Guineas and was the second favorite in the English Derby, but failed to last the distance and was beaten badly in both races. In his three other races that year, he won the Craven and Dante Stakes and placed in the St. James's Palace Stakes.

Phil Bull, in his Timeform publication *Racehorses of 1958*, summed up the colt's European career by writing that "Bald Eagle's inability to rise to the big occasion has been widely attributed to his possession of the sort of temperament that spoiled the racing career of his sire." Bull ended the article by noting that Bald Eagle "has now returned to the United States, where he will presumably stand as a stallion."

Guggenheim had other plans and sent Bald Eagle to New York trainer Woodford C.

			Pharos, 1920	Phalaris Scapa Flow
		Nearco, 1935		
			Nogara, 1928	Havresac II Catnip
	NASRULLAH (GB), b, 1940			
			Blenheim II, 1927	Blandford Malva
		Mumtaz Begum, 1932		
BALD EAGLE, bay colt, March 29, 1955			Mumtaz Mahal, 1921	The Tetrarch Lady Josephine
			Bull Dog, 1927	Teddy Plucky Liege
		Tiger, 1935		
			Starless Moment, 1928	North Star III Breathless Moment
	SIAMA, b, 1947			
			Display, 1923	Fair Play Cicuta
		China Face, 1940		
			Sweepilla, 1931	Sweep Camilla S.

(Woody) Stephens. It took some time, but Stephens had him running and winning with the best of company.

Stephens kept Bald Eagle on grass for his first two starts, then switched him to the dirt. In Bald Eagle's second start on the main track, he won the Suburban Handicap at Belmont Park in July of 1959 under Manuel Yzaca, who became the horse's regular rider. Bald Eagle also won the Saratoga Handicap and closed out the year with victories in the Washington, D.C., International and the Gallant Fox Handicap.

Bald Eagle, who raced in the name of Guggenheim's Cain Hoy Stable, started out strong his five-year-old season in 1960. He beat On-and-On in the one and a quarter-mile Widener Handicap in track record time of 1:59⅗ at Hialeah. A month later, Bald Eagle defeated Amerigo, On-and-On, and Sword Dancer in the Gulfstream Park Handicap, then scored against First Landing and Sword Dancer in the mile Metropolitan Handicap in track-record time of 1:33⅗ in front of a record New York crowd of 70,992.

Bald Eagle's next big win came in September, when he won the mile Aqueduct Handicap over the speedy Intentionally. He closed out the season with a victory in the Washington, D.C., International and was voted champion handicap male.

Bald Eagle, who was retired with a dozen wins from twenty-nine races and earnings of $689,556, entered stud in 1961 at Leslie Combs II's Spendthrift Farm near Lexington. He stood eleven years at Spendthrift before he was sold to French interests after the 1971 breeding season. The sale took place several months after Guggenheim's death in January of that year. Bald Eagle died in France in 1977.

Bald Eagle sired only twelve stakes winners, but two of them became famous. His daughter San San captured the 1972 Prix de l'Arc de Triomphe, and another daughter, Too Bald, developed into a Kentucky Broodmare of the Year, her foals including millionaire Exceller, plus successful stallions Capote and Baldski. Bald Eagle initially was named Nasr after Nasrullah. Guggenheim later changed the name to Bald Eagle because the name Nasr bore too much of a resemblance to that of Egyptian leader Abdul Nasser, who had seized the Suez Canal in 1956. — D. S.

RACE and (STAKES) RECORD						
YEAR	AGE	STS	1ST	2ND	3RD	EARNED
1957	at 2 in Eng	1	1(1)	0	0	$3,897
1958	at 3 in Eng, NA	6	2(2)	0	1(1)	$9,217
1959	at 4 in NA	11	4(4)	3(2)	1(1)	$278,357
1960	at 5 in NA	11	5(5)	2(2)	2(2)	$398,085
Lifetime		29	12(12)	5(4)	4(4)	$689,556

Hill Prince

CHRISTOPHER T. CHENERY'S THE MEADOW near Doswell, Virginia, was the birthplace of many a stakes winner, including one of the greatest champions of them all, Secretariat. However, Hill Prince was the first of the great ones to come from the 2,000-acre farm.

Hill Prince's brilliance wasn't expected, as he came from humble beginnings. His sire, Princequillo, was standing his first season in 1946 at the Hancock family's Ellerslie Stud in Virginia for a $250 fee, and A. B. Hancock Sr. was having trouble filling his initial book. His dam, Hildene, by 1926 Kentucky Derby winner Bubbling Over, had earned but $100

on the track. Their mating, however, produced a dark bay or brown colt who would earn multiple championships under the blue and white blocked silks. Hildene also would produce the $779,577-earner and champion First Landing, plus the dam of champion Cicada, who retired as the leading money-earning female of all time in 1964.

Named a champion at two by *Daily Racing Form* for a near-perfect six-for-seven season, Hill Prince was even more impressive at three, with a classic win in the spring, and with a major effort later in the year against older horses on both coasts. He would be named Horse of the Year for his April-to-December campaign for trainer J. H. (Casey) Hayes.

His first two starts at two were winning efforts at Aqueduct and Monmouth in July of 1949, and he tasted defeat for the only time as a juvenile in his first stakes attempt, the Sapling Stakes at Monmouth. From there, he won his next four starts, including the World's Playground Stakes at Atlantic City and Aqueduct's Babylon Handicap and Cowdin.

He made his three-year-old debut at Jamaica on April 5, 1950, in the Experimental Free Handicap No. 1 at six furlongs and promptly won by one and a quarter lengths. He

			Rose Prince, 1919	Prince Palatine Eglantine
		Prince Rose, 1928		
			Indolence, 1920	Gay Crusader Barrier
	PRINCEQUILLO (GB), b, 1940			
			Papyrus, 1920	Tracery Miss Matty
		Cosquilla, 1933		
HILL PRINCE, bay colt, 1947			Quick Thought, 1918	White Eagle Mindful
			North Star III, 1914	Sunstar Angelic
		Bubbling Over, 1923		
			Beaming Beauty, 1917	Sweep Bellisario
	HILDENE, b, 1938			
			Wrack, 1909	Robert le Diable Samphire
		Fancy Racket, 1925		
			Ultimate Fancy, 1918	Ultimus Idle Fancy

returned ten days later for the second version at one and one-sixteenth miles and put in what would be the worst performance of the campaign with a ninth-place, twenty-length defeat. Under Eddie Arcaro, Hill Prince rebounded nicely, winning the Wood Memorial over Middleground and Next Move.

Sent to Louisville for the Kentucky Derby, Hill Prince developed a fever, but recovered in time to work a mile as fast as the Derby Trial field ran later in the afternoon. Sent off the 5-2 second choice in the Derby, behind the 8-5 Your Host, Hill Prince was within striking distance of Middleground the entire length of the stretch, but could not get past. There was no rest for the strapping colt, as he won the Withers at Belmont the following week before winning the Preakness by five lengths. He reportedly bled while finishing third in the Suburban Handicap, then ran a dull seventh in the Belmont Stakes eleven days later.

After a second-place effort in the Dwyer, Hill Prince was given some time off and returned sharp, rattling off three consecutive wins: the Aug. 26 American Derby at Washington Park, the Sept. 20 Jerome Handicap, and the two-mile Jockey Club Gold Cup on Oct. 7, where he beat older rival Noor at weight-for-age. Sent to California, Hill Prince ran third in both the Thanksgiving Day Handicap and Hollywood Gold Cup, won by Noor, before winning the Sunset Handicap in his final three-year-old effort.

A fissure fracture of his right hind cannon bone put a crimp in his four-year-old season, but Hill Prince managed to make six starts. He won twice, including the New York Handicap under 128 pounds and was second in the Jockey Club Gold Cup. He was voted champion handicapper by *Daily Racing Form* and the Thoroughbred Racing Associations. Hill Prince was elected to Racing's Hall of Fame in 1991.

Standing at Claiborne Farm, Hill Prince sired twenty-three stakes winners. He sired one champion, Bayou, who produced Alluvial, dam of champion Slew o' Gold and 1979 Belmont Stakes winner Coastal. As a broodmare sire, Hill Prince was responsible for champions Dark Mirage and Shuvee. In 1969, Hill Prince was pensioned and sent to The Meadow, where he was euthanized after suffering a heart attack on Jan. 6, 1970. — *E. H.*

RACE and (STAKES) RECORD

YEAR	AGE	STS	1ST	2ND	3RD	EARNED
1949	at 2	7	6(3)	1(1)	0	$46,225
1950	at 3	15	8(8)	2(2)	3(3)	$314,265
1951	at 4	6	2(1)	2(2)	1	$46,900
1952	at 5	2	1(1)	0	0	$14,750
Lifetime		30	17(13)	5(5)	4(3)	$422,140

Lady's Secret

IN 1986, LADY'S SECRET FASHIONED one of the greatest single seasons in horse racing history. She traveled from California to New York, dominating her division and four times taking on many of the nation's best males.

The diminutive filly won ten of her fifteen starts that season, all stakes races, and earned $1,871,053 to be named Horse of the Year and champion mare. She scored eight of her victories in grade I events. Since 1973, when the Thoroughbred Owners and Breeders Association began grading races, no horse has won as many grade I stakes in a single sea-

son. To further put that season in its proper historical context, consider the campaigns of Twilight Tear and Busher. When they were named both champion mare and Horse of the Year, Twilight Tear in 1944 and Busher in 1945, they each won nine stakes races.

"She was the ultimate overachiever," said her trainer, Hall of Famer D. Wayne Lukas. "Early in her career, we didn't think she had superstar potential. In fact, we weren't even sure she would achieve stakes-winner status... But she was very, very tough, and hickory sound."

Although a daughter of the great Secretariat, Lady's Secret didn't look anything like "Big Red." Gray and small and feminine, she probably didn't weigh much more than 900 pounds during her incomparable season of achievement. But she possessed uncommon speed, grace, and grit.

She was bred by Robert H. Spreen at Lukas' farm in Norman, Oklahoma. Lukas had trained the filly's dam, Great Lady M., an erstwhile claimer who went on to win seven stakes and earn $332,008. When Lady's Secret was a yearling, Lukas sold her to Mr. and Mrs. Eugene Klein for $200,000, the trainer recalled.

Until the spring of 1985, Lady's Secret flashed talent and speed, but not the consistent quality and determination that would later earn her the reputation as the "Iron Lady." But

	Nasrullah, 1940	**Nearco** Mumtaz Begum
Bold Ruler, 1954		
	Miss Disco, 1944	Discovery Outdone
SECRETARIAT, ch, 1970		
	Princequillo, 1940	Prince Rose Cosquilla
Somethingroyal, 1952		
	Imperatrice, 1938	Caruso Cinquepace
LADY'S SECRET, gray filly, **April 8, 1982**		
	Nearctic, 1954	**Nearco** Lady Angela
Icecapade, 1969		
	Shenanigans, 1963	Native Dancer Bold Irish
GREAT LADY M., gr, 1975		
	Young Emperor, 1963	Grey Sovereign Young Empress
Sovereign Lady, 1969		
	Sweety Kid, 1963	Olympia Trustworthy II

starting in May, with the Bowl of Flowers Stakes at Belmont, she won eight consecutive stakes, including the Test and the Maskette.

She completed her campaign by finishing second to older stablemate Life's Magic in the Breeders' Cup Distaff. For the year, she had won ten of seventeen and earned $994,349. She wasn't named champion three-year-old filly, though. That honor went to Mom's Command, who swept the so-called Triple Crown for fillies in New York — the Acorn, Mother Goose, and Coaching Club American Oaks. Mom's Command won seven of nine in 1985 and earned $629,148.

Lady's Secret began her championship season by winning three stakes races at Santa Anita: the El Encino, La Canada, and Santa Margarita Invitational. In the Apple Blossom at Oaklawn Park, she was challenged on the early lead by Littlebitapleasure. After disposing of that challenge and running a mile in 1:34⅕, she couldn't withstand the late charge of Love Smitten, who won by a neck while in receipt of eight pounds.

Against males, she finished third in the Metropolitan and Philip H. Iselin Handicaps and second in the Woodward behind the great Precisionist. She won the Whitney by four and a half lengths, defeating Ends Well, Skip Trial, King's Swan, and Cutlass Reality. She was the first female to win the Whitney since Gallorette in 1948.

In the Maskette Stakes in September, while carrying 125 pounds, she won by seven lengths and completed the mile in 1:33⅖, the fastest mile ever run at Belmont Park by a filly or mare. Fifteen days later, while carrying 129 pounds, she won the Ruffian Handicap by eight lengths and three weeks later added the Beldame Stakes, thus completing her second sweep of the fall championship series for fillies and mares in New York.

With regular rider Pat Day aboard, Lady's Secret completed her memorable campaign by winning the Breeders' Cup Distaff, leading from the start through splits of 1:10 for six furlongs and 1:34⅘ for the mile, then completed the mile and a quarter in 2:01⅕ while not fully extended. Lady's Secret was retired the following season. In her career, she won twenty-two stakes races and twenty-five of her forty-five starts while earning $3,021,325. As a broodmare, she has not produced to date a runner of her caliber. — G. W.

RACE and (STAKES) RECORD

YEAR	AGE	STS	1ST	2ND	3RD	EARNED
1984	at 2	8	3(2)	0	1(1)	$92,823
1985	at 3	17	10(10)	5(5)	0	$994,349
1986	at 4	15	10(10)	3(3)	2(2)	$1,871,053
1987	at 5	5	2	1(1)	0	$63,100
Lifetime		45	25(22)	9(9)	3(3)	$3,021,325

Two Lea

CALUMET FARM'S TWO LEA IMPROVED WITH AGE. What is even more remarkable about her success is that she overcame physical problems which compromised her racing. As a yearling she developed ringbone, a condition that usually affects the joints and results in lameness. Delayed from starting early in her two-year-old season, she finally did set foot on a racetrack when the 1948 racing year was on the wane.

It took two tries before Two Lea achieved her maiden victory. At Belmont in September, she bested a field of nine other fillies by four lengths.

In her sophomore year, Two Lea started seven times and won six races. Her first stakes victory was the Princess Doreen Stakes at Arlington Park. Trained by H. A. (Jimmy) Jones, the bay daughter of Bull Lea finished second in the Modesty Stakes against older fillies and mares, her lone defeat of the season.

In the Cleopatra Handicap at a mile, Two Lea was coupled with another Calumet filly, Wistful. Wistful had won the Kentucky Oaks, Pimlico Oaks, and Coaching Club American Oaks. The meeting amounted to a race for bragging rights between the queen of the Midwest and the queen of the East. Two Lea, the top weight at 122 pounds, won and Wistful finished third. At year's end, both Calumet fillies shared championship honors.

Two Lea's penultimate race of 1949 was the Artful Stakes at Washington Park. Top weighted at 124 pounds, Two Lea trailed the field for three furlongs but finished strongly to win the seven-furlong event in 1:21⅘, within two-fifths of equaling the world record.

Santa Anita beckoned the Calumet runners to herald the new decade. Two Lea won the Arcadia Handicap against older fillies and mares. Nine days later she won the nine-furlong Santa Margarita Handicap. Three starts in a month are difficult undertakings. Yet, on

Jan. 28, Two Lea returned to the race-track. Having defeated the best of her sex, she was pitted against the best of the boys. In the Santa Anita Maturity she was part of an entry with Calumet's 1949 Kentucky Derby winner Ponder. Ridden by Eddie Arcaro, Two Lea led until she was caught by Ponder in the stretch. He went on to win by a length as Arcaro eased the filly in the final sixteenth.

Entries for the Santa Anita Handicap contained a Calumet equivalent to an equine dynamo. In the farm's tripartite package were two Derby winners, a Triple Crown winner, and two multiple champions: Citation, Ponder, and Two Lea. Citation carried 132 pounds; Ponder, 124; and Two Lea, 113. None could catch Noor, who was allowed to carry 110. Citation finished second; Two Lea was third, and Ponder closed to finish fourth.

A hard winter campaign followed and Two Lea was given a break until midsummer. She was second in an overnight handicap in July and was heard from no more during the remainder of the year. At year's end, she was named champion older filly or mare.

Ringbone again gave the filly problems, and more than a year and a half passed before Two Lea launched another campaign. She was six and had a good-sized knot on her fetlock, a result of the firing for ringbone. Although she did not win a championship, 1952 was probably her best year racing. From eleven starts she won six races, five of them stakes. In the Vanity Handicap, Calumet fillies finished one-two-three. Two Lea won, Wistful was second, and Jennie Lee finished third. She also defeated males in the Hollywood Gold Cup. In October at Bay Meadows, Two Lea won two of her last three starts, all stakes.

On the track she had started twenty-six times, won fifteen of those, and finished unplaced only twice. She earned $309,250. Two Lea retired to Calumet, and her success as a broodmare rivaled her race record. In 1955 she produced a bay colt by Tom Fool who nearly captured the Triple Crown. In the Belmont Stakes, Tim Tam struggled home second on a fractured sesamoid. She also produced to the cover of Nasrullah the stakes-winning full brothers Pied d'Or and On-and-On. Two Lea died in 1973 at the age of twenty-seven. — T. H.

TWO LEA, bay filly, 1946			
BULL LEA, br, 1935	Bull Dog, 1927	Teddy, 1913	Ajax / Rondeau
		Plucky Liege, 1912	**Spearmint** / Concertina
	Rose Leaves, 1916	Ballot, 1904	Voter / **Cerito**
		Colonial, 1897	Trenton / Thankful Blossom
TWO BOB, ch, 1933	The Porter, 1915	Sweep, 1907	Ben Brush / Pink Domino
		Ballet Girl, 1906	St. Leonards / **Cerito**
	Blessings, 1925	Ohio, 1913	**Spearmint** / Lady Hamburg II
		Mission Bells, 1919	Friar Rock / Sanctuary

RACE and (STAKES) RECORD

YEAR	AGE	STS	1ST	2ND	3RD	EARNED
1948	at 2	3	1	0	2	$3,300
1949	at 3	7	6(3)	1(1)	0	$60,300
1950	at 4	5	2(1)	2(1)	1(1)	$71,100
1951	at 5	0	0	0	0	—
1952	at 6	11	6(5)	3(2)	0	$174,550
Lifetime		**26**	**15(9)**	**6(4)**	**3(1)**	**$309,250**

Eight Thirty

SOMETIMES A HORSE DESERVING OF A CHAMPIONSHIP slips through the cracks. That's what happened to Eight Thirty. He won sixteen of twenty-seven races between 1938 and 1941, with thirteen of those wins coming in stakes, including four in one month as a three-year-old. However, he never topped a year-end championship poll. That does not mean, however, that his accomplishments have gone unrecognized. In 1994, Eight Thirty finally received his due when he was elected to the Racing Hall of Fame.

Bred and owned by George D. Widener and foaled at Widener's Old Kenney Farm (later to become part of Spendthrift Farm) near Lexington, Kentucky, Eight Thirty had been acquired in utero when Widener purchased Dinner Time for $6,000 from the William Robertson Coe dispersal of 1935. Eight Thirty began his racing career at two in June of 1938 at Delaware Park, which had opened only the previous year. In his debut, the colt won a five-furlong maiden race with Eddie Arcaro up. He then won, in succession, the Christiana Stakes at Delaware and the Flash Stakes at Saratoga, both in July. He also had runner-up efforts in the Futurity and Saratoga Special.

At three, Eight Thirty won three races, including the Diamond State Stakes, at Delaware Park before taking on Saratoga. At the historic New York track, he racked up four consecutive victories in a one-month period to establish himself as one of the top runners in training. On Aug. 2, he captured the Wilson Stakes by four lengths, then came back three days later to win the Saratoga Handicap at one and a half miles. He next took the Travers Stakes by five lengths over only two challengers, and four days later, he won the Whitney.

The Saratoga campaign took its toll, however, as Eight Thirty developed soreness in one of his hind legs and was sidelined for the rest of the year. He had won seven of ten starts and earned $39,125.

He returned at four none the worse for wear, winning half of his eight starts that season. All four victories came in stakes. He started off with a victory in the 1940 Toboggan Handicap at Belmont Park, carrying 127 pounds in that race. After a fourth-place finish in the Metropolitan Handicap under 128 pounds, Eight Thirty captured the Suburban Handicap carrying 127 pounds, then ended up third in the Brooklyn Handicap under a 130-pound impost.

After another third in the Butler Handicap at Empire City a week after the Brooklyn, Eight Thirty was sent to Suffolk Downs for the Massachusetts Handicap. He won, equaling Seabiscuit's track record of 1:49 for the nine-furlong event. The third-place finisher in that race, Challedon, would be named champion handicap male that year. Eight Thirty closed out his four-year-old season with a repeat victory in the Wilson Stakes, beating his only competitor by four lengths.

At five, Eight Thirty only started twice but won both outings: the Toboggan, then the Metropolitan under 132 pounds. *The Blood-Horse* of May 31, 1941, reported on the race, stating that Eight Thirty, "handling his heavy impost smartly, ran between the leaders inside the last furlong and began drawing out…he came to the finish two lengths in front, with speed in reserve." Eight Thirty gave thirty pounds to runner-up Bold and Bad.

The Met Mile proved to be Eight Thirty's last race. A few days later, a filling was noticed in one of his ankles, and Widener decided to retire the tough campaigner. Eight Thirty, who was trained by Bert Mulholland for most of his career, compiled a record of twenty-seven starts, sixteen wins, three seconds, and five thirds, with earnings of $155,475.

Eight Thirty was retired to Old Kenney Farm, where he established himself as a successful sire and later, top broodmare sire. He sired forty-five stakes winners, including Sailor, Lights Up, Bolero, and Big Stretch. Among the stakes winners produced by his daughters were Jaipur, Evening Out, Jester, Rare Treat, and First Balcony. Eight Thirty died of natural causes in 1965 at the age of twenty-nine. He had been pensioned since 1958 at Leslie Combs II's Spendthrift Farm. — *J. L. M.*

EIGHT THIRTY, chestnut colt, 1936

- PILATE, ch, 1928
  - Friar Rock, 1913
    - Rock Sand, 1900 — Sainfoin / Roquebrune
    - Fairy Gold, 1896 — Bend Or / Dame Masham
  - Herodias, 1916
    - The Tetrarch, 1911 — Roi Herode / Vahren
    - Honora, 1907 — Gallinule / Word of Honour
- DINNER TIME, ch, 1929
  - High Time, 1916
    - Ultimus, 1906 — Commando / Running Stream
    - Noonday, 1898 — Domino / Sundown
  - Seaplane, 1922
    - Man o' War, 1917 — Fair Play / Mahubah
    - Bathing Girl, 1915 — Spearmint / Summer Girl

RACE and (STAKES) RECORD

YEAR	AGE	STS	1ST	2ND	3RD	EARNED
1938	at 2	7	3(2)	2(2)	1(1)	$19,375
1939	at 3	10	7(5)	1(1)	1	$39,125
1940	at 4	8	4(4)	0	3(3)	$81,450
1941	at 5	2	2(2)	0	0	$15,525
Lifetime		27	16(13)	3(3)	5(4)	**$155,475**

Gallant Bloom

GALLANT BLOOM WAS AN UNASSUMING PACKAGE, wrapped in plain brown paper. But, like a jack-in-the-box, when you opened her up, all hell broke loose. She was a small filly, with a kind, gentle disposition, but when she took on Amazons like Shuvee and Gamely, both future Hall of Famers, the hellcat in her came out.

During her incredible twelve-race winning streak, which spanned three seasons (1968-70), she beat the best fillies and mares in the country with speed, grit, and heart. To demonstrate the esteem in which Gallant Bloom was held, consider that Shuvee in 1969 became racing's second winner of the New York Racing Association's Triple Crown for Fillies, sweeping the Acorn, Mother Goose, and Coaching Club American Oaks. She also romped in the Alabama Stakes and defeated top older fillies and mares in the Ladies Handicap. But when the ballots were in for three-year-old filly honors, she did not receive a single vote, as Gallant Bloom swept the ballot. Even with the presence of Gamely in the older female division that year, Gallant Bloom also was voted champion handicap filly or mare in some polls.

Early in her career, no one could have predicted that the daughter of Gallant Man would be anything more than an inconsistent, speed-crazy sprinter. After winning her first two starts, including the five and a half-furlong National Stallion Stakes at Belmont, the King Ranch filly fell apart, getting beaten a total of fifty-two lengths in her next three starts.

Then suddenly, she awakened from her sleep, winning an allowance race by three lengths before romping by nine in the six-furlong Matron Stakes. When she stretched out to a mile in the Frizette Stakes and was nailed by Shuvee after blowing a three-length lead, her trainer Max Hirsch decided he had to teach the filly how to relax and rate off the pace.

Gallant Bloom responded favorably to Hirsch's patient approach. In an incredible turnaround, she went out and won her next twelve races. During her streak, she won at eight different racetracks, from six furlongs to one and three-sixteenths miles,

GALLANT BLOOM, bay filly, May 22, 1966

GALLANT MAN (GB), b, 1954	Migoli, 1944	Bois Roussel, 1935	Vatout / Plucky Liege
		Mah Iran, 1939	Bahram / **Mah Mahal**
	Majideh, 1939	**Mahmoud**, 1933	Blenheim II / **Mah Mahal**
		Qurrat-al-Ain, 1927	Buchan / Harpsichord
MULTIFLORA, b, 1961	Beau Max, 1947	Bull Lea, 1935	Bull Dog / Rose Leaves
		Bee Mac, 1941	War Admiral / Baba Kenny
	Flower Bed, 1946	Beau Pere, 1927	Son-in-Law / Cinna
		Boudoir II, 1938	**Mahmoud** / Kampala

over surfaces labeled fast, slow, good, and sloppy. She defeated Shuvee three times — in the Gardenia (clinching the two-year-old filly championship), Delaware Oaks, and Gazelle Handicap — and annihilated Gamely by seven lengths in the Matchmaker Stakes.

A month before Gallant Bloom made her three-year-old debut in the six-furlong Liberty Belle Stakes at Aqueduct, Hirsch died at age eighty-eight, and his son Buddy took over the stable. In a final demonstration of her sprinting speed, Gallant Bloom outran the speed demon Miss Swapsco through sizzling fractions of :21⅗ and :44⅗ before going on to victory. After that, Hirsch stretched her out for good and she never looked back.

Her victory over Shuvee in the Gazelle, in which both fillies carried 127 pounds, clinched the three-year-old filly championship. She then went after the handicap title in the Matchmaker, and left two-time Beldame winner Gamely, Top Flight winner Amerigo Lady, and Maskette winner Singing Rain far up the track.

After concluding her three-year-old campaign with a victory in the Spinster Stakes, Gallant Bloom went to Santa Anita and captured the Santa Maria and Santa Margarita Handicaps. Her streak ended at twelve when she returned from California and finished third to Reviewer in the Nassau County Handicap. But she had a chip developing in her ankle and it finally ended her career in her next race, the Suburban Handicap.

After producing four foals in four years, Gallant Bloom produced only one foal in the next seventeen years. Veterinarians were baffled, as they tried unsuccessfully to get her to cycle regularly. She did get in foal to Drone in 1984, but aborted the fetus. Another year, she had a false pregnancy. She finally was turned over to King Ranch foreman Neville Collins as a pet project. He bred her to the seldom-used stallion Opportune, and Gallant Bloom finally produced a foal. In 1992, at the age of twenty-five, Gallant Bloom's great heart gave out and she just lay down in her paddock and died. — *S. H.*

RACE and (STAKES) RECORD

YEAR	AGE	STS	1ST	2ND	3RD	EARNED
1968	at 2	10	6(3)	1(1)	0	$231,400
1969	at 3	8	8(7)	0	0	$220,514
1970	at 4	4	2(2)	0	1(1)	$83,825
Lifetime		22	16(12)	1(1)	1(1)	$535,739

207

Ta Wee

TA WEE WAS THE CHAMPION SPRINTER of both 1969 and 1970 and carried weights remarkable for any 20th Century runner, male or female. In the 1970 Interborough Handicap, Ta Wee bowed out with a victory under 142 pounds. It was her second consecutive win under 140 or more and her sixth career stakes win under as much as 130. Today, 130 pounds is rarely assigned any horse; Ta Wee carried at least that much in every start at four!

Ta Wee was sired by the champion sprinter and top miler Intentionally and was out of the remarkable mare Aspidistra, by Better Self. Aspidistra had been acquired in 1957 for a reported $6,500 at the behest of the employees of W. L. McKnight when they were casting around for a memorable 70th birthday present for the head of Minnesota Manufacturing and Mining (3-M).

Purchased by trainer John Sceusa to be presented to McKnight, the gift horse was risked later for a claiming tag of $6,500. However, she was still owned by McKnight at the time of her retirement, and she later became a distinguished producer for the Tartan Farms operation McKnight was establishing in Florida. In addition to Ta Wee, Aspidistra's stakes winners included the magnificent Dr. Fager, Horse of the Year in 1968, and the mare also became a tail-female ancestress of classic winner and champion Unbridled.

Ta Wee was trained for McKnight's Tartan Stable by Scotty Schulhofer. Dr. Fager, Ta Wee, and Schulhofer all were later inducted into the Racing Hall of Fame, as was John Nerud, who had trained Dr. Fager for McKnight and later took on a key management role in the overall Tartan breeding and racing enterprise.

At three, in her first tour as champion sprinter, Ta Wee ran ten times from January into

					Man o' War
			War Relic, 1938		Friar's Carse
		Intent, 1948			
			Liz F., 1933		Bubbling Over
	INTENTIONALLY,				Weno
	blk, 1956				
			Discovery, 1931		Display
		My Recipe, 1947			Ariadne
TA WEE,			Perlette, 1934		Percentage
dark bay or brown filly,					Escarpolette
March 26, 1966					
			Bimelech, 1937		Black Toney
		Better Self, 1945			La Troienne
	ASPIDISTRA,		Bee Mac, 1941		War Admiral
	b, 1954				Baba Kenny
			Bull Brier, 1938		Bull Dog
		Tilly Rose, 1948			Rose Eternal
			Tilly Kate, 1935		Draymont
					Teak

November, and she won eight races, all stakes. She launched her year winning a division of the Jasmine Stakes and then, after running third in the Mimosa, she scored five consecutive victories, in the Prioress, Comely, Miss Woodford, Test, and Fall Highweight. In the six-furlong Fall Highweight Handicap, the three-year-old Ta Wee carried 130 pounds to defeat King Emperor (131).

The winning streak ended when she was stretched beyond sprint distances and tried on grass, but Ta Wee rebounded to win the Interborough Handicap, at six furlongs. Dr. Fager had won the Vosburgh Handicap in 1967 and 1968, and at three, Ta Wee kept the family string alive, defeating older males in the seven-furlong race.

At four, Ta Wee was mathematically assaulted by racing secretaries of New York and New Jersey, but Tartan management had accepted heavy weights for Dr. Fager and did not shrink from challenges for Ta Wee. The filly won five of seven races from March through October. She began by taking the six-furlong Correction Handicap under 131 pounds. After running second under 134 in the seven-furlong Distaff, she took the six-furlong Hempstead with 132 and the six-furlong Regret Handicap under 136.

Ta Wee then was second again, under 134 in the six-furlong Gravesend Handicap, before closing her career with two more six-furlong events under the highest weights of her career. To win the Fall Highweight, she took up 140 pounds and outran Towzie Tyke, giving him nineteen pounds. Finally, for the Interborough, Ta Wee was assigned 142 pounds. She won at 3-5, giving runner-up Hasty Hitter twenty-nine pounds. Ta Wee's accomplishments earned her a second champion sprinter title. She was retired with fifteen wins in twenty-one starts and earnings of $284,941.

Ta Wee had six foals, of which five were winners and four were stakes winners. To the cover of the sentimentally named Tartan stakes winner Minnesota Mac, Ta Wee produced the graded sprint stakes winner Great Above as her first foal. Great Above later became renowned as the sire of 1994 Horse of the Year Holy Bull and broodmare sire of a later two-time sprint champion, Housebuster. Ta Wee also foaled the stakes winners Entropy, Tax Holiday, and Tweak. — E. L. B.

RACE and (STAKES) RECORD

YEAR	AGE	STS	1ST	2ND	3RD	EARNED
1968	at 2	4	2	0	0	$12,410
1969	at 3	10	8(8)	0	1(1)	$170,663
1970	at 4	7	5(5)	2(2)	0	$101,868
Lifetime		21	15(13)	2(2)	1(1)	**$284,941**

Affectionately

WHEN HALL OF FAME TRAINER HIRSCH JACOBS TALKED, people listened. So in declaring Affectionately "the best horse I've ever trained," that statement took on historic importance, especially since the conditioner's earlier stars included champions Stymie and Hail to Reason. Jacobs bestowed the superlative after Affectionately won the Polly Drummond Stakes for her fifth consecutive win of her two-year-old season.

Affectionately was a three-time champion on the race-track, and her start as a broodmare can only be described as downright spectacular. Few mares produce a stakes winner their first season, but she came up with a Horse of the Year as her first foal.

Affectionately, who traced in female family to Col. E. R. Bradley's foundation mare La Troienne, was bred by the partnership of Jacobs and Isidor Bieber, and was foaled at Dr. Charles Hagyard's farm near Lexington, Kentucky, on April 26, 1960. Five years earlier, Jacobs privately had purchased Affectionately's dam, Searching, from Ogden Phipps for $15,000 at the time Searching was in training and still a maiden. Jacobs thought that Searching's true value would come later as a broodmare, but both he and his partner were in for a surprise. Searching won a dozen stakes and earned $327,381.

Affectionately was campaigned by the Bieber-Jacobs team in the name of Jacobs' wife, Ethel. The daughter of Swaps made her debut in January of her two-year-old season in 1962, winning a three-furlong maiden event. Under Jacobs' guidance, Affectionately rolled through the first part of her two-year-old season, winning nine of her first ten starts, including major engagements in the Sorority Stakes at Monmouth Park and the Spinaway Stakes at Saratoga. In the Matron Stakes at Aqueduct in September, she faced unbeaten Midwest sensation Smart Deb and finished third. Neither filly would win again

SWAPS, ch, 1952	Khaled, 1943	Hyperion, 1930	Gainsborough / Selene
		Eclair, 1930	Ethnarch / Black Ray
	Iron Reward, 1946	Beau Pere, 1927	Son-in-Law / Cinna
		Iron Maiden, 1941	War Admiral / Betty Derr

AFFECTIONATELY, dark bay filly, April 26, 1960

SEARCHING, b, 1952	War Admiral, 1934	Man o' War, 1917	Fair Play / Mahubah
		Brushup, 1929	Sweep / Annette K.
	Big Hurry, 1936	Black Toney, 1911	Peter Pan / Belgravia
		La Troienne, 1926	Teddy / Helene de Troie

that year, but the two were named co-champions.

Affectionately, who was known as the "Queen of Queens" among New York race fans, won stakes over the next two seasons, but it was her added-money victories her five-year-old season that stamped her as something special. Those wins included the Vagrancy, Toboggan, and Top Flight Handicaps. New York racing secretary Tommy Trotter called Affectionately's win in the seven-furlong Vagrancy the high point of the 1965 racing season. Affectionately carried 137 pounds, giving the field seventeen to twenty-eight pounds. In the six-furlong Toboggan, she defeated top male sprinter Chieftain in 1:09⅖ to become the first female to win the race since 1910.

Affectionately's victory in the Top Flight at one and an eighth miles served to establish that she was more than just a sprinter. In a televised race, the daughter of Swaps scored by eight lengths over Steeple Jill, with Old Hat running third. Ironically, the Aqueduct bettors had abandoned their heroine and made Old Hat the favorite. At year's end, Affectionately was champion sprinter and shared championship honors in the handicap mare division with Old Hat.

Affectionately was retired with a record of twenty-eight wins from fifty-two races and earnings of $546,659. Eighteen wins came in stakes, and she also placed in nine added-money races. She had followed Cicada as only the second female to earn $500,000-plus.

Jacobs, who dispersed most of his mares on doctor's orders, kept Affectionately and bred her to Hail to Reason in 1966. The resulting foal, Personality, won the Preakness Stakes and shared 1970 Horse of the Year honors with turf star Fort Marcy.

Affectionately experienced later difficulties as a broodmare and produced only three other foals, one of which started. Her two stakes-winning half-sisters also made marks as broodmares. Admiring (by Hail to Reason) produced stakes winner Glowing Tribute, the 1993 Kentucky Broodmare of the Year. Admiring's full sister, Priceless Gem, produced European champion Allez France. Affectionately died at age nineteen. She was inducted into the Racing Hall of Fame in 1989. — D. S.

RACE and (STAKES) RECORD

YEAR	AGE	STS	1ST	2ND	3RD	EARNED
1962	at 2	13	9(6)	1(1)	3(2)	$216,357
1963	at 3	9	4(1)	1	1	$33,592
1964	at 4	15	8(5)	2	0	$108,994
1965	at 5	15	7(6)	4(4)	2(2)	$187,716
Lifetime		52	28(18)	8(5)	6(4)	$546,659

Miesque

STAVROS NIARCHOS' HOMEBRED MIESQUE started at the top in her racing career, and went up from there. She conquered her European rivals, then crossed the Atlantic to win a Breeders' Cup race not once but two years in a row. Miesque earned championships in every country in which she raced and won the hearts of all who saw her run.

In all, she made sixteen starts, winning twelve (eleven of them stakes, and ten grade/group I events), finishing second three times (all in group I events), and third once (also a group I). Miesque's career earnings of $2,070,163 place her among the leading money-earning fillies and mares.

Miesque had the right credentials to succeed at the highest levels. A daughter of Niarchos' European champion Nureyev and the first foal from multiple French stakes winner Pasadoble, Miesque was placed in the masterful hands of trainer Francois Boutin. She raced only four times at two in 1986. In her first start, she finished third in the group I Prix Morny, then won the Prix de la Salamandre, took a listed stakes at Longchamp, and won the Prix Marcel Boussac. She was named France's champion juvenile.

At three, Miesque won the Prix Imprudence in France in early April, then skipped over to England to trounce the Brits in the General Accident One Thousand Guineas. Back in France, she took the Dubai Poule d'Essai des Pouliches (the French One Thousand Guineas). She next ran into Sheikh Mohammed's top filly Indian Skimmer, who beat her at a distance in the one and five-sixteenths-mile Prix de Diane-Hermes (French Oaks).

Miesque bounced right back and in August took the Prix du Haras de Fresnay-le-Buffard Jacques Le Marois, which re-established her credentials as the best miler in Europe.

She next won the Prix du Moulin de Longchamp, beating male group I winner Soviet Star by two and a half lengths. Back in England she contested the Queen Elizabeth II Stakes. This time, however, Miesque's finishing kick wasn't there. She ran second best to Milligram, who had finished second to Miesque in the Prix Marcel Boussac and One Thousand Guineas.

		Nearctic, 1954	Nearco Lady Angela
Northern Dancer, 1961			
		Natalma, 1957	Native Dancer Almahmoud
NUREYEV, b, 1977			
		Forli, 1963	Aristophanes Trevisa
Special, 1969			
MIESQUE, bay filly, March 14, 1984		Thong, 1964	Nantallah Rough Shod II
		Graustark, 1963	Ribot Flower Bowl
Prove Out, 1969			
		Equal Venture, 1953	Bold Venture Igual
PASADOBLE, b, 1979			
		Barustar, 1960	Fine Top Quinona
Santa Quilla, 1970			
		Neriad, 1964	Princequillo Sea-Change

The decision was made to invade. Miesque was shipped to Hollywood Park for the fourth edition of the Breeders' Cup Mile. Breaking from the fourth post position in the fourteen-horse field, Miesque raced well within the front tier until the stretch, when she took the lead and ran off under a hand ride by Freddie Head to win by three and a half lengths. Her time for the mile was a course record of 1:32⅖. Her accolades at the end of the year amounted to five championship titles: champion three-year-old filly in France and England, champion miler in France and England, and champion U.S. grass mare.

In 1988 at four, Miesque started only four times, and lost only once. She won her debut in the Prix d'Ispahan in late May, then didn't race again until August in the Prix Jacques Le Marois. In that one, she ran off to beat English-based Warning by a length.

In her seventh outing against the colts, Miesque was impeded by traffic and lost by a head to Soviet Star in the Prix du Moulin. In her final career start, Miesque returned to her birthplace, Kentucky, to attempt to become the first horse to win back-to-back Breeders' Cup races. In the field of a dozen horses, Miesque raced about halfway back until the stretch. Then, on the rain-soaked Churchill Downs turf, Miesque drew off to a four-length win, and raced into history.

Boutin said Miesque was not the best horse he had ever trained, but acknowledged her as "definitely the most constant and easiest to train because she is so regular."

Miesque claimed the titles of champion miler and champion older mare in France that year, as well as champion grass mare in the United States. She was retired, and had produced eight foals through 1999, including multiple group I winners Kingmambo, sire of 1999 Belmont Stakes winner Lemon Drop Kid, and East of the Moon, and stakes winners Miesque's Son and Moon Is Up. — *K. H.*

RACE and (STAKES) RECORD

YEAR	AGE	STS	1ST	2ND	3RD	EARNED
1986	at 2 in Fr	4	3(2)	0	1(1)	$139,101
1987	at 3 in Fr ,Eng, NA	8	6(6)	2(2)	0	$1,181,868
1988	at 4 in Fr, NA	4	3(3)	1(1)	0	$749,194
Lifetime		**16**	**12(11)**	**3(3)**	**1(1)**	**$2,070,163**

Carry Back

INAUSPICIOUS BEGINNINGS, hard work, and persistence often pay off at the races, and the career of Carry Back is a prime example. Carry Back was the product of the Maryland-based stallion Saggy and a mare named Joppy — a mating that later in the 20th Century might have produced a truly horrendous name.

Breeder-owner-trainer Jack Price took Joppy in lieu of a board bill owed by a client at his Ohio farm. After breeding her, Price sent Joppy to Ocala Stud in Florida, where the foal was born. With little invested in the colt, Price nonetheless put him to work early. At two, Carry Back raced seven times in Florida between January and April of 1960. Among those starts was

a five-furlong win at Gulfstream Park in then-track record time of :57⅗. Moving north, his triumphs included the Cowdin Stakes at Belmont, the Garden State Stakes, and the Remsen. By the time his two-year-old season was done, Carry Back had faced the starter twenty-one times, with five wins, four seconds, four thirds, and $286,299 to show for his work. The colt ran in the name of Price's wife, Katherine.

He didn't get much of a break after that success, either. Price shipped the colt back to Florida, where he ripped off victories in the Flamingo, the Everglades, and the Florida Derby. He was third in the Fountain of Youth. Shipped back north, Carry Back ran second in the Wood Memorial at Aqueduct, then headed for Churchill Downs as a charismatic hero.

Despite his arduous campaign — and despite drawing post position fourteen — Carry Back went to the post in the eighty-seventh running of the Kentucky Derby as the $2.50-1 favorite under jockey John Sellers. Typically, he lagged behind the early leaders, began passing horses on the turn, and outfinished the second-favorite, Fred Hooper's

CARRY BACK, brown colt, April 16, 1958

SAGGY, ch, 1945
- Swing and Sway, 1938
  - Equipoise, 1928 — Pennant / Swinging
  - Nedana, 1922 — Negofol / Adana
- Chantress, 1939
  - Hyperion, 1930 — Gainsborough / Selene
  - Surbine, 1924 — Bachelor's Double / Datine

JOPPY, br, 1949
- Star Blen, 1940
  - Blenheim II, 1927 — Blandford / Malva
  - Starweed, 1928 — Phalaris / Versatile
- Miss Fairfax, 1943
  - Teddy Beau, 1934 — Teddy / Beautiful Lady
  - Bellicent, 1927 — Sir Gallahad III / Whizz Bang

Crozier, to win by three-quarters of a length in 2:04.

He backed up his Kentucky Derby success with a victory in the Preakness but struggled home seventh, nearly fifteen lengths behind the winner, Sherluck, as the odds-on favorite in the Belmont Stakes. Through 1999, that was the worst finish of any horse trying to complete the Triple Crown "hat trick."

After finally getting a break from training, Carry Back returned to win the Jerome and Trenton Handicaps. Those efforts cemented his title as three-year-old champion of 1961.

Carry Back carried on as a four-year-old. In the Metropolitan Handicap on Memorial Day of 1962, he turned a ten-pound weight advantage into a two and a half-length victory, beating Kelso and other top handicap stars. In that race, he equaled the track record of 1:33⅗. The Met Mile only enhanced Carry Back's popularity and a defeat by Beau Purple in the Suburban Handicap did little to erode his support. Wheeling back in the Monmouth Handicap less than two weeks after the Suburban, Carry Back ran away from both Kelso and Beau Purple to score a three-length victory in track-record time. Carry Back then won the Whitney Stakes at Saratoga and finished fourth in the Aqueduct Stakes.

Price, however, had bigger plans yet for his handicap powerhouse. He sent Carry Back to France for the Prix de l'Arc de Triomphe, only to see him finish a poor tenth on the Parisian grass. The horse finished his four-year-old campaign with five wins, five seconds, and three thirds in nineteen starts. After three years of racing, the colt had gone to the post fifty-six times, earning more than $1.1 million.

Price sent his star to stud in Ocala, Florida, in 1963 — briefly — then returned him to action, starting him out six times with two wins, including the Trenton Handicap, which he also had won two years earlier. Carry Back entered stud for good in 1964, standing first in Kentucky, then at Price's Dorchester Farm in Ocala. He sired twelve stakes winners and the dams of thirty stakes winners. After his breeding career, he was pensioned to the Ocala Jockey Club and euthanized at age twenty-five. Carry Back was elected to the Racing Hall of Fame in 1975. — B. K.

RACE and (STAKES) RECORD

YEAR	AGE	STS	1ST	2ND	3RD	EARNED
1960	at 2 in NA	21	5(3)	4(3)	4(3)	$286,299
1961	at 3 in NA	16	9(7)	1(1)	3(3)	$565,349
1962	at 4 in Fr, NA	19	5(3)	5(5)	3(3)	$319,177
1963	at 5 in NA	6	2(1)	1(1)	1(1)	$70,340
Lifetime		62	21(14)	11(10)	11(10)	$1,241,165

Bimelech

BIMELECH ACHIEVED FAME just by being born, then went on to justify his initial acclaim. Foaled on Feb. 27, 1937, at Col. E. R. Bradley's Idle Hour Stock Farm near Lexington, Kentucky, he was the last colt sired by Bradley's major stallion Black Toney and was a full brother to 1935 champion three-year-old filly Black Helen.

Bradley had named Bimelech after a friend, John Harris, whose close associates called him "Bimelech." The nickname was a shortened version of the Biblical name Abimelech. In keeping with Bradley's tradition of giving his horses names beginning with the letter B, the A was dropped.

Trained by William Hurley, Bimelech became an unbeaten champion two-year-old, plus a dual classic winner and champion three-year-old and a member of the Racing Hall of Fame. He captured the 1940 Preakness and Belmont Stakes, and in the eyes of some, would have won the Kentucky Derby if handled differently.

A victory by Bimelech in the Run for the Roses was a foregone conclusion for Bradley and many

others. Less than two months before the big race, he was installed in the winter books at 3-1, the shortest winter price ever quoted on a Derby favorite up to that time. More astounding was the fact that Bimelech hadn't even started that year.

Bimelech, who had spent the winter at Idle Hour, came out for the Blue Grass Stakes at Keeneland on April 25. It was his first start since he won the Pimlico Futurity the previous fall, and at 1-10 he defeated Joseph E. Widener's speedy Roman by two and a half lengths.

After the victory, Idle Hour general manager Olin Gentry received some advice from rival trainer Ben A. Jones, who had sent out Lawrin to win the 1938 Kentucky Derby. "Your horse is fat, but if he does not run again until the Derby, he'll win it," Jones told Gentry.

Gentry suggested to Hurley it might be wise not to run Bimelech again until the Derby, but Hurley felt differently. "For any other horse it would be, but Bimelech is an iron horse," he said.

Hurley sent out Bimelech in the Derby Trial on April 30, and the Idle Hour colt won by two and a quarter lengths as the 1-10 favorite over Gallahadion. Three days later, on May 3, Bimelech faced Gallahadion in the Kentucky Derby for his third race in eight days. The "iron horse" went off at 2-5 odds, the shortest Derby odds in thirty-five years. Ridden by F. A. Smith, Bimelech held a half-length lead at the eighth-pole, but was passed by Gallahadion and lost by one and a half lengths. It would have been Bradley's fifth Derby winner, and it didn't take long for the "what ifs" to surface.

Bimelech came back to win the fiftieth Preakness as the favorite over Gallahadion on May 11, then ran again seven days later in the Withers Stakes at Belmont Park. It was his fifth race in less than a month, and he finished second. On June 8, he won the Belmont Stakes at 6-5 odds, with Gallahadion finishing behind him once again.

Bimelech raced once more that year before suffering an injury at Saratoga. He started twice during the winter of his four-year-old season before Bradley decided to retire him in March. Bimelech had an aversion to the new starting gates, and Bradley did not want to risk injury. Bimelech entered stud that year at Idle Hour with a record of eleven wins from fifteen races and earnings of $248,745.

Bradley died in August of 1946, and Bimelech was acquired by a syndicate consisting of Greentree Stud, King Ranch, and Ogden Phipps and sent to stand at Greentree near Lexington. Bimelech sired thirty stakes winners, including Better Self, the broodmare sire of the great Dr. Fager. Another of Bimelech's stakes winners, Be Faithful, is the granddam of major sire Never Bend. Bimelech, whose dam, French-bred La Troienne, is referred to as the most important broodmare imported to North America this century, died in 1966. One of five stakes winners produced from La Troienne, Bimelech was elected to the Racing Hall of Fame in 1990, a year before Black Helen was inducted. — D. S.

BIMELECH, bay colt, February 27, 1937			
BLACK TONEY, br, 1911	Peter Pan, 1904	Commando, 1898	Domino / Emma C.
		Cinderella, 1888	Hermit / Mazurka
	Delgravia, 1903	Ben Brush, 1893	Bramble / Roseville
		Bonnie Gal, 1889	Galopin / Bonnie Doon
LA TROIENNE (Fr), b, 1926	Teddy, 1913	Ajax, 1901	Flying Fox / Amie
		Rondeau, 1900	Bay Ronald / Doremi
	Helene de Troie, 1916	Helicon, 1906	Cyllene / Vain Duchess
		Lady of Pedigree, 1910	St. Denis / Doxa

RACE and (STAKES) RECORD

YEAR	AGE	STS	1ST	2ND	3RD	EARNED
1939	at 2	6	6(4)	0	0	$135,090
1940	at 3	7	4(4)	2(2)	1(1)	$110,005
1941	at 4	2	1	0	0	$3,650
Lifetime		15	11(8)	2(2)	1(1)	$248,745

Lure

LURE DEMONSTRATED IMPRESSIVE TALENT from day one, but how he ended up making his mark on racing involved a 180-degree turnaround from that first start.

The son of Danzig matured early, winning his first start in June of his juvenile season (1991) going five furlongs in track record time. But Lure is one of the century's best horses not because of his blazing speed nor his love for the dirt. Rather, it is because of his

prowess on the turf. While he was good on the dirt, he was great on the grass. Nevertheless, he was never a champion. In fact, he is surely on the short list of top runners never to receive an Eclipse Award.

Lure won the Breeders' Cup Mile in both 1992 and 1993, but the Eclipse Award for champion turf male both years went to runners in the Breeders' Cup Turf (Sky Classic, who missed by a nose to Fraise in the Turf in 1992, and Kotashaan, who won the Turf the following year). Neither of those horses received a single vote for the Top 100.

Lure was victorious in his first two starts as a three-year-old at Aqueduct, including an impressive dead-heat with Devil His Due in the Gotham Stakes. But after Lure finished second in the Lexington Stakes and sixth in the Riva Ridge Stakes, trainer Claude R. (Shug) McGaughey III and co-owner Seth Hancock decided to try the colt on the grass.

Lure raced for the Hancock family's Claiborne Farm and William Haggin Perry's The Gamely Corp.; after Perry's death in November, 1993, he raced for Claiborne and Perry's widow, Nicole Perry Gorman.

Lure's pedigree gave him every reason to like the lawn. Besides being by a son of Northern Dancer, his dam, Endear, by Alydar, was a half-sister to the top turf runner Tiller. It took only one start to show his affinity. Three months after the Riva Ridge, Lure won an

			Nearctic, 1954	Nearco / Lady Angela
DANZIG, b, 1977	Northern Dancer, 1961		Natalma, 1957	**Native Dancer** / Almahmoud
	Pas de Nom, 1968	Admiral's Voyage, 1959	Crafty Admiral / Olympia Lou
LURE, bay colt, May 14, 1989		Petitioner, 1952	Petition / Steady Aim
	Alydar, 1975	Raise a Native, 1961	**Native Dancer** / Raise You
ENDEAR, b, 1982		Sweet Tooth, 1965	On-and-On / Plum Cake
	Chappaquiddick, 1968	Relic, 1945	War Relic / Bridal Colors
		Baby Doll II, 1956	Dante / Bebe Grande

allowance race at Belmont by ten and a quarter lengths. A star was born.

Following a second in the Kelso Handicap a month later, Lure won the Breeders' Cup Mile wire to wire by three lengths, shattering the Gulfstream Park course record in the process (1:32⅖, besting the old mark of 1:34). He paid $12.80, a price his backers would certainly not see again. In his subsequent fifteen races, Lure was odds-on a dozen times.

Lure appeared at Keeneland in April of 1993, winning an allowance event to prepare him for a series of four spring races against rival Star of Cozzene. Lure won the first two — the Early Times Turf Classic Stakes and Early Times Dixie Handicap — and Star of Cozzene the latter two, the Early Times Manhattan Stakes and Caesars International Handicap. After winning the Daryl's Joy Stakes at Saratoga, Lure was to start next in the Arlington Million, but boggy turf conditions caused McGaughey to scratch and wait for another day. That day was the Kelso Handicap at Belmont, which Lure won easily in his final prep for a repeat attempt in the Breeders' Cup.

Lure was the heavy favorite for the 1993 Breeders' Cup Mile at Santa Anita, but there was some concern about his post position, twelve, in the thirteen-horse field. But television analyst Mike Battaglia was right when he uttered perhaps the best line on a Breeders' Cup telecast to date, "Lure could win if he started from the parking lot." Lure was forced wide in the first turn, but quickly moved to the lead, took command, and was hand-ridden to a two and a quarter-length victory.

Three straight Mile wins was, unfortunately, not to be. Lure won three of seven starts at five, but finished a disappointing ninth in the '94 Mile, his final start. In all, he made twenty-five starts, won fourteen of them, and finished second eight times to earn $2,515,289.

RACE and (STAKES) RECORD						
YEAR	AGE	STS	1ST	2ND	3RD	EARNED
1991	at 2	3	1	1	0	$20,340
1992	at 3	7	4(2)	2(2)	0	$729,910
1993	at 4	8	6(5)	2(2)	0	$1,212,803
1994	at 5	7	3(3)	3(3)	0	$552,236
Lifetime		25	14(10)	8(7)	0	$2,515,289

Lure was retired to Claiborne Farm near Paris, Kentucky, but because of low fertility, the farm collected on an insurance policy fertility clause. He was purchased by Coolmore Stud in Ireland, but was later returned to stand at Ashford Stud near Versailles, Kentucky. To date, he has sired one winner, French group I winner Orpen. — D. L.

Fort Marcy

GRASS RACING'S INCREASING POPULARITY in North America has been aided by several milestones, not the least of which was the establishment of the Washington, D.C., International at Laurel in 1952. Laurel president John Schapiro proved able to entice a collection of quality horses from Europe and South America for a showdown in the Maryland autumn, and his International gave added prestige to other grass races, old and new.

It was not until nearly two decades after Laurel's first International, however, that a turf championship was created. Even then, it was a shared honor, for 1970 marked the final year before the Eclipse Award format unified North American Thoroughbred championships. Fort Marcy, the grass star, was voted Horse of the Year on the *Daily Racing Form* poll, while the dirt-track star Personality won on the Thoroughbred Racing Associations poll.

In subsequent years, the versatile John Henry won two Horse of the Year titles, the second almost entirely dependent on his grass form. Two all-out grass runners, All Along (1983) and Kotashaan (1993), also have been voted Horse of the Year.

The emergence of Fort Marcy was illustrative of the role grass racing long played in North America and which still is a factor: It was something to try when dirt racing failed. In the midst of his three-year-old season in 1967, Fort Marcy's form had been so desultory that breeder-owner Paul Mellon and trainer Elliott Burch entered him in a horses in training sale at Belmont Park. Harry Albert, whose partnership-owned Gun Bow had chased Kelso unsuccessfully in the International three years earlier, bid $76,000 for Fort Marcy. Trainer Syl Veitch, acting for Mellon, bid in the horse at $77,000. Albert had just missed a bargain; Mellon had just missed losing one.

Converted full time to grass racing, Fort Marcy reeled off four consecutive stakes triumphs. He then lost four in a row, but was named to back up Damascus as very much a second string U.S. representative in the International. Damascus had secured Horse of the Year with resounding victories in such races as the Preakness, Belmont, Travers, Woodward, and Jockey Club Gold Cup. The Laurel race marked his debut on grass, and while the English/Irish classic winner Ribocco might have appeared his most accomplished challenger, it was countryman Fort Marcy that stood him off through a testing drive to score an upset by a nose.

The International introduced Fort Marcy as an actor at the top level of American Turf drama and secured his first grass-course championship. For the next three seasons, he toured American racetracks, seeking the best and most demanding grass distance races. Under Burch's sporting management, he proved as able a traveler as a racer and had major wins in a half-dozen states. He took a second running of the International, plus the Man o' War, Hollywood Park Invitational, Dixie, Bougainvillea, Sunset, and Stars and Stripes. He set one and a half-mile course records of 2:26⅗ in Hollywood Park's Sunset and 2:27⅖ in Pimlico's Dixie.

Fort Marcy was champion or co-champion grass horse three times, in 1967, 1968, and 1970. In his final championship year, when he shared Horse of the Year designation, the tried and true old war horse won five major turf stakes. A son of the Nearco stallion Amerigo out of Mellon's great broodmare Key Bridge, Fort Marcy closed his campaign in gaudy fashion, taking, in succession, the United Nations, Man o' War, and International.

In six seasons, Fort Marcy ran seventy-five times and won twenty-one races, including sixteen stakes, and earned $1,109,791. He lived a long life as a pensioner at Mellon's Rokeby Farm in Virginia, where he died at twenty-seven in 1991. He was elected to the Racing Hall of Fame in 1998. — E. L. B.

AMERIGO (GB), ch, 1955	Nearco, 1935	Pharos, 1920	Phalaris / Scapa Flow
		Nogara, 1928	Havresac II / Catnip
	Sanlinea, 1947	Precipitation, 1933	Hurry On / Double Life
		Sun Helmet, 1940	Hyperion / Point Duty
KEY BRIDGE, b, 1959	Princequillo, 1940	Prince Rose, 1928	Rose Prince / Indolence
		Cosquilla, 1933	Papyrus / Quick Thought
	Blue Banner, 1952	War Admiral, 1934	Man o' War / Brushup
		Risque Blue, 1941	Blue Larkspur / Risque

FORT MARCY, bay gelding, April 2, 1964

RACE and (STAKES) RECORD

YEAR	AGE	STS	1ST	2ND	3RD	EARNED
1966	at 2	10	1	2	1	$5,300
1967	at 3	18	7(5)	2(1)	4(1)	$236,264
1968	at 4	13	3(2)	6(4)	2(2)	$186,667
1969	at 5	13	5(4)	1(1)	3(3)	$226,512
1970	at 6	13	5(5)	4(3)	2(1)	$388,537
1971	at 7	8	0	3(3)	2(2)	$66,511
Lifetime		75	21(16)	18(12)	14(9)	$1,109,791

Gamely

IN A LIFETIME OF RACING, the late William Haggin Perry had many fabulous moments. Obviously, he counted a number of champion Gamely's races among them, for he would later name his breeding operation, The Gamely Corp., in her honor.

Bred by Claiborne Farm and raced in partnership with Perry in his colors, Gamely was certainly aptly named, and in no race did her gameness show more than in the 1968 Inglewood Handicap at Hollywood Park. Just three weeks after a second-place finish to eventual Horse of the Year Dr. Fager in the Californian Stakes, Gamely was sent against the colts again in the Inglewood. Giving weight on the scale, Gamely dueled with Rising Market the entire length of the stretch, winning by a nose. The daughter of Bold Ruler—Gambetta, by My Babu, covered the one and an eighth miles in 1:47⅕.

Three weeks later, also at Hollywood, the four-year-old filly returned against members of her own sex in the Vanity Handicap, the richest race ever run at the track for fillies and mares, with a gross purse of $79,650. She won the one and an eighth-mile race by three-quarters of a length carrying 131 pounds, the most weight ever carried to victory by a distaffer in a California stakes. She not only won, but did so in stakes-equaling time — 1:47⅗ — after being sent, uncustomarily, to the lead because of the slow opening quarter. In the Vanity, Gamely, trained by James W. Maloney, was part of a three-horse entry racing for Perry. Her stablemates, Princessnesian and Desert Law, ran second and third, respectively. Princessnesian carried 128 pounds and Desert Law 115.

Gamely was by no means done for the year. She shipped East to Saratoga to win an overnight under 132 pounds, then took the Diana, though she was disqualified to second.

Then, on closing day at Aqueduct, Gamely, the best of the West, met the best fillies and mares in the East in a great renewal of the Beldame Stakes.

Gamely opened up by four lengths early and was on top by three at the half-mile pole. But she was joined shortly thereafter by Politely and Amerigo Lady, and the real racing began. With Gamely nearest the rail, Politely to her outside, and Amerigo Lady outside of her, the three ran as a team through the stretch. Slight brushing did occur, but a foul claim was disallowed. The result — Gamely by a nose over Politely, with Amerigo Lady a neck back in third. Gamely's Beldame victory assured her the championship as older filly and mare in 1968; she was the Thoroughbred Racing Association's champion three-year-old filly the previous year.

Gamely could have raced as a two-year-old, but she was kept away from the races because she was so big — she was over 16.2 hands. She made her debut in California as a three-year-old in 1967 and won the Princess Stakes and finished second in the Hollywood Oaks and Railbird Stakes. Sent to Saratoga that summer, she won the Test and Alabama Stakes. In a division of the Test, she set a seven-furlong track record of 1:21⅘.

At five, Gamely again began the year on the West Coast and ended it on the East. She repeated her previous year's wins in the Wilshire Handicap and Beldame Stakes, and also won the Santa Monica and Diana Handicaps. She also tried colts, finishing second to Nodouble in the Santa Anita Handicap. She was again voted a champion in some polls.

Gamely retired during the fall of her five-year-old season with sixteen wins in forty-one starts and earnings of $574,961. Her winnings are tops among offspring of the great Bold Ruler, who was king of the sire lists in the 1960s. Gamely also was royally bred on her dam's side. She was produced from stakes winner Gambetta, whose dam, Rough Shod II, produced champions Moccasin and Ridan and major winner Lt. Stevens.

In 1975, at age eleven, Gamely died at Claiborne Farm of a ruptured stomach. She had produced her second live foal and second by Round Table just five days earlier. Her first foal, Cellini, was a group I winner in England.

Hollywood Park, site of many of Gamely's victories, conducts a grade I race in her honor.

— D. L.

Pedigree of GAMELY, bay filly, February 10, 1964

BOLD RULER, dk b, 1954	Nasrullah, 1940	Nearco, 1935	Pharos / Nogara
		Mumtaz Begum, 1932	Blenheim II / Mumtaz Mahal
	Miss Disco, 1944	Discovery, 1931	Display / Ariadne
		Outdone, 1936	Pompey / Sweep Out
GAMBETTA, b, 1952	My Babu, 1945	Djebel, 1937	Tourbillon / Loika
		Perfume II, 1938	Badruddin / Lavendula
	Rough Shod II, 1944	Gold Bridge, 1929	Golden Boss / Flying Diadem
		Dalmary, 1931	Blandford / Simon's Shoes

RACE and (STAKES) RECORD

YEAR	AGE	STS	1ST	2ND	3RD	EARNED
1967	at 3	14	4(3)	3(2)	3(3)	$117,617
1968	at 4	14	7(6)	3(3)	2(2)	$282,742
1969	at 5	13	5(4)	3(3)	1(1)	$174,602
Lifetime		**41**	**16(13)**	**9(8)**	**6(6)**	**$574,961**

Old Rosebud

OLD ROSEBUD IS ONE OF THE GREATEST HORSES to return from injury to compete at racing's highest levels. He was champion two-year-old of 1913, and the leading three-year-old after he won the Kentucky Derby, but he bowed a tendon in his next race and had a two-year lay-off. Old Rosebud returned at six to be champion handicapper.

His trainer, Frank D. Weir, recalled in *The Great Ones* that "Old Rosebud was the kind of horse one sees once in a lifetime. He certainly was the fastest horse I ever trained or saw. If he had been sound, there is no telling how fast he would have run."

Bred by John E. Madden, Old Rosebud was by the first-crop stallion Uncle out of the Himyar mare Ivory Bells. Weir purchased Old Rosebud as a yearling for $500, then resold a majority interest in the gelding to Churchill Downs treasurer, Hamilton C. Applegate. Applegate's family owned a whiskey distillery with its principal label named Old Rosebud; hence the gelding's name.

Old Rosebud came to hand early in his two-year-old year with his first start on Feb. 9, 1913, at Juarez in Mexico in the three and a half-furlong Yucatan Stakes, which he won by six lengths. Old Rosebud went on to start thirteen more times at two, winning eleven times. In May and June of that year, Old Rosebud showed a striking display of brilliance rarely seen — four track records for five furlongs in a twelve-day period.

The gelding continued his streak with victories in the Harold Stakes and Cincinnati Trophy at Latonia, then the Flash Stakes at Saratoga.

Unfortunately for his connections, Old Rosebud's two-year-old season ended prematurely when he pulled up lame after winning the United States Hotel Stakes. Even though he missed the fall stakes races, Old Rosebud was named champion two-year-old.

Ankle problems kept Old Rosebud from racing until two weeks before the Kentucky Derby, in an eight-furlong allowance race in Lexington, which he won easily. He started in the Derby as favorite. His jockey, Johnny McCabe, pushed Old Rosebud to the lead from the gate and the gelding drew off to win by eight lengths.

Three weeks later, Old Rosebud contested the Withers Stakes at Belmont Park, where races at the time still were run clockwise in the English manner. Old Rosebud was unaccustomed to this method of racing and during the race did not change leads coming into the stretch, which caused him to bow a tendon.

It appeared the gelding's career was over, but Weir wasn't about to give up on his champion. After several unsuccessful treatments, Old Rosebud was turned out for two years. The time off worked, and he came back at age six just as strong as when he left.

As a six-year-old of 1917, Old Rosebud finished second in a five and a half-furlong allowance race in his return, at Juarez, in February. Shipped to Oaklawn Park, he set two track records. Sent to Churchill Downs, Old Rosebud lost to Roamer at even weights, but a week later beat Roamer in the mile and a sixteenth Clark Handicap. His other victories included Latonia's Inaugural Handicap as well as the Queens County, Carter, Red Cross, Frontier, Bayview, and Delaware Handicaps.

Old Rosebud broke down again, but a year and a half lay up in Texas helped bring him back at eight. His body was weaker, but he was game. From thirty starts, he won nine times and earned $12,182. At nine, Old Rosebud won a high-weight handicap from eight starts. Weir brought him back again at ten. In his second start, he won a claiming race for his fortieth victory. At the age of eleven, Old Rosebud finished second in a claiming race at Jamaica, then broke down in a six-furlong allowance on May 17, 1922. Old Rosebud couldn't survive this final injury, and on May 23 Weir reluctantly decided to euthanize Old Rosebud, for the old fighter could run no more. — C. C.

UNCLE, ch, 1905	Star Shoot, 1898	Isinglass, 1890	Isonomy / Deadlock
		Astrology, 1887	Hermit / Stella
	The Niece, 1882	**Alarm, 1869**	**Eclipse / Maud**
		Jaconet, 1875	Leamington / Maggie B. B.
IVORY BELLS, br, 1899	Himyar, 1875	**Alarm, 1869**	**Eclipse / Maud**
		Hira, 1864	Lexington / Hegira
	Ida Pickwick, 1888	Mr. Pickwick, 1878	Hermit / Tomato
		Ida K., 1880	King Alfonso / Lerna

OLD ROSEBUD, bay gelding, 1911

RACE and (STAKES) RECORD

YEAR	AGE	STS	1ST	2ND	3RD	EARNED
1913	at 2	14	12	2	0	$19,057
1914	at 3	3	2	0	0	$9,575
1915	at 4	0	0	0	0	—
1916	at 5	0	0	0	0	—
1917	at 6	21	15	1	3	$31,720
1918	at 7	0	0	0	0	—
1919	at 8	30	9	7	5	$12,182
1920	at 9	8	1	2	0	$1,295
1921	at 10	2	1	0	0	$700
1922	at 11	2	0	1	0	$200
Lifetime		**80**	**40**	**13**	**8**	**$74,729**

Bewitch

THE YEAR WAS 1945. Assembled among the mares and foals grazing the lush spring grass between the white fences that divided Warren Wright Sr.'s Calumet Farm were three youngsters who would among themselves earn ten year-end racing championships: Citation, Coaltown, and Bewitch, the lone filly. All three were the offspring of Bull Lea.

As Wright assembled his breeding and racing stock in the early 1930s, he drew from the successful bloodlines of other breeders. From the established H. P. Whitney Stud, Wright purchased for $500 the stakes-placed three-year-old filly Potheen, who produced four stakes winners for Calumet, the best one being Bewitch.

Bewitch made an auspicious debut at Keeneland in April, 1947. In a race for maiden fillies, the Calumet runner assumed the lead from the start and romped to a six-length victory. A week later, she rallied to win by a neck, after surviving a tangled start and interference in the stretch. She then won her first stakes, the Debutante Stakes at Churchill Downs, by eight lengths. This, her first stakes race, began a string of six straight stakes wins.

Along the way on this amazing run of wins, Bewitch defeated future Triple Crown winner and stablemate Citation in the six-furlong Washington Park Futurity. By this time the filly's training duties had been turned over to H. A. (Jimmy) Jones, son of former trainer Ben Jones.

At Belmont Park, Bewitch suffered the only defeats of her juvenile season. The Matron Stakes became her seventh straight stakes win, but she was disqualified for bearing in. In her final start of the year, Bewitch finished third to Citation in the Futurity Stakes. Her record earned her honors as champion juvenile filly.

Fired for osselets and rested over the winter, Bewitch returned to winning form in her first start, the Ashland Stakes at Keeneland. Bucked shins kept the brown filly out of competition until late June. In the Princess Doreen Stakes at Arlington Park, she turned in the worst performance of her career to date, finishing fifth. Redemption followed. In the Modesty Handicap against older fillies and mares, Bewitch carried only 107 pounds to a length and a quarter victory. She followed with a win eleven days later in the Cleopatra Handicap. Tackling the colts for the first time as a three-year-old, she finished third in the Dick Welles Stakes. This loss was followed by a win in the Artful Handicap, her last start at three. She finished the year with four wins and a third in six starts and earnings of $69,000.

Bewitch reclaimed her throne as a champion at four, racing mainly in the Midwest. She won only three stakes, but her accomplishments still earned her honors as champion older mare. Her crowning effort came in the mile Beverly Handicap at Washington Park in which she won by a neck in 1:34⅖ — the fastest mile ever run by a filly.

In New York, she lost the Beldame Handicap and the Ladies Handicap, but secured her position at the head of the class in winning her last start of the year, the Vineland Handicap. In 1950, Bewitch traveled the length and breadth of the country. Although she won only twice in eleven starts, she finished unplaced only once.

In her final year of racing, the six-year-old mare started fifteen times. In twelve of those races, she faced the boys. Racing mainly on the California circuit, Bewitch won twice. Her major victory came against fillies in the Vanity Handicap at Hollywood Park.

Bewitch retired to Calumet Farm with a record of fifty-five starts, twenty wins, ten seconds, and eleven thirds. She had amassed $462,605 in earnings to become the leading money earner among fillies and mares. Bewitch did not replicate herself in her offspring, producing only two foals, both of which died before reaching the races. Bewitch died in 1959 and was buried at Calumet. — *T. H.*

Pedigree of BEWITCH, brown filly, 1945

- **BULL LEA, br, 1935**
  - Bull Dog, 1927
    - Teddy, 1913 — Ajax / Rondeau
    - Plucky Liege, 1912 — Spearmint / Concertina
  - Rose Leaves, 1916
    - Ballot, 1904 — Voter / Cerito
    - Colonial, 1897 — Trenton / Thankful Blossom
- **POTHEEN, br, 1928**
  - Wildair, 1917
    - Broomstick, 1901 — Ben Brush / Elf
    - Verdure, 1910 — **Peter Pan** / Recess
  - Rosie O'Grady, 1915
    - Hamburg, 1895 — Hanover / Lady Reel
    - Cherokee Rose II, 1910 — **Peter Pan** / Royal Rose

RACE and (STAKES) RECORD

YEAR	AGE	STS	1ST	2ND	3RD	EARNED
1947	at 2	10	8(6)	0	1(1)	$213,675
1948	at 3	6	4(4)	0	1(1)	$69,000
1949	at 4	13	4(3)	4(1)	2	$74,400
1950	at 5	11	2(1)	2(2)	6(2)	$32,480
1951	at 6	15	2(1)	4(4)	1	$73,050
Lifetime		55	20(15)	10(7)	11(4)	$462,605

Davona Dale

THE LATE 1970s MARKED A RESURGENCE in the fortunes of famed Calumet Farm. Between 1977 to 1981 the farm received three Eclipse Award championships, and all were won by fillies — Davona Dale, Our Mims, and Before Dawn. The best of these was a big, long-striding bay named Davona Dale.

Rarely does one farm experience the longevity to witness the result of breeding its horses in successive generations. Davona Dale was a product of Calumet breeding through and through. In the first generations, nine of the fourteen names belonged to Calumet homebreds. Davona Dale's sire was Best Turn, who won five stakes for Calumet. Her dam was Royal Entrance, a daughter of Calumet's near Triple Crown winner Tim Tam.

Davona Dale made her debut at Belmont Park on Oct. 23, 1978. Her winning effort set the tone for her career. John Veitch, trainer of the Calumet runners throughout the late '70s, opted for stakes competition for the filly's next start. She took the Holly Stakes at Meadowlands.

Veitch chose the Tropical Park Derby at Calder Race Course to initiate Davona Dale's sophomore campaign and possible Triple Crown bid. With nothing but a work over the track, Davona Dale finished fourth in a strong field of twelve that included ten colts. At Gulfstream Park Davona Dale finished second in the Shirley Jones Stakes to 1978's co-champion juvenile filly Candy Eclair. However, in the Bonnie Miss Stakes, Davona Dale began a win streak of eight races.

She took her act to Fair Grounds, where she won the Debutante Stakes, then won Oaklawn Park's Fantasy Stakes by two and a half lengths.

Davona Dale then was sent to Churchill Downs for the Kentucky Oaks. On a track

		Royal Charger, 1942	Nearco Sun Princess
	Turn-to, 1951		
BEST TURN, dkb/br, 1966		Source Sucree, 1940	Admiral Drake Lavendula
		Swaps, 1952	Khaled Iron Reward
	Sweet Clementine, 1960		
DAVONA DALE, **bay filly,** **May 14, 1976**		Miz Clementine, 1951	**Bull Lea** **Two Bob**
		Tom Fool, 1949	Menow Gaga
	Tim Tam, 1955		
ROYAL ENTRANCE, b, 1965		Two Lea, 1946	**Bull Lea** **Two Bob**
		Sun Again, 1939	Sun Teddy Hug Again
	Prince's Gate, 1957		
		Siena Way, 1952	**Bull Lea** Hydroplane II

soaked by two days of rain, Davona Dale took command in the stretch and coasted to a four and a half-length victory. Two weeks later, Davona Dale easily won the Black-Eyed Susan Stakes at Pimlico.

On May 26, eight days after her Black-Eyed Susan victory and her third race in twenty-two days, the tough filly stepped onto the Belmont Park oval for the Acorn Stakes, which she won by two and one quarter lengths. The day after the June 9 Belmont Stakes, Davona Dale won the Mother Goose. Relishing the added distance of the longer race, Davona Dale demolished her rivals by ten lengths.

If there were to be a Triple Crown winner of any sort in 1979, the onus would fall on the Calumet filly. The final leg was the grueling Coaching Club American Oaks on June 30. Four fillies confronted her in the starting gate, and at the end of the twelve-furlong marathon, Davona Dale romped by eight lengths. Where Spectacular Bid had faltered, Davona Dale had not, winning the filly version of the Triple Crown.

The Saratoga meet loomed on the horizon. Here Davona Dale faced the other co-champion two-year-old filly, It's in the Air, in the Alabama. Davona Dale might have been a little short for the mile and a quarter race, finishing second to the front-running It's in the Air. Next, Veitch entered Davona Dale in the Travers Stakes, in which she ran fourth to General Assembly. She also finished fourth in her final start that season in the Maskette Handicap at Belmont Park. Her accomplishments earned her the Eclipse Award for champion three-year-old filly.

At four, Davona Dale was beset with problems, and finished third in an allowance race in her first start back after an injury. Returning to the origin of her fall from grace, Davona Dale tackled three other fillies in the Ballerina Stakes at Saratoga, prevailing by a length over Misty Gallore with It's in the Air a nose back in third. Once again she attempted the Maskette, a race that would be her final start, and again she finished fourth.

Davona Dale retired to the broodmare ranks at Calumet Farm with eighteen starts and eleven wins. She never finished worse than fourth. Her earnings amounted to $641,612. — *T. H.*

RACE and (STAKES) RECORD

YEAR	AGE	STS	1ST	2ND	3RD	EARNED
1978	at 2	2	2(1)	0	0	$43,355
1979	at 3	13	8(8)	2(2)	0	$555,723
1980	at 4	3	1(1)	0	1	$42,534
Lifetime		**18**	**11(10)**	**2(2)**	**1**	**$641,612**

Genuine Risk

SHE WAS BEAUTIFUL, CLASSY, AND TOUGH, the epitome of the Hollywood heroine in horseflesh. Genuine Risk's life would make a great movie, but as it has been said, truth sometimes is stranger than fiction, and it might be hard for the general public to believe the story wasn't pure fabrication.

Genuine Risk, the second filly ever to win the Kentucky Derby, was bred by Mrs. G. Watts Humphrey Jr. from a birthday-present mare. Humphrey told his wife she could have

a mare as a thirtieth birthday present, as long as she "took the Keeneland fall sale catalogue and picked it out herself, on pedigree and also conformation." Mrs. Humphrey picked the mare Virtuous. The mare's second foal for Mrs. Humphrey was Genuine Risk.

Genuine Risk was selected from the 1978 Fasig-Tipton Kentucky July yearling sale by fourteen-year-old Matthew Firestone, whose parents, Bert and Diana Firestone, paid $32,000 for the nice chestnut by Exclusive Native.

Genuine Risk broke her maiden in her first outing at two, over a sloppy Belmont Park strip in late September of 1979. She started her year late because of bucked shins in the spring. Trained by LeRoy Jolley, she next took an allowance race by seven and a quarter lengths before scoring in the Tempted Stakes by three. In her last start of the year, Genuine Risk won the Demoiselle Stakes by a nose from Smart Angle.

At three, she won a March allowance race at Gulfstream Park, and afterwards was shipped to New York to take an overnight handicap at Aqueduct. Then, Genuine Risk was entered against the colts in the Wood Memorial. She finished a creditable third, and the decision was made to enter her in the Derby. It was the first time since 1959 that a filly had attempted the Derby.

Genuine Risk lined up against the colts at Churchill Downs the first Saturday in May, and was sent away at odds of more than 13-1. Jacinto Vasquez allowed her to settle after breaking from post position ten in the thirteen-horse field. Genuine Risk rolled along near the middle of the pack, but was reserved near the outside to stay clear of traffic. She looped to the lead on the turn for home, opened daylight on the colts, and won the Kentucky Derby by a length.

The second jewel in the Triple Crown will forever be known not as a classic race, but a classic judgment call. Codex, under Angel Cordero Jr., was on the rail coming into the final turn of the Preakness. Genuine Risk was on his outside, beginning her move. Then, much to the crowd's amazement, Codex carried Genuine Risk almost to the middle of the racetrack. As if that weren't bad enough, Cordero hit Genuine Risk three times with his whip. Codex then bumped into her. Genuine Risk couldn't sustain her drive, and she finished four and three-quarters lengths behind Codex. Vasquez filed an objection, but the stewards and the Maryland Racing Commission let the finish stand. Genuine Risk contested the Belmont Stakes, briefly took the lead in the stretch, but was passed near the wire by Temperence Hill.

Genuine Risk suffered from a virus after the Belmont, so she was freshened for three months before taking on her own sex in the Maskette, in which Bold 'n Determined beat her by a nose. In her last race at three, Genuine Risk edged the older Misty Gallore in the Ruffian and was crowned champion filly of her crop.

At four, she won her debut, an April allowance race, then finished third in another allowance event in May in her first start on grass. She made her final appearance in August, winning an allowance race at Saratoga by eight and a quarter lengths. While being aimed for the Woodward, Genuine Risk seemed off, and the Firestones decided to retire their great filly. She was inducted into the Racing Hall of Fame in 1986. Much was expected from Genuine Risk as a broodmare, but it wasn't until 1993 that she had a foal that survived. The arrival of Genuine Reward caused as much of a furor as his dam's victory in the Derby thirteen years earlier. — K. H.

Pedigree

GENUINE RISK, chestnut filly, February 15, 1977

EXCLUSIVE NATIVE, ch, 1965
- Raise a Native, 1961
  - Native Dancer, 1950 — Polynesian / Geisha
  - Raise You, 1946 — Case Ace / Lady Glory
- Exclusive, 1953
  - Shut Out, 1939 — Equipoise / Goose Egg
  - Good Example, 1944 — Pilate / Parade Girl

VIRTUOUS, b, 1971
- Gallant Man, 1954
  - Migoli, 1944 — Bois Roussel / Mah Iran
  - Majideh, 1939 — Mahmoud / Qurrat-al-Ain
- Due Respect II, 1958
  - Zucchero, 1948 — Nasrullah / Castagnola
  - Auld Alliance, 1948 — Brantome / Iona

RACE and (STAKES) RECORD

YEAR	AGE	STS	1ST	2ND	3RD	EARNED
1979	at 2	4	4(2)	0	0	$100,245
1980	at 3	8	4(2)	3(3)	1(1)	$503,742
1981	at 4	3	2	0	1	$42,600
Lifetime		15	10(4)	3(3)	2(1)	**$646,587**

231

Sarazen

ONE OF THE MOST CAPTIVATING ASPECTS OF RACING is to watch a horse from a humble background not only defeat his blue-blooded competitors, but dominate them to become a champion. The gelding Sarazen was such a horse. John E. Madden remarked about Sarazen's plebeian pedigree: "When a man can breed a Quarter Horse to a plow mare and get a horse that can beat everything in America, it's time for me to sell out."

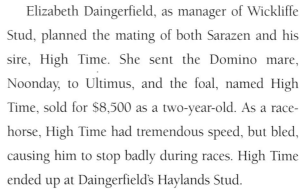

Elizabeth Daingerfield, as manager of Wickliffe Stud, planned the mating of both Sarazen and his sire, High Time. She sent the Domino mare, Noonday, to Ultimus, and the foal, named High Time, sold for $8,500 as a two-year-old. As a racehorse, High Time had tremendous speed, but bled, causing him to stop badly during races. High Time ended up at Daingerfield's Haylands Stud.

In 1920, Dr. Marius Johnston of Lexington, Kentucky, acquired the undistinguished producer Rush Box (by Box). On the advice of Daingerfield, he sent the mare, plus another mare of lowly origins, to High Time. The two resulting foals turned out to be Sarazen and Time Exposure, stakes winners of a total of twenty-two races.

Col. Phil T. Chinn, pinhooker, trainer, and breeder, purchased Sarazen and Time Exposure as yearlings from Johnston for a total of $2,500. Chinn named Sarazen after the famous golfer, Gene Sarazen. In his first start, Sarazen broke his maiden at Hawthorne on July 7, 1923, going five furlongs. He won two more races for the trainer; then Chinn sold the gelding. Chinn recalled in *The Great Ones* that he "made a sucker play — sold the horse to Mrs. Graham Fair Vanderbilt for $35,000 and he was worth $100,000."

Hall of Fame trainer Max Hirsch took over the gelding's conditioning for Mrs. Vanderbilt's Fair Stable. Their purchase paid off immediately, with Sarazen winning the

		Commando, 1898	Domino Emma C.
	Ultimus, 1906		
HIGH TIME, ch, 1916		Running Stream, 1898	Domino Dancing Water
		Domino, 1891	Himyar Mannie Gray
	Noonday, 1898		
SARAZEN, chestnut gelding, 1921		Sundown, 1887	Springfield Sunshine
		Order, 1888	Bend Or Angelica
	Box, 1894		
RUSH BOX, lt b, 1915		Pandora, 1887	Rayon d'Or Blue Grass Belle
		Singleton, 1901	St. Simon Field Azure
	Sallie Ward, 1909		
		Belle Nutter, 1898	Faraday Sarah F.

Champagne Stakes at Belmont Park by two lengths over Aga Khan. He also won the Oakdale Handicap, the National Stakes, and the Laurel Special. He concluded his undefeated two-year-old season with a facile victory in the eight-furlong Pimlico Serial Weight-for-Age Race No. 2 against older horses.

At three, Sarazen turned out to be one of the best of his generation with eight victories from twelve starts and earnings of $95,640. He suffered his first defeat in the Lynbrook Handicap on May 2, a day before the Kentucky Derby. He came back two months later to win the seven-furlong Carter Handicap. His other highlights included winning the Fleetwing, Saranac, Huron, and Manhattan Handicaps.

Sarazen then finished third in the Fall Highweight with top weight of 135 pounds. He bounced back to win the Arverne Handicap, carrying 128 pounds, two pounds less than Zev, the previous season's champion and world's leading money earner who finished second.

Sarazen went into his next race, the ten-furlong International Special No. 3, with handicappers questioning if he could get the distance due to his breeding and small size. In front of 60,000 fans, Sarazen faced the best European three-year-old of 1923, Epinard, plus Chilhowee, Mad Play, and Man o' War's brother My Play. Sarazen was much the best, winning by one and a half lengths in 2:00⅖, almost two seconds faster than the track record. He finished the year as the leading money earner with victories from five to ten furlongs.

Sarazen's continued success at four and five made him atypical — a horse that showed extreme brilliance at two, but maintained his performance later. At four, he won five of ten races. He did almost as well at five, winning four of fourteen races for earnings of $42,970. Unfortunately, Sarazen was a victim of his own success. He was so good that the weights he was forced to carry caused him to sour and lose interest in putting forth his best effort. Jacobs tried everything to correct his behavior, but to no avail. At seven, Sarazen finally was retired with twenty-seven victories from fifty-five starts and earnings of $223,800. His owner, Mrs. Vanderbilt, sent the gelding to Tom Piatt's Brookdale Farm in Kentucky. He died at age nineteen. — C. C.

RACE and (STAKES) RECORD

YEAR	AGE	STS	1ST	2ND	3RD	EARNED
1923	at 2	10	10(6)	0	0	$36,680
1924	at 3	12	8(8)	1(1)	1(1)	$95,640
1925	at 4	10	5(5)	0	1(1)	$48,160
1926	at 5	14	4(4)	1(1)	1(1)	$42,970
1927	at 6	4	0	0	1(1)	$100
1928	at 7	5	0	0	2(2)	$250
Lifetime		55	27(23)	2(2)	6(6)	$223,800

Sun Beau

SUN BEAU HELD THE TITLE of all-time leading money earner for nine years. It wasn't as long as Kelso's reign, but it was close to it.

A homebred for Willis Sharpe Kilmer, Sun Beau had begun his racing career in the Roaring Twenties and finished in the Depression, earning $376,744 from 1927-31. His title of "all-time leading money earner" lasted until March of 1940, when Seabiscuit established a new record.

Like many horses from that era, Sun Beau raced often and sometimes for very little. He started only four times as a two-year-old, but went to the post seventy times over the next four years. He won thirty-three races — seventeen stakes — finished second a dozen times and third ten times under the care of no fewer than eight trainers. His richest payday came in the 1930 Southern Maryland Handicap, with a purse of $34,000 to the winner.

Ironically, Sun Beau never was the overall money leader for a single season, and only twice was he the leading money earner in an age division. In 1930, Sun Beau led all five-year-olds, with $105,005. The following year, he topped the six-year-old division, with $110,925. It was during his six-year-old season that he took the money title from Gallant Fox.

Sun Beau took over from Gallant Fox by collecting the winner's purse of $27,300 in the Arlington Handicap on Aug. 1, 1931. The victory was his third straight and boosted his earnings to $330,044. Sun Beau raced five more times that year, and went out a winner in the Hawthorne Gold Cup, defeating favored Mate, Plucky Play, and Jim Dandy in a select four-horse field. It was Sun Beau's third consecutive win in that race, and since then no other horse has won the race more than twice. Sun Beau, who needed plenty of work between his races, was named champion handicap male in 1931, after sharing the title with Diavolo in 1929 and with Blue Larkspur in 1930.

Sun Beau came to the races a few years after Kilmer's great gelding Exterminator was retired from competition. Kilmer privately had purchased Exterminator shortly before the 1918 Kentucky Derby and was rewarded handsomely when the son of McGee took down the winner's share of $14,700. Exterminator won fifty of 100 races during his career.

Sun Beau's sire, French-bred Sun Briar, was purchased as a yearling by Kilmer for $6,000 at Saratoga. Sun Briar was champion two-year-old male in 1917 and the year's leading money-earning juvenile while racing in Kilmer's orange, brown, and gold silks. Sun Briar, who won the Travers Stakes as a three-year-old, faced Exterminator in the 1919 Champlain Handicap at Saratoga and set a track mark of 1:50 for one and one-eighth miles while giving that rival eight pounds.

Sun Beau also had a connection to a Kentucky Derby winner. Reigh Count, who won the 1928 Run for the Roses, was foaled the same year as Sun Beau, and he, too, was bred by Kilmer. In fact, Reigh Count's sire, Sunreigh, was a full brother to Sun Briar. Kilmer sold Reigh Count as a two-year-old to John D. Hertz, and missed out on part of the glory of another Kentucky Derby winner.

Sun Beau was one of thirty-four stakes winners sired by Sun Briar, and his dam, Beautiful Lady, carried the same Fair Play/Rock Sand cross that was responsible for Man o' War. Sun Beau entered stud in 1932 at Kilmer's Court Manor in Virginia and stood there until he was moved to Christopher T. Chenery's The Meadow near Doswell, Virginia, following his owner's death in 1940. As an eighteen-year-old stallion in 1943, Sun Beau was bred to Chenery's mare Hildene, who produced a colt from that mating. That colt, who was later gelded and given the name Mangohick, was the first of Hildene's five stakes winners, the others including Horse of the Year Hill Prince and champion First Landing.

Sun Beau, who sired five other stakes winners, died in March of 1944 from intestinal problems and was buried on the lawn at Chenery's estate. He was elected to the Racing Hall of Fame in 1996. — D. S.

SUN BEAU, bay colt, 1925	**SUN BRIAR,** b, 1915	Sundridge, 1898	Amphion, 1886 — Rosebery / Suicide
			Sierra, 1889 — Springfield / Sanda
		Sweet Briar II, 1908	St. Frusquin, 1893 — St. Simon / Isabel
			Presentation, 1898 — Orion / Dubia
	BEAUTIFUL LADY, ch, 1916	Fair Play, 1905	Hastings, 1893 — Spendthrift / Cinderella
			Fairy Gold, 1896 — Bend Or / Dame Masham
		Mileage, 1909	Rock Sand, 1900 — Sainfoin / Roquebrune
			Lady Madge, 1896 — Rayon d'Or / Lady Margaret

RACE and (STAKES) RECORD

YEAR	AGE	STS	1ST	2ND	3RD	EARNED
1927	at 2	4	1	0	1	$1,150
1928	at 3	23	8(3)	5(3)	1	$79,909
1929	at 4	14	6(4)	2	4(2)	$79,755
1930	at 5	19	9(4)	3(1)	3(3)	$105,005
1931	at 6	14	9(6)	2(2)	1	$110,925
Lifetime		74	33(17)	12(6)	10(5)	$376,744

Artful

IN HER OWN TIME, Artful was recognized as an outstanding filly. From the vantage point of nearly a century later, her status deserves an added cachet of history: She was in the vanguard among homebreds in the Whitney family's saga of the American Turf.

William Collins Whitney influenced such matters as the presidential campaign that landed Grover Cleveland in the White House, as well as the utilities and mass transit systems of New York City. As Secretary of the Navy under Cleveland, Whitney converted the fleet from wooden to steel ships. In racing, which he entered in 1898, Whitney was joined, then succeeded, by son Harry Payne Whitney, whose success dwarfed his own. The founder's daughter-in-law, Mrs. Payne Whitney, launched the enduring Greentree

Stud. Harry Payne Whitney, in turn, was succeeded by his son, C. V. Whitney, and, as the century turns, the latter's widow, Marylou, and a nephew, Leverett Miller, are current keepers of the tradition.

Present near the beginning of this tradition, Artful was a 1902 filly sired by Hamburg and out of Martha II, by Dandie Dinmont. W. C. Whitney died early in her two-year-old season, and his horses were raced in the name of his son's racing partner, Herman Duryea, following the tradition by which respect for the dead was expressed in that era without sacrificing a stable. The stable topped the owners' list for the third time in four seasons; subsequent Whitney generations topped that list a dozen times. Artful was trained by John W. Rogers, who launched the filly's public career at the scene of many a significant debut, Saratoga. While that upstate New York track had a proud history of Thoroughbred racing dating from the Civil War era, its rejuvenation near the last turn of the

		Hindoo, 1878	Virgil Florence
	Hanover, 1884		
HAMBURG, b, 1895		Bourbon Belle, 1869	Bonnie Scotland Ella D.
		Fellowcraft, 1870	Australian Aerolite
	Lady Reel, 1886		
Artful, brown filly, 1902		Mannie Gray, 1874	Enquirer Lizzie G.
		Silvio, 1874	Blair Athol Silverhair
	Dandie Dinmont, 1882		
MARTHA II, b, 1895		Meg Merrilies, 1874	Macgregor Meteor
		Rayon d'Or, 1876	Flageolet Araucaria
	Louise T., 1885		
		Spark, 1878	Leamington Mary Clark

century was another matter to which William Collins Whitney's hand had been set, to general satisfaction.

Artful finished second in her debut behind stablemate Dramici, who, under the quaint custom of the day, had been "declared" to win by the stable. The *Daily Racing Form* chart discerned that "Artful, a genuine crackerjack, hard held and close up throughout, finished as easily and could probably have won."

Next time out, Artful was again accompanied by a "declared" winner from the stable, finishing second to Princess Rupert. Again, the *Racing Form* chart referred to Artful as an obvious "crackerjack."

As a maiden filly, Artful got into the climactic Futurity Stakes at 114 pounds, receiving thirteen from the colt Sysonby and the filly Tradition. Whether Rogers and Whitney had been orchestrating the "crackerjack's" early defeats to avail themselves of this condition is not to be proven ninety-five years later. Neither, however, is the notion to be discounted.

The Futurity marked the first victory of Artful's career, and she was not to know defeat again. Sysonby was reported to have been drugged by his groom, which admittedly took some of the glitter off Artful's victory. Still, the field for that edition of the Futurity was regarded as so strong that her defeating the likes of Oiseau, Tradition, and Agile was clearly an exceptional effort. Four days later, Artful was held at 1-15 and outclassed her field to win the Great Filly Stakes, and then, after a break of six weeks, she concluded her juvenile season by winning the White Plains Handicap under 130 pounds.

The day after the White Plains, the Whitney horses were sold at auction, and Harry Payne Whitney bought Artful for $10,000. The price perhaps indicated a general belief that she was a sprinter, but at three Artful won two sprints as preparation for the Brighton Handicap, then won that one and a quarter-mile event under 103 pounds. Artful won from a field including the great filly Beldame and the good colts Ort Wells and Delhi.

Artful foaled three moderate winners and later was sent to England, where she produced one foal. She then was returned to this country where she failed to produce further offspring, although bred annually through the age of twenty-three. She died at twenty-five in 1927. She had won six of eight races to earn $81,125. — E. L. B.

RACE and (STAKES) RECORD

YEAR	AGE	STS	1ST	2ND	3RD	EARNED
1904	at 2	5	3(3)	2	0	$57,805
1905	at 3	3	3(1)	0	0	$23,320
Lifetime		8	6(4)	2	0	**$81,125**

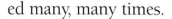

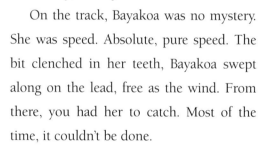

Bayakoa

THE IMAGE IS INDELIBLE. Laffit Pincay's whip raised high in his left hand, his mouth wide open in obvious elation. Beneath him strides the source of his exultation, the great Bayakoa, ears pressed back, tongue lolling from the side of her peculiar parrot-mouth, her bay body in full splendor. It was just a single moment, but one that was repeated many, many times.

On the track, Bayakoa was no mystery. She was speed. Absolute, pure speed. The bit clenched in her teeth, Bayakoa swept along on the lead, free as the wind. From there, you had her to catch. Most of the time, it couldn't be done.

What made this Argentinean flash so beloved to the racing world, though, was her undeniable courage. At the height of her majesty, Bayakoa was simply unstoppable, carrying the burgundy and gray colors of Janis and Frank Whitham to victory in some of the nation's most celebrated races.

Her tale began in South America. Right from the start, Bayakoa exuded class. Quality performances in group I events early on eventually caught the eye of Ron McAnally, the man who would mold Bayakoa into a powerhouse. For McAnally, one trip to Argentina was all it took. He loved what he saw, and brought the bay mare to Southern California during her three-year-old year. A few months later as a four-year-old, the daughter of Consultant's Bid won a Hollywood Park allowance race.

Sound as an oak she was, but Bayakoa was too nervous for her own good. A war she waged with some inner demon caused her nearly to self-destruct on numerous occasions. Bayakoa would wring herself dry with anxiety. What was left, her heart and soul, she

		Bold Ruler, 1954	**Nasrullah** / Miss Disco
	Bold Bidder, 1962		
CONSULTANT'S BID, b, 1977		High Bid, 1956	To Market / Stepping Stone
		Fleet Nasrullah, 1955	**Nasrullah** / Happy Go Fleet
	Fleet Judy, 1963		
BAYAKOA (Arg), bay filly, October 10, 1984		Solid Miss, 1952	Solidarity / Henpecker
		Nashua, 1952	**Nasrullah** / Segula
	Good Manners, 1966		
ARLUCEA (Arg), b, 1974		Fun House, 1958	The Doge / Recess
		Right of Way, 1957	Honeyway / Magnificent
	Izarra, 1964		
		Azpeitia, 1957	Corindon II / Bidasoa

would empty onto the racetrack. Pacifying the big mare was quite a chore for McAnally and his able staff, all of whom kept her environment as tranquil as could be. In the afternoons, Pincay provided the gentle touch, soothing the mare he says is the best he ever sat on.

Considering Bayakoa's borderline insanity, her career can only be looked upon as astounding. From early 1989 through the fall of 1990, Bayakoa was no less than spectacular. The Spinster Stakes, the Hawthorne, the Santa Margarita, and the Milady Handicaps — each she won twice. Gems like the Ruffian, Apple Blossom, Santa Maria, and the Vanity Handicaps — Bayakoa captured every one of them, as well. All in all, she snared fifteen major stakes during this run, twelve of them in grade I company.

Her exploits during those two dynamic seasons saw Bayakoa become the first mare in nineteen years, since Shuvee in 1971, to be honored with back-to-back Eclipse Awards as North America's outstanding older female. Both of her championship campaigns were climaxed with triumphs in the Breeders' Cup Distaff. The first, a fantastic display at Gulfstream Park in 1989, was repeated the following year at Belmont Park. Only three others — Miesque, Lure, and Da Hoss — have ever won two Breeders' Cup events.

Unfortunately, her second Distaff will forever be shrouded in sadness. What was billed as a showdown between the Argentinean sensation and champion Go for Wand, a shooting star in her own right, ended tragically. Go for Wand, in the heat of battle, broke her leg and fell. Bayakoa crossed the finish alone. By the time Bayakoa reached the end of the line a few months later, she had amassed over $2.8 million. Her success — twenty-one wins from thirty-nine starts, seventeen in stakes — stretched over six racing seasons and two continents, a testament to her durability.

Expectations were rightfully high as she began her next calling as a broodmare, but her foals never matched their mother's ability. Sadly, Bayakoa died from laminitis in 1997. She was only thirteen. One year later, her phenomenal career was honored as she was elected to the Racing Hall of Fame. — C. H.

RACE and (STAKES) RECORD

YEAR	AGE	STS	1ST	2ND	3RD	EARNED
1987	at 2-3 in Arg	8	3(1)	3(2)	0	$76,442
1988	at 4 in NA	7	2(1)	2	0	$73,200
1989	at 5 in NA	11	9(8)	1(1)	0	$1,406,403
1990	at 6 in NA	10	7(7)	2(2)	0	$1,234,406
1991	at 7 in NA	3	0	1(1)	0	$71,250
Lifetime		39	21(17)	9(6)	0	**$2,861,701**

Exceller

EXCELLER PUT TOGETHER A YEAR in which he won six grade I stakes, defeated two Triple Crown winners in the same race, and was the leading money-earner among older horses. Even with all that, it wasn't enough to sway Eclipse Award voters in his favor. That happened in 1978 when Exceller was a five-year-old, and the title of champion older male went to four-year-old Seattle Slew. Like Gallant Man two decades earlier and Lure in the 1990s, millionaire Exceller remains one of the sport's top horses never to have been honored with a championship.

What was particularly disturbing to owner Nelson Bunker Hunt and trainer Charlie Whittingham was that Exceller had defeated Triple Crown winners Seattle Slew and Affirmed in that year's Jockey Club Gold Cup at Belmont Park. It was the first time two Triple Crown winners had run in the same race, and it was Exceller, making up a twenty-two-length deficit, who prevailed by a nose over Seattle Slew in the one and a half-mile race. Ridden by Bill Shoemaker, Exceller had outlasted Seattle Slew's final challenge in the closing yards to even the score to one victory each. Seattle Slew had won the one and a quarter-mile Woodward Stakes two weeks earlier at Belmont Park. Affirmed's chances in the Jockey Club Gold Cup were compromised after the colt's saddle slipped.

Exceller then was returned to his Southern California base and closed out the year with his sixth grade I win that season, capturing the Oak Tree Invitational Stakes on grass as the 3-10 favorite. Exceller's grade I wins in the first part of the year came on dirt in the Hollywood Gold Cup Handicap under 128 pounds, and on grass in the Hollywood Invitational Handicap under 127 pounds, the Sunset Handicap under 130 pounds, and the

San Juan Capistrano Handicap under 126 pounds. Exceller had earned $879,790 that year, and was accorded one honor by *Daily Racing Form*.

Exceller who was bred in Kentucky by Mrs. Charles Engelhard, had experienced his first taste of turf racing while competing in Europe as a two-year-old and excelled at lengthy distances. He won at fifteen and a half furlongs in both the Prix Royal-Oak (the French equivalent of the St. Leger Stakes) and the Grand Prix de Paris. He also won the Grand Prix de Saint-Cloud at twelve and a half furlongs and the Coronation Cup (in England) at twelve furlongs. In perhaps his biggest confrontation overseas, he ran third to The Minstrel and Orange Bay in the King George VI and Queen Elizabeth Diamond Stakes.

Exceller arrived in North America his four-year-old season and won the Canadian International Championship Stakes in the fall. Following his near-championship season in 1978, he raced four times as a six-year-old, but failed to win. He was retired with fifteen wins from thirty-three starts and earnings of $1,674,587, and entered stud at John R. Gaines' Gainesway Farm near Lexington, Kentucky. Syndicated for $375,000 a share, the second-highest syndication price at that time, he stood his first season for $75,000.

A son of Vaguely Noble, Exceller was the richest of five stakes winners produced from the Bald Eagle mare Too Bald, the 1986 Kentucky Broodmare of the Year. Hunt had purchased Exceller through Lee Eaton for $25,000 at the 1974 Keeneland July yearling sale from Claiborne Farm, agent for Mrs. Engelhard. While Exceller was in training, Hunt sold an interest in the horse to Dr. Herbert Schnapka. In 1968, Hunt in partnership had won the 1968 Prix de l'Arc de Triomphe with Vaguely Noble.

Unlike Vaguely Noble, who also stood at Gainesway, Exceller failed to excel at stud, and was sent to Sweden for the 1991 breeding season. In the spring of 1997, Exceller's owner, Gote Ostlund, sent the stallion to a slaughterhouse because he could not pay for his upkeep. Later that fall, Exceller's son, Pirion, won that country's St. Leger. The news of Exceller's slaughter led to the creation of the Exceller Fund to rescue horses and place them in good homes. — *D. S.*

Pedigree

EXCELLER, bay colt, May 12, 1973

VAGUELY NOBLE (GB), b, 1965	Vienna, 1957	Aureole, 1950	Hyperion / Angelola
		Turkish Blood, 1944	Turkhan / Rusk
	Noble Lassie, 1956	**Nearco**, 1935	Pharos / Nogara
		Belle Sauvage, 1949	Big Game / Tropical Sun
TOO BALD, dkb/br, 1964	Bald Eagle, 1955	**Nasrullah**, 1940	**Nearco** / Mumtaz Begum
		Siama, 1947	Tiger / China Face
	Hidden Talent, 1956	Dark Star, 1950	Royal Gem II / Isolde
		Dangerous Dame, 1951	**Nasrullah** / Lady Kells

RACE and (STAKES) RECORD

YEAR	AGE	STS	1ST	2ND	3RD	EARNED
1975	at 2 in Fr	4	1	0	2(2)	$13,755
1976	at 3 in Fr	6	4(3)	1	0	$320,786
1977	at 4 in Fr, Eng, NA	9	3(3)	2(2)	2(2)	$375,256
1978	at 5 in NA	10	7(7)	1(1)	0	$879,790
1979	at 6 in NA	4	0	1(1)	2(2)	$85,000
Lifetime		33	15(13)	5(4)	6(6)	**$1,674,587**

241

Foolish Pleasure

HE WAS THE UNDEFEATED TWO-YEAR-OLD CHAMPION of 1974 and won the following year's Kentucky Derby. In the 1976 Suburban Handicap he defeated the great Forego. And he was the first Thoroughbred millionaire to have been sold at public auction. Despite

those achievements, however, Foolish Pleasure was best known for his role in one of racing's most tragic incidents: the death of the filly Ruffian.

Bred in Florida by Waldemar Farms, Foolish Pleasure was purchased by trainer LeRoy Jolley on behalf of Tennessee businessman John L. Greer for $20,000 at the 1973 Fasig-Tipton Saratoga select yearling sale. A son of What a Pleasure, Foolish Pleasure was produced from the Tom Fool mare Fool-Me-Not.

In his career debut, Foolish Pleasure raced to within one and a half seconds of Hialeah's track record for five furlongs, getting that distance in :59 in a four and a half-length victory. Moved right up into stakes company, the bay colt rolled to a ten-length triumph. That was the first of six consecutive stakes victories for Foolish Pleasure, who completed the year undefeated in seven starts. Voted champion two-year-old male, Foolish Pleasure became the winter-book favorite for the 1975 Kentucky Derby.

Foolish Pleasure began his three-year-old campaign winning a betless exhibition at Hialeah Park under Jacinto Vasquez. The colt extended his undefeated string to nine when he held off a fast-closing Prince Thou Art while lugging out in the stretch in the Flamingo Stakes. As the 1-5 favorite in the Florida Derby, Foolish Pleasure engaged in a duel with Sylvan Place as both were passed by Prince Thou Art for a three and a quarter-length victory. Two days after Foolish Pleasure's first loss, it was discovered that the frogs on both front hooves had been peeled back during the race. After recovering from the injury,

Foolish Pleasure rallied late to defeat Bombay Duck by a head in the Wood Memorial at Aqueduct.

Breaking from post position three as the 19-10 Derby favorite, Foolish Pleasure gamely split rivals rounding the second turn and ran by Avatar and Diabolo to win by one and three-quarters lengths. In the Preakness, 23-1 longshot Master Derby held off a late bid by Foolish Pleasure to win by a length. Despite the defeat, Foolish Pleasure was accorded 13-10 favoritism in the Belmont Stakes, but lost by a neck to Avatar.

With Ruffian dominating her competition, the New York Racing Association put up $350,000 for a special race pitting the three male classic winners against the filly. Avatar's connections declined the invitation, ending the classic winner concept for the race. NYRA officials reportedly awarded money to Master Derby's owner to withdraw the Preakness winner, leaving a Foolish Pleasure-Ruffian match race carded for July 6.

With Vasquez committed to ride Ruffian, the 2-5 favorite, Braulio Baeza was aboard Foolish Pleasure. The colt broke on top in the one and a quarter-mile race, with Ruffian leaving the gate from the rail. Ruffian quickly assumed a short lead that she held after a quarter-mile. After three-eighths of a mile, Ruffian suddenly swerved to the outside, slightly bumping Foolish Pleasure. The filly had fractured the sesamoids in her right foreleg, was pulled up in distress, and later euthanized. Foolish Pleasure continued around the course.

With five victories from eleven starts, Foolish Pleasure finished second to Wajima in balloting for the Eclipse Award. In his final season of competition, Foolish Pleasure won half of his eight starts in 1976, including a nose decision over Forego in the Suburban. Foolish Pleasure retired to Greentree Stud with sixteen wins in twenty-six starts, four runner-up efforts, and three third-place finishes, for earnings of $1,216,705.

Foolish Pleasure became leading first crop sire of 1980. Relocated three times during his stud career, he sired forty-one stakes winners, including champions Baiser Vole, Bayford, and What Nonsense. He also was the sire of the dams of forty-four stakes winners, including champions Caitano and Nydrion.

Foolish Pleasure died at Horseshoe Ranch in Dayton, Wyoming, on Nov. 17, 1994. — R. M.

			Nasrullah, 1940	Nearco / Mumtaz Begum
		Bold Ruler, 1954		
	WHAT A PLEASURE, ch, 1965		Miss Disco, 1944	Discovery / Outdone
			Mahmoud, 1933	**Blenheim II** / Mah Mahal
		Grey Flight, 1945		
FOOLISH PLEASURE, bay colt, March 23, 1972			Planetoid, 1934	Ariel / La Chica
			Menow, 1935	Pharamond II / Alcibiades
		Tom Fool, 1949		
	FOOL-ME-NOT, b, 1958		Gaga, 1942	Bull Dog / Alpoise
			Tourbillon, 1928	Ksar / Durban
		Cuadrilla, 1943)		
			Bouillabaisse, 1935	**Blenheim II** / Becti

RACE and (STAKES) RECORD

YEAR	AGE	STS	1ST	2ND	3RD	EARNED
1974	at 2	7	7(6)	0	0	$284,595
1975	at 3	11	5(3)	4(3)	1(1)	$716,278
1976	at 4	8	4(3)	0	2(2)	$215,832
Lifetime		26	16(12)	4(3)	3(3)	$1,216,705

Beldame

AUGUST BELMONT II BRED BELDAME, and she won while carrying his colors. But ironically, the talented filly achieved her greatest glory during the time she was leased to Newton Bennington, one of Belmont's friends and business associates.

The lease agreement was reached before the end of Beldame's juvenile campaign in 1903. Belmont was a busy and important man, with projects like building Belmont Park and New York City's subway system on his mind. Besides, he wasn't getting along well with the filly's trainer, John J. Hyland.

The two men disagreed about the seriousness of a skin problem Beldame developed at Saratoga. Hyland said the eruptions were only mosquito bites, but Belmont thought she  was suffering from hives or shingles. Beldame ran sixth in an overnight race, finishing eight lengths behind the eventual two-year-old filly champion, Hamburg Belle. Then Belmont insisted that Beldame be declared from the Futurity, and an angry Hyland announced that he was quitting at the end of October — a promise he kept.

When Hyland departed, Beldame was already a two-time stakes winner. She made her first start for Bennington and trainer Fred Burlew in November, beating colts easily in a six-furlong overnight race. It proved to be a good omen.

With the new team in charge, the chestnut daughter of Octagon was magnificent at three. She lost only twice in fourteen starts, both times to older males, and she was honored as the champion filly of her division. Short or long, it didn't matter. She was virtually unbeatable at any distance.

A masculine type who had a mind of her own, Beldame also stood out because of her finicky eating habits. She had a marked aversion to oats, and would never consume more

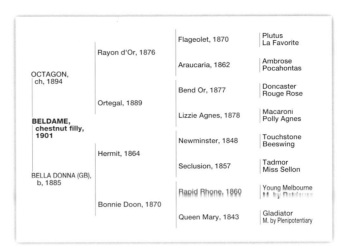

			Flageolet, 1870	Plutus La Favorite
	Rayon d'Or, 1876		Araucaria, 1862	Ambrose Pocahontas
OCTAGON, ch, 1894			Bend Or, 1877	Doncaster Rouge Rose
	Ortegal, 1889		Lizzie Agnes, 1878	Macaroni Polly Agnes
BELDAME, chestnut filly, 1901			Newminster, 1848	Touchstone Beeswing
	Hermit, 1864		Seclusion, 1857	Tadmor Miss Sellon
BELLA DONNA (GB), b, 1885			Rapid Rhone, 1860	Young Melbourne M. by Birdcatcher
	Bonnie Doon, 1870		Queen Mary, 1843	Gladiator M. by Plenipotentiary

than three quarts a day. But she loved ear corn. Seven or eight ears were laid on her manger every day, and she always stripped them clean to the cob.

Perhaps Beldame's finest effort of 1904 came in the Saratoga Cup, when she was installed as the 9-5 favorite over four-year-old Africander, who had won the Belmont Stakes and set a track record in taking the Saratoga Cup during a championship campaign the previous year. The field also included 1903 American Derby winner The Picket and 1902 Lawrence Realization winner Major Daingerfield. They might as well not have shown up. Beldame, who carried 108 pounds under the weight-for-age conditions, charged to the front and romped. Beldame also was impressive in the First Special at Gravesend. She won in hand by two lengths, repelling a stiff challenge from another Saratoga Cup winner, Caughnawaga.

Five days later, Beldame closed out her 1904 campaign with a victory in the Second Special, giving two actual pounds to Broomstick and soundly defeating Africander and five-year-old McChesney. Other highlights of the season included a two-length triumph in the Carter Handicap against older males while under a stout hold. She left her female rivals reeling in the Gazelle, Alabama, and other races.

In one particularly memorable effort, she ran off with rider Gene Hildebrand as the 2-5 favorite before the Ladies Stakes and galloped around until finding a gap that led back to her barn. However, she apparently suffered no ill effects from her experience. Returned to the track, Beldame broke on top, led throughout, and won while being eased at the end.

For the 1905 season, the filly returned to August Belmont II, but remained in Burlew's barn. In the Suburban, the important handicap of the year, she carried top weight by scale, 123 pounds, and defeated Delhi to become only the second filly to capture the race. She also took the Standard Stakes.

After she retired from racing, Beldame's earnings were reported differently. According to a race-by-race tabulation in *Goodwin's Guides*, her total was $102,135. *The American Racing Manual* credited her with $102,570. However, one thing was certain, she was only the third filly, following Miss Woodford and Firenze, to earn more than $100,000. — *D. B. B.*

RACE and (STAKES) RECORD

YEAR	AGE	STS	1ST	2ND	3RD	EARNED
1903	at 2	7	3(2)	1(1)	1(1)	$21,185
1904	at 3	14	12(10)	1(1)	1(1)	$54,100
1905	at 3	10	2(2)	4(3)	2(2)	$26,850
Lifetime		**31**	**17(14)**	**6(5)**	**4(4)**	**$102,135**

Roamer

FROM THE HUMBLEST OF BEGINNINGS came a great horse. Roamer was sired by the farm teaser, and his dam was a blind English-bred claiming mare. The story goes that one or the other of them jumped a fence to accomplish the mating, thus the name of the offspring. Roamer was a Thoroughbred of the old school who won at distances from four and a half furlongs to one and three-quarters miles, set or equaled eleven track records, won twenty-four stakes and placed in twenty-seven others, was undisputed champion at three and four, and top-class competitor at five, six, and seven.

Americans found a champion in a slightly built, commonly bred gelding who beat the odds. Roamer was bred by the sons of Col. E. F. Clay, who with his partner and brother-in-law Col. Catesby Woodford, sent out such 19th Century champions as Hanover, Miss Woodford, Ben Brush, and Runnymede. The Clays sent out Roamer for the first time on May 1, 1913, in a maiden race at Lexington, and he won by five. Roamer came out behind eventual champion juvenile colt Old Rosebud a couple of times in Louisville, then raced his way to New York.

Once there, one of the brothers, Woodford Clay, dropped Roamer into a $1,000 selling race. It cost him $2,005 to keep his horse when someone else put in a claim. The winning purse had amounted to only $380. A few days later, Andrew Miller's trainer Jack Goldsborough offered $2,500 for Roamer. Clay jumped at the money, and Roamer carried Miller's cardinal silks with white sash and black cap in ninety races.

Miller was a classmate of Teddy Roosevelt at Harvard, founded *Life* magazine, became a steward of The Jockey Club in its early years, and helped purchase and revive Saratoga racetrack in 1900. He had previously raced Major Daingerfield, leading money earner of 1902.

Roamer won the Saratoga Special over Col. E. R. Bradley's Black Toney at two, but didn't manage to score another victory that year. At three, that all changed.

Roamer's five records that year included a victory in the one and an eighth-mile Washington Handicap at Laurel in American record time of 1:49⅗. He was the leading money earner that year with $29,105 while winning twelve of sixteen races. He concluded his three-year-old season with six consecutive victories.

The winner of eight of thirteen races at four, Roamer carried 128 pounds to victory in the Brookdale Handicap at Aqueduct and the Saratoga Handicap. He equaled the track record in the former, and won by ten lengths in the latter.

The 15.2-hand gelding won only once in thirteen outings at five, but his seconds under top weight in six handicap races marked him the best of his division. At six, Roamer's former rival from his foal crop — Old Rosebud — returned to the races after a two-year absence. The two met seven times, with Old Rosebud proving the best three times and Roamer winning twice. Roamer gave weight four times.

At seven, Roamer was ranked behind four-year-old Cudgel, but ran some of his best races, including the mile Queens County Handicap under top weight. He also equaled Empire City's one and an eighth-mile record of 1:51 in taking the Empire City Handicap.

After Roamer won his third Saratoga Handicap, the racing public demanded the gelding challenge Salvatore's record mile of 1:35⅕. Roamer was given a "pacemaker," two-year-old named Lightning, and promptly left him a couple of strides away from the Saratoga gate. Regular rider Andy Schuttinger brought the gelding around two turns and came under the wire in 1:34⅘ without urging.

At eight, Roamer suffered a slight leg problem and won only one of six outings. He was turned out, fully expected to return at nine. On New Year's Eve, Miller suffered a fatal heart attack. A few hours later, Roamer slipped on ice in his paddock, broke his leg, and had to be euthanized. — K. H.

KNIGHT ERRANT, br, 1901	Trenton, 1881	Musket, 1867	Toxophilite / Mare by West Australian
		Frailty, 1877	Goldsbrough / Flora McIvor
	St. Mildred, 1890	St. Simon, 1881	Galopin / St. Angela
ROAMER, bay gelding, 1911		Lady Fitz-James, 1878	Scottish Chief / Hawthorn Bloom
	Bona Vista, 1889	Bend Or, 1877	Doncaster / Rouge Rose
ROSE TREE II, b, 1896		Vista, 1879	Macaroni / Verdure
	Fanny Relph, 1892	Minting, 1883	Lord Lyon / Mint Sauce
		Elm, 1885	Consternation / Elmina

RACE and (STAKES) RECORD

YEAR	AGE	STS	1ST	2ND	3RD	EARNED
1913	at 2	17	4(1)	6(1)	1	$8,480
1914	at 3	16	12(9)	1(1)	2(2)	$29,105
1915	at 4	13	8(7)	1(1)	0	$15,320
1916	at 5	13	1(1)	6(6)	1(1)	$5,705
1917	at 6	17	7(4)	4(4)	2(2)	$16,501
1918	at 7	16	6(5)	6(6)	2(2)	$21,950
1919	at 8	6	1	2	1	$1,767
Lifetime		**98**	**39(26)**	**26(20)**	**9(7)**	**$98,828**

Blue Larkspur

COL. E. R. BRADLEY WAS A WORLDLY ENTREPRENEUR whose bent was generally toward the gaming industry, and he preferred being the house to trying to beat it. His success with such installations as the posh Beach Club in Palm Beach allowed diversity of investment, such as an interest in the Fair Grounds racetrack and later in Hialeah.

Advised by a physician that fresh air and some country living were a good antidote to too many days and nights in gambling parlors — however luxurious — Bradley also developed Idle Hour Stock Farm outside Lexington and began assembling an outstand-

ing collection of mares and stallions. The Kentucky Derby emerged as a beguiling target to any in the racing business, especially a fellow with a Kentucky farm and an honorary Kentucky title. Before Calumet Farm came into power, Bradley was the most successful at turning out Derby winners, winning the classic four times from 1921 through 1933.

Ironically, the Derby eluded both Bimelech and Blue Larkspur, arguably Bradley's two best colts. Bimelech was unbeaten until the 35-1 Gallahadion collared him in the 1940 running. Eleven years earlier, Blue Larkspur, the story goes, was done in by a bizarre combination of mud and appendicitis. The mud was that which lay heavily over the Churchill Downs strip on Derby Day; the appendicitis was that which lay heavily upon the mind and body of trainer Derby Dick Thompson. In Thompson's absence, the assistant neglected to have Blue Larkspur shod in stickers, and he struggled home fourth behind Clyde Van Dusen.

To that point, Blue Larkspur might have been styled a hard-luck horse whenever the big ones were on the line. The previous fall, he apparently had been kicked before the start of the Belmont Futurity, in which he finished eighth of twenty-four. On lesser days, Blue

BLACK SERVANT, br, 1918	Black Toney, 1911	Peter Pan, 1904	Commando / Cinderella
		Belgravia, 1903	Ben Brush / Bonnie Gal
	Padula, 1906	Laveno, 1892	Bend Or / Napoli
		Padua, 1886	Thurio / Immortelle
BLOSSOM TIME, br, 1920	North Star III, 1914	Sunstar, 1908	Sundridge / Doris
		Angelic, 1901	St. Angelo / Fota
	Vaila, 1911	Fariman, 1900	Gallinule / Bellinzona
		Padilla, 1900	Macheath / Padua

BLUE LARKSPUR, bay colt, 1926

Larkspur had already established the reputation of a high-class colt. He was a son of Bradley's stallion Black Servant and the North Star III mare Blossom Time. The latter was out of Vaila, one of a number of important Bradley imports (La Troienne was another). Bradley liked inbreeding, and Blue Larkspur was inbred to the mare Padua, second dam of Black Servant and third dam of Blossom Time.

At two, before the Futurity, Blue Larkspur had won in his second start and took consecutive stakes decisions over Jack High, in the Juvenile, National Stallion, and Saratoga Special. Jack High reversed the order in the Hopeful, in which Blue Larkspur carried 130 pounds and was hampered by traffic. Blue Larkspur won four of seven tries at age two.

Blue Larkspur returned at three to defeat Clyde Van Dusen in a prep race before his Derby misfortune. In the one-mile Withers Stakes, Blue Larkspur closed with such a mighty rush to win that he became the betting favorite for the one and a half-mile Belmont Stakes — despite the off going and a common prejudice against any Domino-line colt getting the trip. Blue Larkspur kicked the reputation of being unable to handle wet going as he won the Belmont handily, with old rival Jack High third. He almost came a cropper again in a big one, though, for he was kicked at the start once more. This time, he won the race, but a leg filled, and he ran a fever for several days.

Blue Larkspur later won the Arlington Classic before a bowed tendon ended his season. He was able to make only three starts at four before the leg failed again, but his two victories, in the Stars and Stripes Handicap and Arlington Cup, enhanced his position as a colt of exceptional class. He had won ten of sixteen races to earn $272,070, at the time the third-highest total of any American runner in history.

In the stud, Blue Larkspur remained exceptional. He got fifteen percent stakes winners (forty-four), and his daughters included such influential broodmares as Myrtlewood, Blue Delight, and Bloodroot. His daughters produced 114 stakes winners, including champions Twilight Tear, Durazna, Real Delight, By Jimminy, Bull Page, and Ancestor. Blue Larkspur died in 1947 and was elected to the Racing Hall of Fame in 1957. — E. L. B.

RACE and (STAKES) RECORD

YEAR	AGE	STS	1ST	2ND	3RD	EARNED
1928	at 2	7	4(3)	1(1)	1	$66,970
1929	at 3	6	4(3)	1(1)	0	$153,450
1930	at 4	3	2(2)	1	0	$51,650
Lifetime		16	10(8)	3(2)	1	$272,070

RANK	NAME	BIRTH YEAR	OWNER	BREEDER	TRAINER
1	Man o' War	1917	Samuel D. Riddle	August Belmont II and Nursery Stud (Ky)	Louis Feustel
2	Secretariat	1970	Meadow Stable	Meadow Stud (Va)	Lucien Laurin
3	Citation	1945	Calumet Farm	Calumet Farm (Ky)	Ben A. Jones and H.A. (Jimmy) Jones
4	Kelso	1957	Bohemia Stable	Mrs. Richard C. du Pont (Ky)	Dr. John Lee and Carl H. Hanford
5	Count Fleet	1940	Mrs. John D. Hertz	Mrs. John D. Hertz (Ky)	G.D. Cameron
6	Dr. Fager	1964	Tartan Stable	Tartan Farms (Fl)	John Nerud
7	Native Dancer	1950	Alfred G. Vanderbilt	Alfred G. Vanderbilt (Ky)	W.C. Winfrey
8	Forego	1970	Lazy F Ranch	Lazy F Ranch (Ky)	Frank Y. Whiteley Jr.
9	Seattle Slew	1974	Tayhill Stable	Ben S. Castleman (Ky)	William H. Turner and Douglas Peterson
10	Spectacular Bid	1976	Hawksworth Farm	Mrs. William Jason and Mrs. William Gilmore (Ky)	Grover G. (Bud) Delp
11	Tom Fool	1949	Greentree Stable	Duval Headley (Ky)	John M. Gaver
12	Affirmed	1975	Louis Wolfson	Harbor View Farm (Fl)	Lazaro S. Barrera
13	War Admiral	1934	Glen Riddle Farm	Samuel D. Riddle (Ky)	George Conway
14	Buckpasser	1963	Ogden Phipps	Ogden Phipps (Ky)	W.C. Winfrey and Eddie A. Neloy
15	Colin	1905	James R. Keene	James R. Keene (Ky)	James G. Rowe Sr.
16	Damascus	1964	Mrs. Thomas Bancroft	Mrs. Thomas Bancroft (Ky)	Frank Y. Whiteley Jr.
17	Round Table	1954	A.B. Hancock Jr. and Travis M. Kerr	Claiborne Farm (Ky)	Moody Jolley and William Molter
18	Cigar	1990	Allen Paulson	Allen Paulson (Md)	William I. Mott
19	Bold Ruler	1954	Wheatley Stable	Wheatley Stable (Ky)	James (Sunny Jim) Fitzsimmons
20	Swaps	1952	Rex C. Ellsworth	Rex C. Ellsworth (Cal)	Meshach (Mesh) Tenney
21	Equipoise	1928	C.V. Whitney	Harry Payne Whitney (Ky)	Fred Hopkins and T.J. Healey
22	Phar Lap (NZ)	1926	David J. Davis and H.R. Telford	A.F. Roberts (NZ)	Tommy Woodcock
23	John Henry	1975	Dotsam Stable	Golden Chance Farm (Ky)	Ronald McAnally
24	Nashua	1952	Belair Stud and Leslie Combs II syndicate	Belair Stud (Ky)	James (Sunny Jim) Fitzsimmons
25	Seabiscuit	1933	Wheatley Stable and Charles S. Howard	Wheatley Stable (Ky)	James (Sunny Jim) Fitzsimmons and Tom Smith
26	Whirlaway	1938	Calumet Farm	Calumet Farm (Ky)	Ben A. Jones
27	Alydar	1975	Calumet Farm	Calumet Farm (Ky)	John H. Veitch
28	Gallant Fox	1927	Belair Stud	Belair Stud (Ky)	James (Sunny Jim) Fitzsimmons
29	Exterminator	1915	J. Cal Milam and Willis Sharpe Kilmer	F.D. (Dixie) Knight (Ky)	J. Cal Milam, Henry McDaniel, J. Simon Healy, Will McDaniel, F. Curtis, Bill Knapp, Eugene Wayland, Will Shields, and John I. Smith
30	Sysonby	1902	James R. Keene	James R. Keene (Ky)	James G. Rowe Sr.
31	Sunday Silence	1986	Dr. Ernest Gaillard, Arthur Hancock, and Charles Whittingham	Oak Cliff Thoroughbreds Ltd. (Ky)	Charles Whittingham
32	Skip Away	1993	Carolyn Hine	Anna Marie Barnhart (Fl)	Hubert (Sonny) Hine
33	Assault	1943	Robert J. Kleberg Jr.	King Ranch (Tx)	Max Hirsch
34	Easy Goer	1986	Ogden Phipps	Ogden Phipps (Ky)	Claude R. (Shug) McGaughey III
35	Ruffian	1972	Locust Hill Farm	Mr. and Mrs. Stuart S. Janney (Ky)	Frank Y. Whiteley Jr.
36	Gallant Man	1954	Ralph Lowe	Aga Khan III and Prince Aly Khan (Eng)	John Nerud
37	Discovery	1931	Adolphe Pons and Alfred G. Vanderbilt	Walter J. Salmon Jr. (Ky)	John R. Pryce and J.H. Stotler
38	Challedon	1936	William L. Brann	Branncastle Farm (Md)	L.J. Schaefer
39	Armed	1941	Calumet Farm	Calumet Farm (Ky)	Ben A. Jones and H.A. (Jimmy) Jones
40	Busher	1942	Col. E.R. Bradley and L.B. Mayer	Idle Hour Stock Farm (Ky)	J.W. Smith and George Odom
41	Stymie	1941	King Ranch and Ethel D. Jacobs	Max Hirsch (Tx)	Max Hirsch and Hirsch Jacobs
42	Alysheba	1984	Dorothy and Pamela Scharbauer	Preston Madden (Ky)	Jack C. Van Berg
43	Northern Dancer	1961	E.P. Taylor	E.P. Taylor (Can)	Horatio Luro
44	Ack Ack	1966	Forked Lightning Ranch	Harry F. Guggenheim (Ky)	Frank A. Bonsal and Charles Whittingham
45	Gallorette	1942	William L. Brann	Preston M. Burch (Md)	Edward A. Christmas
46	Majestic Prince	1966	Frank M. McMahon	Leslie Combs II (Ky)	John Longden
47	Coaltown	1945	Calumet Farm	Calumet Farm (Ky)	Ben A. Jones and H.A. (Jimmy) Jones
48	Personal Ensign	1984	Ogden Phipps	Ogden Phipps (Ky)	Claude R. (Shug) McGaughey III
49	Sir Barton	1916	John E. Madden and Cmdr. J.K.L. Ross	John E. Madden and Vivian A. Gooch (Ky)	W.S. Walker and H. Guy Bedwell
50	Dahlia	1970	Nelson Bunker Hunt	Nelson Bunker Hunt (Ky)	Maurice Zilber

RANK	NAME	BIRTH YEAR	OWNER	BREEDER	TRAINER
51	Susan's Girl	1969	Fred W. Hooper Jr.	Fred W. Hooper Jr. (Fl)	J.W. Russell, Thomas W. Kelly, J.L. Newman, and Ross Fenstermaker
52	Twenty Grand	1928	Greentree Stable	Greentree Stable (Ky)	Thomas W. Murphy, James G. Rowe Jr., William Brennan, and Cecil Boyd-Rochfort
53	Sword Dancer	1956	Brookemeade Stable	Brookmeade Stable (Va)	Elliott Burch
54	Grey Lag	1918	Max Hirsch and Harry F. Sinclair	John E. Madden (Ky)	Max Hirsch and Sam Hildreth
55	Devil Diver	1939	Greentree Stable	Greentree Stable (Ky)	John L. Gaver
56	Zev	1920	Rancocas Stable	John E. Madden (Ky)	Sam C. Hildreth
57	Riva Ridge	1969	Meadow Stable	Meadow Stud (Ky)	Lucien Laurin
58	Slew o' Gold	1980	Equusequity Stable	Claiborne Farm (Ky)	John O. Hertler and Sidney Watters Jr.
59	Twilight Tear	1941	Calumet Farm	Calumet Farm (Ky)	Ben A. Jones
60	Native Diver	1959	Mr. and Mrs. L.K. Shapiro	Mr. and Mrs. L.K. Shapiro (Cal)	M.E. (Buster) Millerick
61	Omaha	1932	Belair Stud	Belair Stud (Ky)	James (Sunny Jim) Fitzsimmons and Cecil Boyd-Rochfort
62	Cicada	1959	Christopher T. Chenery	Meadow Stud (Ky)	J.H. (Casey) Hayes
63	Silver Charm	1994	Robert and Beverly Lewis	Mary Lou Wootton (Fl)	Bob Baffert
64	Holy Bull	1991	Warren A. Croll Jr.	Pelican Stable (Fl)	Warren A. Croll Jr.
65	Alsab	1939	Mrs. Albert Sabath	Tom Piatt (Ky)	August Swenke
66	Top Flight	1929	C.V. Whitney	Harry Payne Whitney (Ky)	Tom Healey
67	Arts and Letters	1966	Paul Mellon	Paul Mellon (Va)	Elliott Burch
68	All Along (Fr)	1979	Daniel Wildenstein	Dayton Ltd. (Fr)	Patrick Biancone
69	Noor (Eng)	1945	Charles S. Howard (estate)	Aga Khan III (Eng)	Burley Parke
70	Shuvee	1966	Mrs. Whitney Stone	Whitney Stone (Va)	Willard C. Freeman
71	Regret	1912	Harry Payne Whitney	Harry Payne Whitney (NJ)	James G. Rowe Sr.
72	Go for Wand	1987	Christiana Stables	Christiana Stables (Pa)	William Badgett Jr.
73	Johnstown	1936	Belair Stable	A.B. Hancock (Ky)	James (Sunny Jim) Fitzsimmons
74	Bald Eagle	1955	Harry F. Guggenheim	Harry F. Guggenheim (Ky)	W.C. (Woody) Stephens
75	Hill Prince	1947	Christopher T. Chenery	Christopher T. Chenery (Va)	J.H. Hayes
76	Lady's Secret	1982	Mr. and Mrs. Eugene V. Klein	Robert H. Spreen (Ok)	D. Wayne Lukas
77	Two Lea	1946	Calumet Farm	Calumet Farm (Ky)	H.A. (Jimmy) Jones
78	Eight Thirty	1936	George D. Widener	George D. Widener (Ky)	W.F. Mulholland
79	Gallant Bloom	1966	Robert J. Kleberg Jr.	King Ranch (Ky)	W.J. Hirsch
80	Ta Wee	1966	Tartan Stable	Tartan Farms (Fl)	F.S. (Scotty) Schulhofer
81	Affectionately	1960	Ethel D. Jacobs	Bieber-Jacobs Stable (Ky)	Hirsch Jacobs
82	Miesque	1984	Flaxman Holdings	Flaxman Holdings (Ky)	Francois Boutin
83	Carry Back	1958	Mrs. Jack Price	Jack A. Price (Fl)	Jack A. Price
84	Bimelech	1937	Col. E.R. Bradley	Idle Hour Stock Farm (Ky)	H.J. (Dick) Thompson
85	Lure	1989	Claiborne Farm and Nicole P. Gorman	Claiborne Farm and The Gamely Corp. (Ky)	Claude R. (Shug) McGaughey III
86	Fort Marcy	1964	Rokeby Stable	Paul Mellon (Va)	Elliott Burch
87	Gamely	1964	William Haggin Perry	Claiborne Farm (Ky)	James W. Maloney Jr.
88	Old Rosebud	1911	Col. Hamilton, C. Applegate, and Frank D. Weir	John E. Madden (Ky)	Frank D. Weir
89	Bewitch	1945	Calumet Farm	Calumet Farm (Ky)	Ben A. Jones
90	Davona Dale	1976	Calumet Farm	Calumet Farm (Ky)	John M. Veitch
91	Genuine Risk	1977	Diana Firestone	Mrs. G. Watts Humphrey Jr. (Ky)	LeRoy Jolley
92	Sarazen	1921	Col. Phil T. Chinn and Fair Stable	Dr. Marius E. Johnston (Ky)	Col. Phil T. Chinn and Max Hirsch
93	Sun Beau	1925	W.S. Kilmer	Willis Sharp Kilmer (Va)	A.G. Blakeley and J. Whyte
94	Artful	1902	Harry Payne Whitney	William Collins Whitney (Ky)	John W. Rogers
95	Bayakoa (Arg)	1984	Mr. and Mrs. Frank Whitham	Haras Principal (Arg)	Ronald McAnally
96	Exceller	1973	Belair Stud and Nelson Bunker Hunt	Mrs. Charles W. Engelhard (Ky)	Charles Whittingham
97	Foolish Pleasure	1972	John L. Greer	Waldemar Farms (Fl)	LeRoy Jolley
98	Beldame	1901	August Belmont II; lessee, Newton Bennington	August Belmont II (Ky)	John J. Hyland and Fred Burlew
99	Roamer	1911	Woodford Clay and Andrew Miller	Clay Brothers (Ky)	French Brooks and A. Jack Goldsborough
100	Blue Larkspur	1926	Col. E.R. Bradley	Idle Hour Stock Farm (Ky)	H.J. (Dick) Thompson

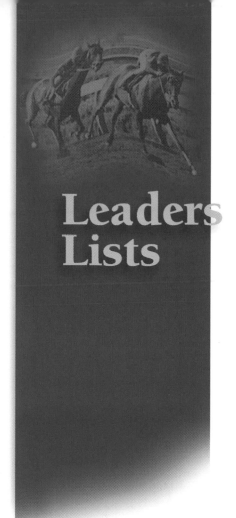

Leaders Lists

MOST WINS

Rank	Horse	Starts
17	Round Table	**43**
39	Armed	**41**
88	Old Rosebud	**40**
4	Kelso	**39**
23	John Henry	**39**
99	Roamer	**39**

UNBEATENS

Rank	Horse	Starts
15	Colin	**15**
48	Personal Ensign	**13**

ONCE BEATENS

Rank	Horse	Starts
7	Native Dancer	**22**
1	Man o' War	**21**
30	Sysonby	**15**
35	Ruffian	**11**
46	Majestic Prince	**10**

MOST STARTS

Rank	Horse	Starts
41	Stymie	**131**
29	Exterminator	**100**
99	Roamer	**98**
25	Seabiscuit	**89**
23	John Henry	**83**
39	Armed	**81**
60	Native Diver	**81**
88	Old Rosebud	**80**
86	Fort Marcy	**75**
93	Sun Beau	**74**

KENTUCKY DERBY WINNERS

Rank	Horse	Year
2	**Secretariat**	1973
3	**Citation**	1948
5	**Count Fleet**	1943
9	**Seattle Slew**	1977
10	Spectacular Bid	1979
12	**Affirmed**	1978
13	**War Admiral**	1937
20	Swaps	1955
26	**Whirlaway**	1941
28	**Gallant Fox**	1930
29	Exterminator	1918
31	Sunday Silence	1989
33	**Assault**	1946
42	Alysheba	1987
43	Northern Dancer	1964
46	Majestic Prince	1969
49	**Sir Barton**	1919
52	Twenty Grand	1931
56	Zev	1923
57	Riva Ridge	1972
61	**Omaha**	1935
63	Silver Charm	1997
71	Regret	1915
73	Johnstown	1939
83	Carry Back	1961
88	Old Rosebud	1914
91	Genuine Risk	1980
97	Foolish Pleasure	1975

(bf—Triple Crown winners)

NUMBER OF HORSES

20

15

10

5

1900s

MULTIMILLIONAIRES

Rank	Horse	Earnings	Rank	Horse	Earnings
18	Cigar	$9,999,815	58	Slew o' Gold	$3,533,534
32	Skip Away	$9,616,360	76	Lady's Secret	$3,021,325
63	Silver Charm	$6,944,369	95	Bayakoa	$2,861,701
42	Alysheba	$6,679,242	10	Spectacular Bid	$2,781,608
23	John Henry	$6,591,860	85	Lure	$2,515,289
31	Sunday Silence	$4,968,554	64	Holy Bull	$2,481,760
34	Easy Goer	$4,873,770	12	Affirmed	$2,393,818

GALLOPING GELDINGS

Rank	Horse
4	Kelso
7	Forego
22	Phar Lap
23	John Henry
29	Exterminator
39	Armed
60	Native Diver
86	Fort Marcy
88	Old Rosebud
92	Sarazen
99	Roamer

TOP TRAINERS

Name	No. of Horses
Ben A. Jones and H. A. (Jimmy) Jones	7
James (Sunny Jim) Fitzsimmons	6
Max Hirsch	3
Claude R. (Shug) McGaughey III	3
Frank Y. Whiteley Jr.	3
Charles Whittingham	3

BEST OF THE BREEDERS

Name	No. of Horses
Calumet Farm	9
Claiborne Farm (with partners)	4
John E. Madden (with partners)	4
Meadow Stud	4
Belair Stud	3
Idle Hour Stock Farm	3
Ogden Phipps	3

THE BIG YEARS
(BY FOALING DATE)

Year	No.
1966	6
1945	4
1964	4
1984	4

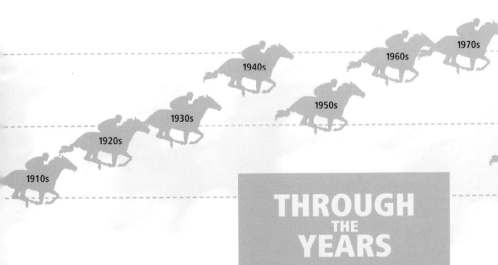

THROUGH THE YEARS

Photo Credits

Man o' War (*Keeneland; Keeneland/Cook*); Secretariat (*NYRA/Bob Coglianese; Anne M. Eberhardt*); Citation (*The Blood-Horse*); Kelso (*The Blood-Horse*); Count Fleet (*The Blood-Horse; Mack Hughes*); Dr. Fager (*NYRA/Bob Coglianese; The Blood-Horse*); Native Dancer (*Bert Morgan; The Blood-Horse*); Forego (*Milton Toby; The Blood-Horse*); Seattle Slew (*Tim Chapman; Anne M. Eberhardt*); Spectacular Bid (*Milton Toby; Barbara D. Livingston*); Tom Fool (*Bert Morgan; Aqueduct Photo*); Affirmed (*Lexington Herald-Leader; The Blood-Horse*); War Admiral (*The Blood-Horse; Morgan Photo Service*); Buckpasser (*NYRA/Mike Sirico; Jim Raftery/Turfotos*); Colin (*The Blood-Horse*); Damascus (*NYRA/Mike Sirico; NYRA/Paul Schafer*); Round Table (*Hawthorne Race Course; Allen F. Brewer Jr.*); Cigar (*Barbara D. Livingston*); Bold Ruler (*Bert Morgan; Allen F. Brewer Jr.*); Swaps (*Courier-Journal; Allen F. Brewer Jr.*);

Equipoise (*The Blood-Horse*); Phar Lap (*The Blood-Horse*); John Henry (*Arlington Park Photo*); Nashua (*The Blood-Horse*); Seabiscuit (*The Blood-Horse*); Whirlaway (*Belmont Park Photo*); Alydar (*Barbara D. Livingston*); Gallant Fox (*H. C. Ashby*); Exterminator (*Keeneland/Cook*); Sysonby (*The Blood-Horse*); Sunday Silence (*Dan Johnson*); Skip Away (*Bill Denver*); Assault (*The Blood-Horse*); Easy Goer (*Skip Dickstein*); Ruffian (*NYRA/Bob Coglianese*); Gallant Man (*Bert Morgan*); Discovery (*The Blood-Horse*); Challedon (*The Blood-Horse*); Armed (*The Blood-Horse*); Busher (*Washington Park Photo*); Stymie (*The Blood-Horse*); Alysheba (*Four Footed Fotos*); Northern Dancer (*Tony Leonard*); Ack Ack (*The Blood-Horse*); Gallorette (*Bert Morgan*); Majestic Prince (*The Blood-Horse*); Coaltown (*Washington Park Photo*); Personal Ensign (*Dan Johnson*); Sir Barton (*Keeneland/Cook*); Dahlia (*Ruth Rogers*); Susan's Girl (*The Blood-Horse*); Twenty Grand (*The Blood-Horse*); Sword Dancer (*Turfotos*);

Grey Lag (*The Blood-Horse*); Devil Diver (*Bert Morgan*); Zev (*The Blood-Horse*); Riva Ridge (*The Blood-Horse*); Slew o' Gold (*The Blood-Horse*); Twilight Tear (*The Blood-Horse*); Native Diver (*The Blood-Horse*); Omaha (*The Blood-Horse*); Cicada (*Turfotos*); Silver Charm (*Barbara D. Livingston*); Holy Bull (*Skip Dickstein*); Alsab (*The Blood-Horse*); Top Flight (*The Blood-Horse*); Arts and Letters (*NYRA/Bob Coglianese*); All Along (*Skip Ball*); Noor (*The Blood-Horse*); Shuvee (*NYRA/Bob Coglianese*); Regret (*Keeneland/Cook*); Go for Wand (*Dan Johnson*); Johnstown (*Caufield & Shook*); Bald Eagle (*The Blood-Horse*); Hill Prince (*The Blood-Horse*); Lady's Secret (*Skip Dickstein*); Two Lea (*The Blood-Horse*); Eight Thirty (*Belmont Park Photo*); Gallant Bloom (*Jim Raftery/Turfotos*);

Ta Wee (*Jim Raftery/Turfotos*); Affectionately (*Turfotos*); Miesque (*Steve Stidham*); Carry Back (*The Blood-Horse*); Bimelech (*Turf Pix*); Lure (*Barbara D. Livingston*); Fort Marcy (*Mike Sirico*); Gamely (*The Blood-Horse*); Old Rosebud (*Sutcliffe Pictures*); Bewitch (*Washington Park Photo*); Davona Dale (*NYRA/Bob Coglianese*); Genuine Risk (*Lexington Herald-Leader*); Sarazen (*Keeneland/Cook*); Sun Beau (*The Blood-Horse*); Artful (*Widener Collection*); Bayakoa (*Four Footed Fotos*); Exceller (*The Blood-Horse*); Foolish Pleasure (*Lexington Herald-Leader*); Beldame (*Keeneland/Cook*); Roamer (*Sutcliffe Pictures*); Blue Larkspur (*The Blood-Horse*)

The Panel

Acknowledgments

Editor
Jacqueline Duke

Assistant Editor
Judy L. Marchman

Artist
Brian Turner

Writers
Deirdre B. Biles
Edward L. Bowen
Catesby Clay Jr.
Tom Hall
Evan Hammonds
Craig Harzmann
Steve Haskin
Kimberly Herbert
Kristin J. Ingwell
Bob Kieckhefer
Tom LaMarra
Dan Liebman
Ron Mitchell
Ray Paulick
David Schmitz
Pohla Smith
Gary West
Jill Williams

Copy Editors
Lisa G. Coots
Patricia Dolan
Ellen Kiser
Patricia Ranft
Debbie B. Tuska
Diane I. Viert

Researchers
Linda Manley
Jo McKinney
Jay Wallace

Photo Research
Amy M. Leinbach

HOWARD BATTLE

Keeneland's racing secretary since 1973, Battle had held that position at other tracks including Arlington, Detroit, and Saratoga. He also works on the Breeders' Cup Racing Secretaries and Directors Panel, Experimental Free Handicap Committee, and the Graded Stakes Committee.

LENNY HALE

Hale is the vice president of the Maryland Jockey Club. He previously worked at the New York Racing Association for seventeen years as racing secretary, director of racing, and senior vice president.

JAY HOVDEY

A two-time Eclipse Award-winner, Hovdey is executive columnist with *Daily Racing Form*. He previously worked as senior correspondent for *The Blood-Horse* magazine and has received numerous other awards for his writing, including the Walter Haight Award.

WILLIAM R. NACK

Nack, a six-time Eclipse Award-winner, started his Turf writing career at *Newsday* in 1972 and now is a senior writer for *Sports Illustrated*. He is best-known for his book chronicling the life of Secretariat, *Big Red of Meadow Stable*.

PETE PEDERSEN

Pedersen, the senior racetrack steward in California, has worked at nearly every track on the West Coast in his more than fifty years in racing. He now is primarily based at Santa Anita.

JENNIE REES

Rees, who has two Eclipse Awards to her credit, is a racing writer and columnist for the Louisville *Courier-Journal*. She also serves as a director of the National Turf Writers Association.

TOMMY TROTTER

Longtime racetrack steward Trotter has worked in the racing industry since 1945 and has held positions at Fair Grounds, Gulfstream Park, Delaware Park, and Turf Paradise among others. He assigned 137 pounds to Forego for the Marlboro Cup, and said he got a "good feeling" when the gelding won under the impost.

Also from
The Blood-Horse, Inc.

Matriarchs: Great Mares of the 20th Century

Country Life Diary (revised edition)

Kentucky Derby Glasses Price Guide

Four Seasons of Racing

Cigar: America's Horse

Crown Jewels of Thoroughbred Racing

Whittingham

Royal Blood